Additional Praise for *Creative Velocity*

Leslie draws from a lifetime of practical professional experiences to celebrate human creativity and demystify what we think of as out-of-the-box thinking. This book is a practical primer. Creativity isn't magic; it's a chemical reaction that she distills into a mix of habits, processes, and mindset shifts that lead to breakthrough results.

—Richard Stern
CEO, TuneIn

This book is a must-read for anyone seeking to harness creativity as a core skill in today's fast-evolving world. Leslie Grandy masterfully argues that creativity is not a talent reserved for a few but a vital skill that can be nurtured and developed in everyone. What sets *Creative Velocity* apart is its practical approach—Grandy doesn't just offer theories but provides powerful exercises and frameworks that empower readers to unlock their creative potential. Whether you're a Fortune 500 CEO trying to unlock growth, an entrepreneur, or a creative professional, this book offers a roadmap to cultivating creativity that will transform individuals and organizations.

—Jason Baumgarten
Global Head of CEO and Board Practice,
Spencer Stuart

Whether you seek the creative confidence to innovate or have already had success pushing boundaries, *Creative Velocity* can unlock your imaginative potential. I'd recommend this book even to the most successful creative minds because the exercises serve as an invaluable reminder to flex mental muscles in unique ways. Everyone can benefit from new perspectives to look at old problems.

—Jeffrey D. Shulman
Professor of Marketing, Michael G. Foster School of Business
at the University of Washington;
Podcaster; Filmmaker

What if creativity wasn't just for artists but for everyone—from engineers to executives? *Creative Velocity* redefines creativity as a skill that anyone can master. Packed with insights from highly productive innovators, this book provides a practical roadmap for unleashing your creative potential and accelerating breakthrough ideas. Whether you're leading a team or just getting started, *Creative Velocity* will inspire you to think bigger, work smarter, and achieve more.

—Jim Louderback,
Editor and CEO, Inside the Creator Economy

Creative Velocity is the cheat code for unlocking innovative potential. In this book, Leslie Grandy has masterfully synthesized research, her own experiences, and the wisdom of successful leaders from across industries to provide actionable strategies answering the age-old question: how do you overcome the roadblocks to "thinking outside the box" and unlock individual and team innovative potential?

—Karim Meghji
Chief Product Officer, Code.org

Creative Velocity is a masterpiece of insight and inspiration. It distills the most actionable findings from the science of creativity and, through engaging interviews with top business leaders, demonstrates how these insights can drive revolutionary success across diverse industries. With numerous hands-on exercises that help boost creative thinking, it makes good on its premise that creativity is not some mythical talent reserved for the few but rather can come from anywhere, from anyone. As a business school faculty member who studies and teaches creativity to countless managers each year, Leslie Grandy's book is an essential handbook that I recommend to anyone who appreciates the power of ideas to create a better status quo but doesn't quite know how to get there.

—Crystal Fahr
Professor of Management, Michael G. Foster School of Business
at the University of Washington

Creative Velocity is a fresh, innovative, and deeply compelling analysis of the central value of innovative thought and action that draws on the author's extensive professional experience. Her book offers powerful techniques to enhance personal and team creativity, supported by useful end-of-chapter individual and group exercises. A recurring focus on incorporating generative AI into creative processes provides added practical benefit. Leslie Grandy's book represents something increasingly rare in the field: a truly novel perspective on an often-misunderstood concept, with a clear, actionable path to realizing the benefits of her insights.

—William Koehler, PhD
Dean, Sloane School of Business and Communication;
Professor of Management, Regis College

CREATIVE VELOCITY

CREATIVE VELOCITY

PROPELLING *BREAKTHROUGH IDEAS* IN THE AGE OF *GENERATIVE AI*

LESLIE GRANDY

WILEY

Published by John Wiley & Sons, Inc., Hoboken, New Jersey.
Published simultaneously in Canada.

For general information on our other products and services or for technical support, please contact our Customer Care Department within the United States at (800) 762-2974, outside the United States at (317) 572-3993 or fax (317) 572-4002.

Wiley also publishes its books in a variety of electronic formats. Some content that appears in print may not be available in electronic formats. For more information about Wiley products, visit our web site at www.wiley.com.

Library of Congress Cataloging-in-Publication Data is Available:

ISBN: 9781394283439 (cloth)
ISBN: 9781394283446 (ePub)
ISBN: 9781394284481 (ePDF)

Cover Design: Wiley
Cover Image: © bankphoto/Adobe Stock
Author Photo: Courtesy of the Author

SKY10100185_031825

To my husband, Jay, whose love has been my greatest source of strength. This book is a tribute to your support and encouragement throughout our unconventional journey together. Thank you for always standing by me, cheering me on, and believing in my creative capacity. You are my hero.

Contents

Creativity is everyone's superpower

Creativity is the lifeblood of humanity. It isn't a gift reserved for the chosen few. It is not about talent or privilege. It's within us all, waiting to be encouraged, nurtured, and indulged. Creativity thrives on attention and is fed by curiosity. It fractures under the weight of pessimism, fear, and doubt. Ambiguity is creativity's playground. Mistakes and failure are the fuel that creativity needs. It is how we solve problems, imagine possibilities, and manifest our future. Creativity allows us to dismantle outdated constructs and reimagine how things work to improve the quality of the human experience. When we access our creative soul, we can embrace the fuzzy front end and messy middle while anticipating the joy of unexpected discoveries from imperfect exploration to uncover novel ideas.

Introduction

"You can't use up creativity. The more you use, the more you have."

—Maya Angelou

Imagine a workplace where the air is charged with sparks of creativity and the buzz of exciting possibilities. Envision a team in which engineers, product managers, data analysts, accountants, customer care agents, sales teams, and operations leaders are empowered to be as creative as designers. Picture an environment where everyone approaches their work with an open mind, free from expert bias, and fueled by the desire to be their best self. You'd think this place would be a great place to work alongside creative minds who are free from stress and inspired to solve big, meaty problems. And you'd be right – studies confirm that creativity doesn't just make us happier, it makes us more productive, too. Creativity, happiness, and productivity are all correlated.

As a leader, I've seen the transformative power of creative thinking firsthand. However, when I challenge my teams to dream bigger and stretch their imaginations beyond the day-to-day, I often meet resistance. "I don't have the time to think big," they argue, or "I don't have the opportunity to be creative in my job," or even, "Isn't that what the design team is supposed to do?" I insist that creativity is indispensable for surmounting the market's latest challenge, carving out new ventures, and navigating the day-to-day hurdles with agility and vision. By championing creative thought, I have aimed to dismantle the barriers of cognitive fixedness and expert bias that narrow their thinking, to kindle a fire of creative confidence that empowers them to aim higher in order to broaden the team's collective perspective, and to increase their capacity to imagine novel solutions to challenging problems.

Creative velocity refers to the ability to quickly and efficiently originate new and innovative ideas that are both useful and valuable. It measures one's capacity to produce the maximum amount of creative output in the least amount of time, which occurs when there are minimal creative barriers and sufficient time spent in a productive flow state.

Through interviews with successful creative thinkers—including Scott Belsky, a partner at A24, an independent film studio, and former executive vice president at Adobe; Jason Silva, storyteller, futurist, and Emmy-nominated television host; and Scilla Andreen, cofounder and chief executive officer (CEO) of IndieFlix and the Impactful Group—you will learn how creative confidence has served as the foundation for creative velocity. Their stories illustrate the importance of an inclusive and open mind, a comfort with ambiguity, a willingness to be self-reflective, and a commitment to always be learning. Maintaining creative velocity requires continuous cultivation of the cognitive skills that fuel it and a commitment to making the time and space to attend to it. After reading the interviews at the end of each chapter, you will find some common themes among this diverse group of people; they possess a surprising level of self-awareness, curiosity, and resilience. And you will find that they endorse and leverage many of the techniques discussed in the book. Most important, they understand how to accept failure, purposefully recharge and activate their creative spirit, regulate their emotions, and achieve a flow state. As Silva admits in Chapter 8, "The relationship between creativity and mood regulation is an important one for me."

Companies often think that building an innovation lab filled with unconventional meeting spaces for brainstorming and hiring a team of people whose job it is to invent will change the trajectory of their business and help them achieve creative velocity. Anointing a special team to be the company's inventors undermines the creative confidence of everyone else in the business required to execute the idea. Consequently, it is common that ideas that emerge from these labs don't materialize commercially because the business operators kill them, usually due to expert bias and a "that will never work" mentality that becomes a self-fulfilling prophecy. In his interview in Chapter 4, Scott Ehrlich, the chief innovation officer at Sinclair, points out, "There are different kinds of negative feedback, particularly in a company. It's not actually the idea but what that idea represents that is threatening. Negative feedback could mean fear." That fear can translate into a lack of creative thinking across job functions that are not normally perceived as imaginative and kills innovation, hindering the organization's ability to achieve creative velocity.

For a company to achieve creative velocity, most employees should share a reasonable level of creative confidence, also known as *creative self-efficacy*. Employees with creative confidence are more likely to initiate and engage in innovative processes and be open and willing to propose new ideas and solutions, an essential first step toward achieving creative velocity. Reaching creative velocity requires employees who feel empowered and confident in their creative abilities and who can use them to solve customers' problems, maximize productivity, face unexpected market challenges, and tackle new business opportunities. Companies that exhibit creative velocity have a pipeline of new ideas to explore, test, and iterate, high employee engagement, and the ability to adjust to unexpected events quickly. In my experience, which is also supported by multiple research studies, employees working in an environment that values their creativity show higher satisfaction and retention scores.

This book goes beyond theory and shares practical insights from C-level executives and entrepreneurs who have discovered that thinking differently is a strength, not a weakness. The individuals interviewed for this book all believe that certain cognitive attributes are crucial for achieving creative velocity. An open mindset, characterized by a willingness to consider new ideas, perspectives, and experiences, is foundational to developing the skills outlined in this book. It is necessary to support the six essential traits of these productive creative thinkers: discernment, flexibility, curiosity, resilience, reflection, and equanimity. Therefore, it's important to approach this book with an open mind as the first step to successfully training yourself to utilize the techniques in each chapter. The exercises at the end of each chapter allow you to practice these methods to help you creatively address business challenges, improve customers' outcomes, and rethink how work is done. Creative thinking isn't an inborn talent but a muscle that strengthens with exercise and is honed through deliberate practice and open-minded exploration.

You can develop and practice the skills and techniques in each chapter on your own or in a group, with or without AI as a partner. Training your brain to solve problems creatively is like learning to cook. You can use a single tool and still make something delicious to eat or combine the tools and techniques to produce more complex recipes. For example, building functional flexibility (Chapter 1) can expand your capacity for imagining mixtures (Chapter 2) and analogies (Chapter 3) and make it easier to disrupt the status quo (Chapters 4 and 5). Similarly, emotions (Chapter 6) and habits (Chapter 7) can impede or activate a flow state (Chapter 8), which is why equanimity is a foundational trait to help you reach peak creative performance.

All these techniques benefit from a playful attitude (Chapter 9), and taken together, they can enhance your storytelling abilities (Chapter 10) because playfulness encourages flexibility in thinking, another trait required to achieve creative velocity.

The Myths of Creativity

Creativity is often surrounded by misconceptions and myths that make it difficult to unleash our creative potential. From my adolescence through my early thirties, I found myself trapped in this web of falsehoods, struggling to navigate my way through it.

The first myth that took root in my beliefs was that creativity is synonymous with artistic talent. This notion seamlessly paved the way for the second myth I embraced: the belief that creativity was a gift bestowed at birth. I believed that this innate talent distinguished the creatively endowed from the rest of us. Both myths became closely tied in my mind to the third fallacy—the idea that creativity manifests solely through art. I was convinced that somewhere within me was buried an untapped well of creativity, waiting for the perfect medium to unleash it.

Driven by these beliefs, I embarked on a quest to uncover my hidden talent, taking piano, sculpting, acting, painting, and even dancing lessons. Yet, each venture ended in disappointment and disillusionment. My fingers stumbled over piano keys, lacking rhythm and musicality. My attempts at acting were met with scathing reviews, my artwork rarely rose above the level of refrigerator art, and my poor dancing bruised my body and soul. The diagnosis was swift and unforgiving: I was left-brained, sentenced to a life governed by logic and precision, a realm supposedly anathema to the creative spirit claimed by those of the right-brained persuasion.

The negative feedback I'd receive about my performances and string of failed artistic endeavors slowly chipped away at my creative confidence. Doubt crept in, undermining my dreams of ever identifying as a creative person.

It wasn't until later in life, working alongside some of the most innovative and creative minds—some of whom I interviewed for this book—that I had an epiphany. This significant realization changed my perception of creativity forever. Through their wisdom and my own experiences, I discovered that creativity isn't an elusive trait tucked away in the genetic code of the fortunate few. Creativity is accessible to anyone willing to embark on the journey to access it. And it needs to be nurtured, developed, and expanded with conscious intention.

Creative thinking can improve our approach to problems, transform complex processes, drive digital and physical product development, and reimagine how individuals conduct everyday activities like grocery shopping or paying for parking. The universe of creative people is not limited to those who can sculpt or sing a beautiful ballad or design a breathtaking space. It includes everyday people, like the person who in 1955 invented Velcro®; the ophthalmologist who realized he could replace a natural, cloudy lens from cataracts with a synthetic lens to restore vision in 1949; and the woman who invented and patented the windshield wiper in 1903. It was that realization that changed my life.

Furthermore, recent research has shown that the brain is far more complex than this simplistic right-brain/left-brain myth I had subscribed to. In fact, neuroscientists have found that creativity involves the simultaneous activation of both hemispheres and multiple regions within each hemisphere.[1] Groundbreaking discoveries in neuroscience demonstrate that creativity doesn't stay limited to one brain hemisphere. Instead, it emerges from the performance of both hemispheres, engaging multiple regions in a coordinated concert of neural activity. This revelation means that creativity grows and flourishes with the involvement of both hemispheres.

The myth of the "right-brained" artist or the "left-brained" logician obscures a more profound truth: creativity is a universal skill that engages the full spectrum of the brain's capabilities. The interplay among these varied regions forms the bedrock of creativity. While the right hemisphere has traditionally been activated by new and unfamiliar things, tying it intimately to creative endeavors, recent psychological research shifts the narrative. It suggests that the utility of an idea—its applicability and effectiveness—is as critical to the definition of creativity as its novelty. While generating novel ideas is essential to the creative process, evaluating their practicality and potential usefulness is equally important. By tapping into the analytical strengths of the left hemisphere, individuals can effectively assess an idea's value and feasibility, helping to ensure that only the most promising ideas are pursued.

Indeed, creative thought demands a rich array of cognitive functions—problem-solving, critical analysis, adaptability, curiosity, and the ability to forge connections across disparate domains. Creativity is equally about leveraging the capacity of one's imagination and designing innovative solutions to the tangible challenges that pervade science, business, and the activities of daily life. The act of creativity calls for a blend of analytical precision, intuitive leaps, and the flexibility to move between diverse modes of thinking that can adapt as the situation demands.

Throughout my career, I've observed how pervasive myths about creativity can limit teams, dampening their ambition to think expansively. From enduring numerous uninspired startup pitches to evaluating the contributions of countless employees, I've come to understand that creativity demands more than just the generation of new ideas. Indeed, this insight gains weight when considering not all patents have value. A deluge of inventive concepts may showcase an individual's imaginative prowess, yet without practical application, such ideas often fall by the wayside, deemed useless or pointless. The true formula for creativity includes a mix of all these variables: imagination, originality, value, and feasibility. The first two leverage the right brain, and the latter two lean into the left brain.

Humanity's prowess for creative thought has guided our species' constant adaptation and evolution. The cornerstone of fostering creativity lies in actively pursuing novel experiences, embracing the allure of the unknown, and approaching ideas with curiosity rather than immediate judgment. In the diverse roles I have occupied across various companies and industries, I have fostered a mindset that thrives on experimentation, values learning from blending perspectives, and is adept at viewing the world through a kaleidoscope of lenses—principles that have been instrumental in igniting and nurturing the creative energy within me.

From being an aspiring artist with unfulfilled dreams to making a mark in the world of technology innovation, my journey is a testament to the endless possibilities of creative skills. It challenges the notion that creativity is an innate gift and champions the idea that it is a craft that can be honed and enriched through dedication. The burgeoning body of scientific inquiry into creativity bolsters the view that every individual harbors the potential for creative thought. This starkly contrasts with a 2021 study that found that 58% of the participants believed that creative accomplishments usually result from sudden inspiration.[2]

In the contemporary discourse on creativity, few psychologists or research scientists in the twenty-first century believe that creativity comes from spontaneous brilliance, although there is some evidence that "eureka moments" exist. The people I interviewed at the end of each chapter have a common understanding of this point. They believe that certain preconditions—some of which are unique to them—must exist to increase the likelihood of having an "aha moment." By being aware of this context, they believe it is possible to intentionally increase the probability of having epiphanies. However, these light bulb moments are usually the result of prior knowledge and thoughts that have been simmering in the subconscious. This suggests that being open to new ideas and allowing them time to develop can inspire more profound creative ideas. Having an open mind that encourages the exploration of novel concepts is a common trait among the people I interviewed.

The myths surrounding creativity can act as barriers, obscuring our path to realizing our creative velocity. Yet, by debunking these myths and embracing creativity as a skill that can be cultivated, we unlock the door to boundless innovation. Dismissing the notion that creativity is the exclusive domain of the arts or a fixed trait, we can nurture this ability through targeted practice and engagement in activities that stimulate our cognitive faculties. By adopting a growth mindset and demonstrating grit and resilience, we can dispel these misconceptions, tapping into our innate creative energies to devise solutions and pioneer advancements in any endeavor.

Create. Generate. Make.

The notion that creativity encompasses the generation of ideas that are both novel and valuable echoes the sentiments of French mathematician Henri Poincaré, who posited, "To create consists precisely in not making useless combinations and in making those which are useful, and which are only a small minority. Invention is discernment, choice."[3] This perspective underscores a crucial aspect of creativity that AI, despite its advancements, struggles to replicate: the ability to discern which ideas are valuable and useful with ethics, empathy, genuine consciousness, and an understanding of the human experience.

The difference between "generative AI" and the "creative use of AI" goes beyond semantics. There is a significant distinction in capability and intention, particularly as AI becomes more ingrained in our daily lives. The ease of generating content quickly challenges the essence of human creativity. Though AI can produce new content, streamline tasks, and introduce diverse viewpoints, it falls short of the human capacity to understand usefulness, style, resonance, and taste. Unlike humans, AI lacks an understanding of art, literature, and music in their nuanced and subtle forms. And often, what makes these works meaningful lies within a metaphor, a figure of speech, or a symbol of an intangible feeling. It also may lie within our personal values. The content it generates, devoid of the human touch, can miss the authenticity and emotional resonance that define genuinely inspirational works. For instance, an AI might compose a poem with impeccable meter and rhyme. Yet, for the present, it will likely fail to capture the soul-stirring pathos or evoke the deep, genuine emotional response characteristic of poetry crafted by a human hand and borne from human experience.

Generate and *create* are often used interchangeably, but they convey distinct concepts. *Generate* implies producing something through a predefined set of rules or algorithms, a process inherently systematic and bounded by the parameters of existing data and models. On the other hand, *create* signifies a leap into the unknown, the birth of something new and original, not merely an iteration of what already exists but a true innovation, unfettered by the constraints that guide AI's output.

While *make* is used synonymously with *generate* or *create* in casual conversation to denote the act of production, it's essential to recognize its broader applicability. As the most versatile among the trio, *make* encompasses a wide array of activities. It can imply constructing, producing, or assembling something, whether from disparate parts or existing materials, aligning it more closely with *generate* in terms of its emphasis on the process rather than the novelty of the outcome. Additionally, *make* can signify the act of bringing something into existence or causing an event to occur, further broadening its scope of use.

Although the act of making can and often does involve creativity, it doesn't inherently require originality—a cornerstone of creativity. This distinction is crucial, as it underlines that the essence of creativity lies in its dedication to originality. While "making" might benefit from creative input, creativity should not be assumed to be present in the act of making anything. A good example of making something without creativity is following a box recipe to make a cake and bringing nothing new to the process.

Co-creating with Generative AI

AI's prowess in swiftly navigating through extensive datasets to unearth patterns, trends, and correlations is invaluable, particularly in market research, where understanding consumer behavior is critical. While AI accelerates the discovery of insights, the human role becomes crucial in navigating the complexities of intellectual property, ensuring authenticity and impact, and addressing biases. Thus, AI and human creativity form a symbiotic relationship, blending computational might with the nuanced application of curiosity, intuition, and discernment.

A pivotal role that humans play when collaborating with AI on ideation is ensuring the ongoing refinement of the problem statement provided in the prompts. The effectiveness of your AI collaboration hinges on the quality of the prompts and datasets used for its training. While AI can propose solutions, it falls upon humans to frame the right questions and precisely define the problem space. This requires a deep understanding of context, audience, and the desired impact of the creative endeavor. Humans play a vital role in steering AI toward outcomes that resonate with customer expectations and business objectives. The human touch should not influence results but rather inform the partnership through relevant inputs, practical constraints, and identification of necessary elements. Moreover, human input is indispensable when it comes to embodying brand values and catering to specific audience tastes. When co-creating with generative AI, using human discernment to evaluate the options is critical, principally because AI, despite its vast capabilities, lacks the understanding of human intricacies and cultural subtleties.

Scott Belsky, author, founder, former executive vice president at Adobe, and partner at A24, whose interview appears in Chapter 10, shares, "As the process part of creativity—chipping away at the stone or mixing the colors or iterating the pixels—becomes less of an obstacle, the other parts of creativity—the original idea, judgment, the innovations in process, and the story—become more important than ever."[4] Artificial intelligence may contribute to the volume of ideas and the narrative. Still, it cannot generate and infuse meaning into its output due to a limited understanding of the nuances of word choice, cultural distinctions, the compound nature of personal experiences, and the causes of emotional response.

Each chapter provides tips on partnering with generative AI when practicing these creative thinking techniques. By using the exercises at the end of each chapter, you will learn various approaches you can use to build creative confidence with or without AI as your partner. Some of them may be easier to convert to AI prompts than others. That is because the intent of this book is not to make you a better AI collaborator, although that is more than likely to happen. Instead, the goal is to unlock your creative confidence in your personal and professional lives by equipping you with various methods to accelerate your capacity to propel breakthrough ideas and achieve creative velocity.

CHAPTER 1

The MacGyver Mindset

"With a little bit of imagination, anything is possible."
—Angus MacGyver

In the 1980s, throughout the popular television series *MacGyver*, the title character is admired for his resourcefulness and talent for solving problems using everyday items. His imagination and ingenuity help him solve complex problems, catapulting the narrative forward with his cognitive skills. In one episode of the show, MacGyver used a ballpoint pen case to fix a car's fuel line. In another, he plays back an old phonographic record on a black cylinder using a piece of paper and a safety pin. In another example of functional flexibility, MacGyver fixed a broken rowing boat using a stick with a fork, a sleeping bag cover, some ropes, and a tarpaulin. MacGyver consistently escaped difficult situations by repurposing objects beyond their intended use, using his extensive knowledge, problem-solving mindset, and cognitive skills. The term "MacGyver" has become a part of our cultural vocabulary. Merriam-Webster defines it as the ability "to make, form, or repair something using whatever is conveniently on hand."[1] This skill involves looking beyond the intended uses of objects and repurposing their components to create inventive solutions.

MacGyver's success depended on many of the creative thinking skills we will cover in this book. For example, he demonstrated combinational and improvisational creativity, rule-breaking, and opposite thinking to tackle challenges, all of which will be discussed in later chapters. A lateral thinker, MacGyver was able to make associations between seemingly unrelated concepts. For example, in episode 6 of season 2, co-written by Kerry Lenhart and John Sakmar, whose interview appears at the end of this chapter, MacGyver used red wine to charge a battery. His ability to think on his feet and maintain an open mind when under stress were critical to his problem-solving skills. He was undeterred when faced with constraints because he was extremely confident in his understanding of how things worked and in his ability to improvise solutions with limited resources on hand. MacGyver was never hindered by knowledge of an object's conventional functionality when working toward his goals. He was naturally comfortable deconstructing the object to its simplest form, combining it with other items, or modifying elements of it to achieve a different purpose.

In the 1930s, German psychologist Karl Duncker identified the cognitive bias that blocks one's ability to repurpose objects beyond their intended use. By the 1940s, the term *functional fixedness*[2] gained traction with social scientists. Since then, researchers have investigated the causes of this bias and explored the circumstances that can help people avoid it and adopt a MacGyver mindset, which accelerates creative velocity. They discovered that the ability to creatively repurpose items depends upon flexible thinking and an open mind.

Functional fixedness arises from ingrained beliefs and rigid mindsets about how things work based on prior knowledge and experience. Researchers learned that while we use these beliefs as a mental shortcut, they narrow our vision and imagination over time.[3] Functional fixedness strengthens as we get older and can become part of our cognitive operating system. It can cause us to become focused or stuck on traditional and established solutions, preventing us from considering new and improved alternatives. This can hinder our ability to come up with creative ideas and may even make it difficult for us to consider innovative approaches to solving problems. The good news is there are techniques you can use to break fixations that will prevent you from seeing novel solutions.

For example, doodling engages our brain in a different activity, disrupting habitual thought patterns, which can help increase our functional flexibility. It encourages us to think beyond the usual associations with objects or tools. Doodling allows more abstract, free-flowing connections to form. Pat Copeland, whose interview appears in Chapter 9, has said, "Doodling serves as a stress reliever and gives us a view of our unconscious thoughts." This low-stress way of exploring our subconscious can open our minds to consider unconventional uses for familiar objects. In addition, the visual-spatial aspects of doodling can facilitate making novel associations and connections that can overcome a fixation on a single idea or approach. And since doodling is often described as aimless, it permits unexpected mixtures of shapes and forms without the pressure to produce a viable outcome. When we're less anxious about "getting it right," we're more open to exploring alternative solutions and breaking free from functional fixedness.

In a research study that explored the role of AI in extending human creativity, Northwestern researchers noted, "A key component of creativity involves abstraction, the process of learning how to make sense of information by identifying the conceptual components which are relevant" for meaning, mechanics and purpose.[4] Observing and analyzing objects, focusing specifically on their structure and potential for reuse, is foundational for overcoming functional fixedness and helpful when using analogic thinking, explored in more detail in Chapter 3.

In Chapter 4, you will learn more about the SCAMPER technique, a methodology that also benefits from breaking down an idea into its core components to challenge existing assumptions about its structure and encourage a fresh perspective. Introduced in the 1970s, SCAMPER prompts different actions to take to reformulate a novel solution that looks different than the current sum of a solution's parts. The "P" part of the SCAMPER methodology considers what can be "put to other use." Abstraction facilitates repurposing by increasing awareness of an object's components, their relationships within the design space, and how they collectively contribute to the overall utility and experience. This opens the mind to considering other ways to utilize or modify the parts and is essential to busting the bias of functional fixedness.

Design thinking is based on foundational tools such as ethnographic research, problem reframing, and experimentation, which help to avoid being stuck in conventional thinking. When engaging in design thinking, it is essential to abstract the specific problem at hand to eliminate cognitive bias and reduce attachment to a specific approach when creating potential solutions. By framing the challenge in a less concrete manner, it becomes possible to explore a wider range of potential solutions and overcome functional fixedness.

Ethnographic research, observing and understanding your target customer behaviors, is foundational to design thinking, and often reveals how customers develop workarounds and shortcuts in their current processes. Your lead customers are often the most motivated to MacGyver a solution if it makes their life easier. Design thinking requires you to be open to the broadest view of the problem space, as MacGyver would, which ensures you don't miss unconventional solutions hidden in plain sight. You may realize that the original issue you were trying to address is just a symptom of a different, deeper underlying problem, or you may find a solution from a different domain that can be applied to a new context. The objective of this approach is to be open to seeing more than the limited set of solutions you are considering.[5] Whether you use design thinking or SCAMPER, the important thing is to recognize the existence of conscious and unconscious biases that can constrain your capacity to generate initial ideas by limiting your openness to unexpected approaches.

When you hear a colleague say "This is how we have always done things" or "This is how things work," it may signal that the person is fixated on a specific way something functions and is resistant to considering alternative approaches. It can also indicate a closed mindset, which limits the possibilities they'd be willing to explore to identify novel solutions. These types of statements suggest a lack of cognitive flexibility and a resistance to looking at the challenge in a new way. After initially validating their fixed mindset, it will take a conscious effort to help them overcome that fixation because the conventional approach won't work. The goal is to move the person into a mental impasse when they realize for themself that the conventional approach isn't the only option.

Insight problems are one tool that can help challenge someone's specific assumptions or fixed mindset. They are a type of problem that requires a sudden restructuring or shift in perspective to solve. These problems are often difficult to solve using only logic and require visual, spatial, mathematical, or verbal skills. This type of problem requires restructuring the stated issue to overcome a mental block and reach a novel or counterintuitive solution. When trying to move a fixated person to a new perspective, begin by presenting a scenario or task that initially seems to require the functionally fixated use of the item. Then, slowly reframe the problem such that the functionally fixated solution is inadequate or impractical.

An example of an insight problem is the "Surgeon Riddle": A child is brought into the emergency room after a serious accident. The surgeon on duty looks at the child and exclaims, "I can't operate on this child; he is my son!" However, the surgeon is not the child's father. How is this possible? Of course, the surgeon is the child's mother. This problem requires letting go of gender bias, unconsciously assuming the surgeon must be a man.

You can reframe the problem and expand the solution set by providing an approach that challenges a fixated person's assumptions. In the 2015 article "Find Innovation Where You Least Expect It," published in the *Harvard Business Review*, Dr. Tony McCaffrey, a cognitive psychologist who has studied functional fixedness, suggests that one way around functional fixedness is to change how you describe the problem or the object. By reframing the issue, as you do when using design thinking, you can change the context of the solution.

For example, consider the Titanic collision. McCaffrey points out that if the goal had been reframed as "keep people out of the water" instead of just "save people," more solutions might have been considered, potentially leading to more survivors.[6] McCaffrey goes on to describe alternative approaches to only seating people in lifeboats, such as building a platform out of doors and lashing them to the lifeboats so more people could be saved than could fit in the lifeboat. Another idea was to use the tires from the 40 or so cars on the ship to create a raft upon which a mattress or door could be placed. McCaffrey even suggests that the lifeboats might have ferried people from the sinking ship to the iceberg, where they could have stayed dry while waiting for help to arrive. However, this solution would have required the passengers and crew to see the iceberg as a savior and not the enemy, which, under the stress of the situation and with the initial framing of the problem, was highly unlikely.

Generic Parts Technique

To overcome a tendency toward functional fixedness, McCaffrey suggests deconstructing the issue or object into discrete elements, which allows one to see it in its most general terms. His methodology, the Generic Parts Technique, depends upon the reduction of any issue or item to its simplest, most generalized description and the least defined use, repeatedly posing two questions: "Can this be decomposed further?" and "Does this description imply a use?"[7] With his colleague, Jim Pearson, McCaffrey studied the impact of generating generic descriptions of the elements on creative velocity and discovered that the group using this Generic Parts Technique (GPT) was better able to solve insight problems than the control group that was not taught this method.

Design fixation, a form of functional fixedness, occurs when designers exclusively focus on an object's intended function and their previous experience while neglecting other possibilities. This can happen when designers lean too heavily on existing or prior art, especially when they are under pressure to solve a problem quickly. Falling in love with an idea or an approach can also make it difficult to move beyond the initial design, causing the designer to become blind to its shortcomings or to new approaches. To protect against this, designers should consider less obvious aspects of the design and consider features that are easy to overlook. For instance, how does this affect the senses? How could the shape be transformed? How might the materials be changed? The SCAMPER methodology covered in more detail in Chapter 4 can potentially help overcome design fixation by prompting designers to explore different types of modifications and transformations to an existing design or concept.

As the Titanic example illustrates, sometimes the barrier to innovative solutions is a fixation on the goal. Goal fixedness arises from how the target outcome is defined and can limit consideration of adjacent or related ideas that don't seem to specifically address the stated outcome. This type of fixedness reflects a cognitive bias that causes an individual to narrowly focus on a specific goal, neglecting other important factors or alternative paths to achieve that goal. It can negatively impact the process of defining and articulating effective problem statements when teams embark on exploring, designing, and identifying novel solutions. Fixating on a goal, like fixating on an object's function, can narrow your field of vision. McCaffrey and Pearson point out that framing a problem in more general terms, using hypernyms, and choosing words that do not limit or imply the solution can invite new possibilities.

Hypernyms are words that represent a broader, more general category or concept. For example, the word *attach* covers a set of more specific terms, like connect, glue, staple, tape, pin, clamp, and more. *Hyponym* is the term that describes these more specific words. If your problem statement or object description uses hyponyms instead of hypernyms, you will not open doors to a wider range of potential solutions. Hypernyms can help remove unnecessary details, making the problem statement easier to understand. They can also make it easier to deconstruct an object as the sum of its most generic parts, enabling new solutions to emerge.

The purpose of the Generic Parts Technique is to abstract a concept or object to dissect the problem into its constituent parts. The first step is to describe the topic in general terms using hypernyms to describe broader categories. For example, if you're out hiking and injure your leg, you may need to make a makeshift splint out of what you have on hand, like MacGyver. To explore all possible solutions to this problem, you could start by creating a general statement such as, "I need to design a flexible and easy-to-apply support structure that can be used in various situations to restrict the movement of a nonfunctional limb." The basic components for this would then include an adjustable restrictive enclosure, an immobilization component, and an attachment mechanism. Now you can envision how to address each of these needs using the resources available to you.

Exquisite Corpse Technique

My friend Kate Collins introduced me to the Exquisite Corpse technique, which originated with the Surrealist artists in Paris in the 1920s. Participants add to a composition in sequence, by following a specific rule and by only seeing the end of what the previous person contributed. Players create, in turn, an image on a sheet of paper, fold it to conceal most of their work, and then pass it to the next player for a further contribution. No one knows what comes before or after their work. The game was originally played by writers with words, not pictures, which is the source of the technique's name. The phrase "Le cadavre exquis boira le vin nouveau" ("The exquisite corpse shall drink the new wine") was collaboratively created using this technique, leading to the French name "cadavre exquis."[8]

This technique also demonstrates the effectiveness of the "yes and" approach in generating new ideas. Breaking free from a linear mindset and preconceived notions about how the parts combine to create the final image is crucial for overcoming functional fixedness. The game's random collaborative process creates unexpected and bizarre combinations, reflecting the Surrealists' intention to embrace the irrational and unconscious. Evolving from a parlor game, Exquisite Corpse is not limited to combining words in a Mad Libs–style format. Individuals can draw the elements directly on the paper or produce a collage to create the figure. The game's emphasis on spontaneity, chance, and collaboration, as well as the unexpected output, makes it accessible to artists as well as nonartists.

The benefit of the Exquisite Corpse exercise is that it taps into the unconscious creative process, leaving linear thinking aside. The technique produces unexpected results that defy traditional logic. To encourage this, the technique has very few rules beyond not sharing your work before the figure is complete. Contributors are encouraged to use abstract shapes and patterns rather than realistic images to inspire more creative and unconventional combinations. This also allows for the use of metaphors to communicate abstract concepts about the figure. For instance, the pattern or color chosen can communicate tension, style, or emotion. A fluffy white cloud positioned as the hair on the head of the corpse might communicate the character being created is spacey or absent-minded. Or choosing to cut out a pair of angel wings instead of arms could imply a mythical creature. Using watches as eyes, for example, has layered meaning here. Using a timepiece may convey the character's age and, simultaneously, can communicate the act of observing, or watching, attentively.

Allowing each contributor to the project the private time to think, imagine, and create helps to suspend judgment and criticism, thus creating an environment where unconventional and innovative ideas can thrive. This approach can help overcome functional fixedness because no contributor is tied to the prior art.

Figure 1.1 Exquisite Corpse Art Project.
©2024 Borg-Olivier, Collins, Storch, Thygesen

Additionally, it fosters a playful mindset, which we will explore further in Chapter 9, by acknowledging that there is no single correct answer. It reduces the stress that hinders creativity, as contributors are required only to comply with a very limited set of rules. Kate described her experience in art class building the Exquisite Corpse, shown in Figure 1.1, as liberating. However, she mentioned that she and her classmates had to first get comfortable with the strange and nonsensical possibilities for how the final product might appear.

As Kerry Lenhart, one of the writers interviewed at the end of this chapter, points out, "Creatively, I think we all stand on the shoulders of those who created before us, people who inspired us. When MacGyver creates his various objects, he uses found bits and pieces scavenged from objects built by others. Often, when John and I are creating projects, we scavenge ideas rather than objects. And, like MacGyver, we hope we are using them in new and unexpected ways."

Partnering with Generative AI

When working with generative AI tools, it's important to consider their limitations as collaborators in developing functional flexibility. These tools lack a deep understanding of the complexities of human experience, which can hinder their ability to recognize or adapt to functional fixedness. While partnering with these tools for a generic parts technique exercise may be feasible, engaging them in an exquisite corpse exercise could prove more challenging.

That is because the process of co-creating with generative AI is characterized by its linear and logical nature, making it suitable for the systematic problem-solving approach of Generative Parts Technique. The structured format of such exercises necessitates clear prompts and systematic approaches to building, which aligns well with the capabilities of generative AI tools.

Using structured methodologies to remove fixations can improve a co-creation partnership with AI. An example of a generative AI tool that can help guide you through the process of abstracting a problem and ideating solutions is the Supermind Ideator, built on ChatGPT and developed by the MIT Center for Collective Intelligence's Design Lab. It leverages a methodology that suggests "moves" people can make to accelerate their creativity. This approach's "basic design moves" align well with the generic parts technique; queries prompt you to zoom in and out of the problem and then explore analogies that might provide the cue for a solution.[9] Looking at both the generalized and detailed perspectives of the specific problem can help break functional fixedness and open novel paths to a solution. This approach to partnering with the generative AI gives your computational partner the responsibility of providing you with challenging questions to help break the box you feel you may be stuck in creatively.

When trying to let go of design or goal fixation, you may find generative AI tools are less flexible than you would have hoped. This can be due to the nature of the prompt used to co-create. The more specific the brief you use in your prompt, the narrower the field of vision your generative AI partner will take. Researchers in Australia have found that generative AI tools may restrict exploration based on vocabulary provided in the prompts and that "the effectiveness of co-ideation with AI rests on participants' chosen approach to prompt creation and on the strategies used by participants to generate ideas in response to the AI's suggestions."[10] The research showed that providing abstractions to the problem can improve the effectiveness and diversity of the AI output. Using hypernyms instead of hyponyms can help abstract the problem when you craft your prompts.

How effectively you define the problem schema to your AI partner carries a lot of the weight of your success when co-creating with computational tools. The problem schema refers to the details and vocabulary used to structure a challenge or task so the AI can process, analyze, and respond constructively to the prompt. You might ask AI for help generating ideas, but if you frame your creative boundaries too narrowly, your AI partner could produce ideas that don't consider disruptive solutions that may still meet your needs. Intention and purpose should guide the AI's approach without building in the fixations and biases that limit exploration.

It might challenge your natural tendency to be ambiguous and nonspecific, but this is essential to removing any intrinsic bias in how you express the issue to avoid fixation. It is also crucial not to fixate on any one idea that emerges. Take your time wandering through the ideation process and evolving the initial output.

Interview with Kerry Lenhart and John Sakmar

I met John and Kerry in 1994 when they were scouting locations in Seattle for a Fox Network medical drama series they created called *Medicine Ball*. At the time, I was working at the Washington State Film Office supporting TV series and film productions, like *Northern Exposure* and *Sleepless in Seattle*. Kerry and John have had an illustrious career in television since the mid-1980s, writing for and producing series including *MacGyver, Boston*

(continued)

Public, Ally McBeal, Chicago Hope, Psych, Mr. and Mrs. Smith, and, more recently, *Kingdom Business* on BET. During their time working on *MacGyver*, they shared that they were relied upon for their capacity to create "MacGyverisms."

1. As writers on the show, what does it mean to "Think like MacGyver?"

To think like MacGyver, you have to get into an ingenious, inventive, and problem-solving mindset. You want to be as creative, knowledgeable, analytical, resourceful, improvisational, and calm under pressure as you can. I wish there was a cool acronym to encapsulate those, but I can't think of one. They're all important, and they all work together. They're all parts of the whole that make MacGyver, MacGyver.

To think like MacGyver means thinking *creatively*. It takes imagination and innovative thinking to find unconventional solutions to problems.

To think like MacGyver means thinking *knowledgeably*. Drawing on a broad base of knowledge, particularly in science, engineering, and general mechanics, to inform decision-making.

To think like MacGyver means thinking *analytically*. Assessing situations quickly and effectively to understand the core issues and potential solutions.

To think like MacGyver means thinking *resourcefully*. Looking at the resources you have with fresh eyes. Thinking about other ways they could be used. Being open to repurposing everyday objects to serve new functions.

To think like MacGyver means thinking *improvisationally*. Adapting to new challenges on the fly, thinking outside the box to devise practical solutions in real time.

And finally, to think like MacGyver means thinking while remaining *calm under pressure*. Maintaining your composure and clear thinking helps you effectively solve problems even in high-stress or emergency situations.

In a nutshell, to think like MacGyver is to be a quick-thinking, inventive problem-solver who can navigate complex situations with limited resources by leveraging creativity, knowledge and adaptability.

2. **Do you have a personal favorite "MacGyverism" from the episodes you contributed to? What makes it stand out to you, and what was the creative process behind it?**

The first episode that John and I wrote was episode 6 of season 2. It was called "Jack of Lies" and introduced the character Jack Dalton. Jack was an old friend of Mac-Gyver's and needed his help to rescue a friend being held hostage in South America. MacGyver learns that this friend is being held captive inside a heavily guarded monastery filled with cloistered monks. MacGyver manages to break into the monastery but is discovered and pursued by Colonel Antunez, the murderous villain of the episode. As Antunez searches the monastery for MacGyver, he sees that all the monks inside are wearing floor-length hooded robes. Suspecting that MacGyver has disguised himself in a robe, he begins to pull the hoods from monks so he can see their faces.

Eventually, Antunez enters a room where one vulnerable monk, his back to Antunez, stands alone. Antunez approaches . . . reaches for the hood to pull it back . . . and is caught completely off-guard when the monk punches him in the face! How does this monk throw a roundhouse punch without even turning around? We discover that the "monk" is indeed MacGyver. But he was *not* standing with his back to Antunez as it appeared. He was actually *facing* Antunez, but wearing the robe backwards!

The thing that John and I loved about this MacGyverism was the simplicity of it. We had been told by executive producers on the show that every MacGyverism

(*continued*)

didn't need to involve MacGyver mixing chemical compounds gleaned from everyday objects to make an explosive. Or involve complicated mechanics to build a rocket launcher or booby-trap from gathered pieces of discarded or disassembled machinery. What makes MacGyver, the character, special, is that he can look at *any* object and see how it can be used in ways that were not intended. A monk's robe is not intended to be worn backwards, and MacGyver used that to his advantage.

This particular MacGyverism was inspired by Buster Keaton. I have a collection of his silent movies, and he's known to be a genius for inventing silent film "gags." In one movie I had seen, Buster needed to hide from someone who was chasing him. He put on a long trench coat, pulled the collar up over his head, and hung himself from a wall hook alongside other coats. Then he pulled his feet up and simply blended in with the other empty coats! We loved this idea so much that we actually used it in the same episode above; MacGyver hung himself up on a wall hook alongside other empty robes. After that, John and I simply brainstormed to think of other ways we could make use of the robe. The backward robe was what we came up with, but it was Buster Keaton's genius that put our train of thought on the right track.

3. How do you re-energize your creative spirit during periods of frustration or stagnation? Where do you find inspiration?

Inspiration can be found anywhere if you look for it. And, more often, when you don't. You can't force inspiration. Or make it happen. You can certainly put yourself in an environment that is more *conducive* to inspiration striking.

Sometimes I'll browse books at a bookstore. Or a library. Both for inspiration and to see what's trending. What are people reading? What do they like? What genres are popular? Same can be said for movies. A spontaneous matinee might seem like an indulgence or "playing hooky," but one scene, or plot device, or style of filmmaking, or actor's performance, or song, or musical moment might spark something.

To re-energize your creative spirit during periods of frustration or stagnation, try a change of scenery. Or environment. If possible, get away. Go outdoors. Go for a walk. Go on a hike. To the beach. Up a mountain. When you "get away from it all"—and if you're quiet—you might be surprised what you find. What inspires you. Speaks to you. Away from distractions and foolishness, you might actually have an epiphany. Keep your senses open. It sounds counterintuitive, but when you rest, your brain keeps working. Making connections. You might be surprised by what pops into your head.

Switching gears is also good. If "task A" is vexing you, frustrating you, stymieing you, don't force it. Pivot to "task B." It's amazing how your brain will "work on" task A and offer a solution when you're not focused on it. Not forcing it. Let inspiration *happen*. Naturally.

4. **How important is failure or the acceptance of failure in cultivating creativity?**

What is creative failure? John and I have pitched countless ideas that we have loved. We think they would make amazing television shows. Yet, in spite of our best efforts, no one has bought the idea and asked us to develop it into a script. Is that failure? If we were to *accept* that as failure we would need to ignore everything we believe; everything that our gut is telling us about the value of our creation; everything that *we* love about our creation. At times like this we sit back and evaluate; are *we* crazy or is everyone else? Is it an issue of right idea, wrong audience? Or is it simply a bad idea?

(continued)

How we define failure can also impact how we handle it. If you walk into a room looking for your keys and they are not the first place you look, have you failed? You look someplace else. Not there either? Now have you failed? Let's say you look a dozen more places, but you still haven't found the keys. Now have you failed? Maybe at this time you realize that you must be looking in the wrong room so you search a different one. Still no keys. But in this new room you find your tennis shoes.

The tennis shoes remind you that you played tennis last night. Aha! You go into your closet and find your keys in the side pocket of your tennis bag. Success! Now, if you had stopped searching after the first place you looked, that would have been a failure. You could say that every place you looked and didn't find the keys was a failure. But they weren't. They were all necessary steps leading you to where you would eventually find the keys.

That's the way I feel about creativity; you haven't failed until you give up. Sure, it's not always possible to cling to an idea or concept as long as you'd like because there are deadlines to work with and people other than yourself to please. But don't think of it as failure; it's a course correction. Years of *experience* has taught us that we're not going to run out of ideas; whether we like it or not, we can always "accept failure" and do the note. And maybe create something even better.

5. **Everyone knows a famous story about a flash of brilliance—a eureka moment when innovation happened. Has that happened to you? What were the circumstances and the idea?**

It may sound counterintuitive, but a flash of brilliance sometimes comes *after* you've "done your homework." It often comes after you've surveyed the landscape, read the room, gotten a lay of the land, noticed what's in the Zeitgeist, or considered the competition. Other times, a flash of brilliance is truly a response to creative problem-solving. They say, "Necessity is the mother of invention." And we have discovered that often leads us to flashes of brilliance.

On *MacGyver*, we knew that the actor playing the title character (played by Richard Dean Anderson) was being pushed to the limits, long hours, stunt work, appearing in every scene, carrying the show single-handedly. In a flash of brilliance, we imagined a guest character—Jack Dalton—as a friend/buddy/sidekick for MacGyver who proved to be so good and so well-liked that he was brought back 18 times. This gave the Mac-Gyver actor some much-needed and well-deserved relief and gave us fresh fuel for storylines.

Exercises

INSIGHT PROBLEM
Scenario:
Three friends decide to rent a hotel room for the night. The room costs $30, so they each contribute $10. Later, the hotel manager realizes that the room rate should have been $25. He gives the bellhop a $5 bill to return to the guests. The bellhop, being dishonest, pockets $2 and gives each guest back $1. Now, each guest has paid $9 for the room, totaling $27. The bellhop has $2.

Challenge:
Adding these together, we get $29. Where is the missing dollar?
The answer to this challenge appears in the back of the book.

PRACTICE THE GENERIC PARTS TECHNIQUE (GPT)

Exercise 1: Everyday Objects
1. **Object Selection:** Pick a common household object, like a blender, a teakettle, or a lamp.
2. **Break It Down:** List all the parts of the object. Can any of these parts be further broken down?

3. **Functional Inventory:** List the elements or components of the item at the most atomic level.

4. **Reimagine Functions:** Consider each item listed has a typical function. Now, imagine it in a more generic category. What other functions could it have in this broader sense?

Exercise 2: Scenario-Based Problems

1. **Problem Setup:** Describe a typical situation that requires a solution, such as pulling up a dandelion weed.

2. **Identify Needs**: List the basic needs to resolve the situation. For example, it must be long enough to get the whole root.

3. **Identify the Tool:** Imagine a new tool that could potentially solve the problem, but there's a catch: it must be adapted from existing products that were not originally designed for this intended use.

4. **Apply Generic Parts Technique:** Break down the tool into its parts and consider how each part's generic functionalities can address the problem creatively.

Exercise 3: Open-Ended Exploration

1. **Choose a Hypernym:** Pick a broad category like "carrier" or "connector."

2. **Imagine Unusual Applications:** Think of situations where a typical item like a carrier or connector might not be readily available. How could you use the generic concept of carrier or connector to address the situation creatively using everyday objects and accomplish the same action? What is required for an item to functionally be considered a "carrier" or "connector"?

PRACTICE THE EXQUISITE CORPSE TECHNIQUE (GROUP)

This group exercise is adapted from a similar one on the Museum of Modern Art website.[11] You can do this exercise as a drawing or as a collage. You will need three to four players. I recommend first attempting it as a collage as described here so you are not constrained by your or your teammate's drawing skills.

As a group, you will contribute to the design of a creature without seeing what the others have contributed. When you repeat this exercise, choose a different figure or structure to create.

♦ **Collect scissors, glue, and an 8.5 × 11 sheet of paper.**

♦ **Take a piece of paper and fold it into the same number of equal parts as there are contributors.**

♦ **Grab a stack of random magazines, newspapers, or junk mail you don't mind cutting up.**

♦ **As you browse the media you have collected, look for evocative shapes, colors, patterns, and images that capture your imagination.** Feel free to cut them into unexpected shapes to help communicate the part of the body.

♦ **Build a collage on the top section of the paper** to create the head of an imaginary character. Limit the time each person has to collect the items and build their section to no more than 15 minutes.

♦ **Fold your image back to conceal it.** Extend the base of your character's neck over the edge of the fold so that your collaborator will know how to connect their image to yours.

♦ **Pass the paper on to a collaborator.** Keep your image hidden and have them add a body to your figure in the middle section of the page.

♦ **Repeat.** Pass the paper to a third person, concealing the first two sections of the page, and have them add the legs and feet. If you are working with four collaborators, then hide that section and pass it to a fourth person to add the feet. Remember to carry over just the end of your section through the fold into each new section so the following person knows where to start.

♦ **Unfold the page and reveal your collaborative image.** Reflect upon each collaborator's choices.

CHAPTER 2

When X Meets Y

"There is no such thing as a new idea. We simply take a lot of old ideas and put them into a sort of mental kaleidoscope."
—Mark Twain

Humans constantly assess similarities and differences—assessing whom they socialize with, whose recommendations to take, and what online reviews matter. These assessments are intended to make us comfortable by leveraging things we are familiar with to make decisions in daily life. Everyone has this skill, yet it is not always a skill people consciously deploy to generate new ideas. As far back as the eighteenth century, philosopher David Hume recognized that the human imagination naturally could manipulate ideas and impressions in various ways, such as uniting, compounding, or composing them into entirely new ideas.[1]

"When X Meets Y," also known as a mixture description or combination, involves taking two familiar concepts, genres, products, or ideas (X and Y) and imagining what it would look like if they were combined or if elements of one were introduced into the other. This blending prompts creative thinking and can lead to innovative or novel ideas that might not have been discovered through linear thought processes. This technique is a good launchpad for activating your creative muscles. Instead of starting from a blank slate, you can use existing concepts as building blocks, making the creative process more accessible and less intimidating.

Mixture descriptions serve as a dynamic tool in crafting compelling narratives, effectively harnessing vivid imagery to encapsulate a vision's core. This technique, pivotal in both business pitches and creative storytelling, such as film scripting, leverages the fusion of disparate disciplines, concepts, and elements to inspire and activate one's audience.

The concept of mixtures extends beyond merely fusing physical products; it also encompasses integrating disparate services to forge novel and enticing customer experiences. A prime example of this innovative synergy is the melding of car maintenance and detailing with valet parking services. This combination caters to drivers who find their vehicles stationary for prolonged periods, whether at home or the office. Companies like Driveway, Wrench, and Roda have redefined convenience by marrying valet services with the labor-intensive tasks of car maintenance. They offer solutions where cars are serviced on-site at a customer's location or through a valet system that manages the pickup and return of vehicles post-repair. Roda takes it a step further by providing the flexibility to have vehicles picked up from and returned to different locations, revolutionizing the traditional car repair experience, which typically involves driving to a service location and waiting or finding alternate transportation until the vehicle is ready.

Utilizing mixture descriptions to articulate the essence of movies and startups has long been a popular strategy. It grounds the audience in familiar references while simultaneously surprising them with an amalgamation of seemingly discordant elements. Take, for instance, Fox Network's promotion of *Scream Queens*, described as a blend of *Glee* and *American Horror Story*,[2] but situated within the confines of a university setting. The specificity that both components originate from the creative mind of Ryan Murphy alters the perception differently than a blend labeled "*Glee* meets *Scream* [the movie]" would because the style and tone of the movie directed by Wes Craven would predict a different output. Adding qualifiers, such as "set in a university," introduces new dimensions and contexts, enriching the original mix with attributes previously unassociated with either element.

While this approach can lead to innovative ideas, its success often depends on execution and the ability to find a meaningful and coherent way to integrate the elements of X and Y. The viability of the mixture idea is not the only thing that matters. The usefulness of the combined idea must be apparent to the target audience, and the cost of accessing that value must be proportional. Mixtures may seem novel and still fail to resonate with audiences or users due to a lack of coherence in the combination or poor execution.

Although not every mashup transforms into a groundbreaking innovation, even those deemed of lesser value can ignite the fuse for subsequent, novel ideas. Embracing discomfort is essential within the creative journey. During the ideation phase, dismissing a combination is tempting due to its seemingly outlandish nature or team members' skepticism about its apparent impracticalities. However, this approach enhances the ideation process by expanding the range of possible combinations considered, potentially leading to more innovative and creative outcomes. Shutting down these initial, wild ideas prematurely can inadvertently close the door to potential creative breakthroughs.

One of the most formidable challenges in crafting mashups is bridging the gap between disparate elements and navigating the discomfort arising from their incongruity. This process demands an open-minded exploration and the courage to venture beyond conventional boundaries, recognizing that the potential for genuine innovation lies within the tension of unlike combinations. Roger Martin, author of *The Opposable Mind*, writes about great leaders, "They have the predisposition and the capacity to hold in their heads two opposing ideas at once. And then, without panicking or simply settling for one alternative or the other, they can creatively resolve the tension between those two ideas by generating a new one that contains elements of the others but is superior to both. This process of consideration and synthesis can be termed integrative thinking."[3]

Combinational or Combinatorial?

You can increase the novelty and velocity of ideas just by connecting seemingly unrelated concepts and discovering similarities that can lead to breakthrough solutions. Maria Popova, author and publisher of *The Marginalian*, writes on the topic of creativity, "In order for us to truly create and contribute to the world, we have to be able to connect countless dots, to cross-pollinate ideas from a wealth of disciplines, to combine and recombine these pieces and build new castles."[4]

Combinational creativity focuses on combining ideas—usually from the same or nearby domains—in new ways and describes how individuals mentally reorganize existing knowledge to generate creative outcomes. Combinational creativity has been the source of centuries of innovation. More recently, the Swiffer Sweeper is a good example of combinational creativity. Combining the concept of a wet mop with disposable dry dusting cloths that attract dirt, dust, and hair off the floors is a cleaning innovation that eliminates the use of a dustpan and broom, as well as a sponge mop. Simply changing the cloths, converts the Sweeper from dry to wet.

Combinatorial creativity, on the other hand, is often discussed in the context of innovations where breakthroughs are achieved by synthesizing diverse knowledge and ideas from different domains. Unlike combinational creativity, which focuses on combining ideas usually from the same or nearby domains, combinatorial creativity is frequently associated with significant innovations that arise from the intersection of distinct fields. Combinatorial products can be game-changing despite being created out of existing products.

A centuries-old combinatorial product, the Gutenberg press was a combination of a screw press designed for oil and wine production with movable type previously developed centuries earlier in China using porcelain. The formulation of oil-based ink suitable for printing on paper was modified to work with the new press technology. Combining existing solutions alone would not have ensured legibility and scale.[5] By synthesizing these disparate elements from different domains (winemaking, ink production, and earlier printing techniques), Gutenberg created a revolutionary device that dramatically increased the speed and efficiency of book production, leading to the widespread dissemination of knowledge and information. This combination of diverse ideas and technologies exemplifies combinatorial creativity.

Since the difference is somewhat nuanced, combinational creativity and combinatorial creativity are often used interchangeably in discussions about the creative process. Both terms describe new ideas or innovations that are created by combining existing ideas, knowledge, or elements in new ways. The core principle behind both concepts is that creativity is not about conjuring something entirely new from nothing but rather about recombining what already exists into novel forms or solutions. The practice of blending distinct entities to spawn innovation is one of the most accessible and versatile forms of creativity. Seventy-seven percent of all patents granted between 1790 and 2010 are coded by a combination of at least two technology codes.[6]

The founder of Ring, which marries a video camera and a doorbell, explains the benefit of this type of compound creativity. "In my early days as an inventor, I realized the importance of developing a product that people were already familiar with," Jamie Siminoff explains. "By giving a new purpose to something that already existed, I could avoid what I refer to as 'over-invention,' which is essentially creating something so unique and new that consumers need an in-depth explanation to understand it."[7]

Mixture descriptions serve as a foundational mechanism in combinatorial creativity by providing a structured way to think about how disparate elements can be combined. Looking at the core components of a solution using the Generic Parts Technique, for example, and then understanding what each element does, how each one works, and what its intended purpose is can simplify the process of choosing what to combine. This can also provide a vocabulary and a conceptual framework for imagining how the blending of these elements might occur, facilitating the creative process. Mixture descriptions inherently involve thinking across traditional domain boundaries, a hallmark of combinatorial creativity. By exploring how elements from unrelated areas can be combined, mixtures can lead to breakthrough innovations that arise from cross-domain insights.

Twists and Qualifiers

When thinking about combinations, it may be helpful to consider twists and qualifiers as the seasoning that adds flavor. They encourage deep exploration of a concept, considering its implications, variations, and potential in a more nuanced way. A twist or qualifier adds complexity and depth to the initial combination. This can lead to a richer investigation of the idea and uncover possibilities that might not have been immediately apparent. Twists refer to unexpected or surprising changes to a combination of ideas. Twists can introduce an element of novelty by further juxtaposing seemingly unrelated concepts in an unconventional manner. For example, the Long Wharf Supply Company is a clothing company that combines the "buy one, give one" model with sustainably made clothing from oyster shells; rather than providing clothing to someone in need, the charitable twist is that the company contributes funds from product sales through charitable partnerships to the reseeding of coastal oyster reefs that naturally filter seawater.

On the other hand, qualifiers refer to additional constraints, conditions, or specifications that are applied to an existing combinational idea or concept to re-focus it. Qualifiers act as modifiers of the combined idea, usually to make the combined idea attractive to a specific market segment. For example, Kardia introduced a medical-grade electrocardiogram (EKG), the KardiaMobile Card, and turned a piece of high-end medical equipment into a portable consumer device. In 2012, Bluetooth and heart rate monitors were first combined to send readings from electrodes attached to a human torso to a doctor's cell phone.[8] The qualifier in the KardiaMobile case was the miniaturization to enable accessibility to consumers. Combining Bluetooth with miniaturized versions of EKG components, the credit card–sized device uses a single lead design to record a medical-grade EKG in seconds on its accompanying mobile app. KardiaMobile Card users can detect AFib, Bradycardia, and Tachycardia giving them more control of their health care.

Qualifiers add an unexpected element that can significantly differentiate a new idea. They often increase an idea's relevancy to a particular community or audience. Qualifiers can help bring an innovative solution into focus, but they can also complexify it. The introduction of additional attributes or context can add layers of depth that can just as easily enhance or detract from the original combination. By identifying and addressing potential shortcomings in the original combination, in this case the lack of portability, the right qualifier can help ensure that the idea has value and purpose to a new audience. An effective qualifier can make an idea more meaningful, differentiated, and resonant. On the other hand, the twist should fuel further creative thinking by introducing a new dimension into the process that is not immediately obvious.

An effective twist or qualifier can uplevel or disrupt a mixture of two ideas. But how do you know what makes a good twist or qualifier? First, it is important to have a deep understanding of the audience for whom the idea is intended. This helps ensure the idea is relevant and coherent in the context of the target customers' needs. It should provide an angle that is not immediately obvious, inviting people to see the combination in a new light. Ideally, the twist should fulfill a need or address a gap that wasn't addressed by the initial combination of X and Y, and, more importantly, its addition should represent something neither X nor Y brought to the mixture.

Playing with constraints, scale, and context can reveal unexpected insights or opportunities. In her interview in the next chapter, Denny Post, the former chief marketing officer (CMO) of T-Mobile and chief executive officer (CEO) of Red Robin, proposes that "working within a set of constraints is where the smartest work gets done." She believes that constraints, like twists and qualifiers added to a mixture, force you to go deeper into the problem space, and they can help create focus on the most important challenge to address or customer to serve. The strategic use of qualifiers and innovative twists can introduce disruptive elements or emphasize critical attributes, such as "X meets Y, tailored for seniors," offering a novel thematic direction or grounding the fusion in a distinct feature.

Adding elements that challenge the expected combination of ideas or concepts often encourages rethinking how they can be integrated or applied. Twists have the power to pivot the narrative, incorporating fresh ideas into the mix that might not have been initially apparent. For instance, The Mirror workout platform ingeniously melds the functionality of traditional home fitness equipment with the interactivity of live online classes, all within the guise of a conventional mirror. The Mirror also includes a camera for an instructor to see you, making it a two-way experience. This clever bidirectional twist turns a mirror into a piece of fitness equipment for at-home workouts, redefining home fitness paradigms.

Beyond the realms of entertainment and technology, mixture descriptions have revolutionized service experiences. The inception of drive-in diners and drive-in movies, marrying the quintessential American pastimes of dining and cinema with the burgeoning automotive culture of the early twentieth century, exemplifies such innovation. As these hybrid experiences gained traction, entrepreneurs sought unique twists—like roller-skating car hops—to distinguish and enhance their offerings.

One of the most prevalent combination products, the all-in-one printer, fax, and copier, was hailed by the *Los Angeles Times* in a 1994 article titled "The Cutting Edge: COMPUTING / TECHNOLOGY / INNOVATION: Multipurpose Machine Combines Printer, Copier, Fax in a Compact Space."[9] The twist that accelerated the value of this invention was the inclusion of digital technology, which opened the door for new capabilities to be added and integrated, like scanning (which was added in the early 2000s), Wi-Fi and network connectivity, and image manipulations.

Blending Distant Domains

The essence of crafting impactful mixture descriptions lies in the significant difference, or the delta, between the combined elements, referred to as X and Y. Merging two entities that share too much similarity seldom paves the way for groundbreaking ideas. Instead, such combinations often culminate in hybrid products representing a compromise rather than a true innovation. The Spork serves as a quintessential example of this principle. Joining a spoon and a fork ends up creating a utensil that features a diminished spoon bowl and truncated tines—a compromise that, while offering convenience to some users, may not justify its existence across all scenarios.

Superficial blends like the Spork tend to yield innovations that only slightly deviate from their origins. These can lead to products that might encroach upon the market share of their predecessors or, at best, carve out a niche market. This is particularly true when the combination merely tweaks the original items without significantly enhancing them or when the hybrid product dilutes the most valuable features of each original. True innovation requires a bolder approach, seeking combinations where the juxtaposition of X and Y unleashes new functionalities, solves unaddressed problems, or taps into unexplored markets, transcending incremental improvements.

In 1941, a Swiss engineer named George de Mestral was out hunting with his dog. He noticed that his pants and dog's hair were covered in a burdock plant. His curiosity about how things work led him to study the burdock under a microscope, and he found thousands of tiny hooks that powerfully bound themselves to nearly any fabric, including his pants and his dog's hair. De Mestral had an idea to combine the hooks he had seen in the burdock with simple loops of fabric. The tiny hooks would catch in the loops and create a powerful connection.[10] He imagined combining a burr and fabric into a fastener, but it was not until 20 years later that the invention found its usefulness. NASA was struggling to keep objects attached to walls while floating in orbit. About the time they discovered the VELCRO® Brand fastener system, fashion designers did, too, and the invention took off.

It is essential to look for pairings that have structural similarities but come from different domains to maximize the distance between the combined elements and increase the chances of an original outcome. Finding a distant domain that provides a strong counterpoint to the base domain involves several considerations. First, it is essential to look for underlying principles, mechanisms, or processes that are common to both domains but manifest in different ways. Then, identify what strengths or capabilities are missing or underdeveloped in the base domain and look for distant domains where those strengths are noticeable. For example, if the base domain lacks a native mobile experience, it might make sense to look to social media or gaming for inspiration. Solutions to complex problems often come from unexpected places. By applying knowledge or methodologies from one domain to another, it's possible to find unique solutions that wouldn't be visible from within the problem domain itself.

Combinational creativity is a robust framework that enriches the creative process, with or without the aid of generative AI. Suitable for individual and team endeavors, it enhances ideational fluency and ignites the imagination. The potency of the resulting ideas is directly proportional to the disparity between the elements being combined—the greater the difference, the more radical the ideas. Conversely, the innovations tend to be more incremental when the elements share a closer relation, as seen with the Spork. Surface-level combinations typically involve entities within the same domain or category that share attributes, making idea generation somewhat more straightforward due to the apparent structural similarities and when a twist or qualifier may infuse new value. However, conceiving ideas that blend services or products with deeper, less obvious connections demands a more profound understanding of each component's underlying mechanics, processes, and architecture.

Partnering with Generative AI

In a 1996 interview with *Wired* magazine, Steve Jobs declared, "Creativity is just connecting things. When you ask creative people how they did something, they feel a little guilty because they did not really do it, they just saw something. It seemed obvious to them after a while. That is because they were able to connect experiences they have had and synthesize new things."[11] For example, the Apple Watch can be described as marrying a watch and a mobile phone, and the iPhone is the marriage of a computer and a cell phone. Combinational creativity is achieved by associating ideas that were previously unlinked or indirectly linked, which makes it an excellent framework for partnering with generative AI. By examining the merging of different disciplines, concepts, and objects, generative AI prompts can take this process to the next level, producing fresh and innovative ideas to evaluate.

A collaboration with a generative AI tool to explore a possible combination of products or services must begin with a clear statement of the outcome you are hoping to achieve. This can look like a problem statement, a design challenge, or a description of what success looks like. Providing a set of clear objectives to your AI partner at the beginning of the collaboration is a foundational best practice. Offering additional insight about the domain, target audience, relevant trends, and mandatory considerations leads to more applicable output. You can also prompt the generative AI tool to consider new variables to test for limitations and flexibility of the proposed ideas.

A sample prompt might be, "I want you to generate innovative ideas by combining these three unique concepts in unexpected ways to solve this problem [define problem schema.] For each idea, explain how the different elements are integrated, why they were chosen to be combined, and what unique value or solution it could offer. After generating five ideas, analyze them for feasibility and suggest which one has the most potential for further development."

"What if" questions effectively trigger refinements to any novel idea that doesn't quite resonate on first read. You can always include potential twists directly into the initial prompt; however, adding them to a combination in stages allows for iterative ideation. As you iterate, you can pull forward the elements of the initial idea you like while identifying any missing aspects that were not captured originally. Leverage Gen AI to suggest additional combinations and variations. For example, input a list of technologies and ask the AI to generate possible combinations and applications. Getting the base combination balance tuned first can help you better understand the value of the twist or qualifier, and you can again iterate in stages by applying different twists to compare the relative impact.

The success of your partnership with Gen AI depends on several key factors. It's important to provide clear prompts that effectively frame your collaboration. By strategically utilizing twists and qualifiers, you can maximize the benefit of your partnership. To achieve this, start off by exploring broad and unconventional ideas. Once you have a pool of ideas, refine and qualify the ones that seem most intriguing. For instance, a prompt might say "I am seeking a way to do A. What innovative product or service could result from merging concepts from X industry with those from Y sector that can solve for A?" This can be a launchpad for groundbreaking insights and ideas.

These techniques enable you to add nuance and complexity to the AI-generated ideas, creating a richer and more diverse set of concepts. However, it's important to remember that human creativity is still essential in this process. By working collaboratively with generative AI, you can build upon its ideas, expand your thinking, and explore truly innovative "when X meets Y" concepts that challenge your assumptions and open up new avenues for exploration.

Interview with Tony Fadell

I met Tony Fadell when I worked at Apple in 2005, leading the Americas Online Stores team. When Apple launched a new product, there was a meticulously managed internal communication process, which had different groups like customer care and e-commerce sales briefed on a need-to-know basis about whatever upcoming

(continued)

product innovation Apple was bringing to market. In those briefings, Tony was—and he remains—an inspiring storyteller. As SVP of the iPod Division, he led the team that created the first 18 generations of the iPod and the first three generations of the iPhone. Throughout his career, Tony has authored more than 300 patents. In 2010, Tony co-founded Nest Labs, the company that pioneered the "Internet of Things," and the manufacturer of the Nest Learning Thermostat. Google acquired Nest Labs for $3.2 billion in 2014. In May 2016, TIME named the Nest Learning Thermostat, the iPod and the iPhone three of the "50 Most Influential Gadgets of All Time." Tony is also *The New York Times* bestselling author of *Build: An Unorthodox Guide to Making Things Worth Making,* and is the Principal at Build Collective, an investment and advisory firm coaching deep tech startups. Tony continues to foster innovation through his investments in sustainable and environmentally friendly businesses. From tackling food security, sustainability, transportation, energy efficiency, weather, robotics, and disease to empowering small business owners, entrepreneurs, and consumers, the startups in Build Collective's portfolio are improving lives and prospects for the future.

1. **In a world of generative AI, what is the role of human creativity?**

   The only thing that has changed with generative AI is how quickly you can find inspiration. Using generative AI when doing design, can offer you inspiration. But at the end of the day, you, as the human in the mix, need to meaningfully understand your customers, the problems they face, and the solutions you can offer. You need to meaningfully understand where they're coming from. Meaningfully means you have insights about these customers' profiles and needs, and then you can turn them into real solutions. You can't just take what other people have regurgitated and what LLMs will regurgitate. Meaningfully also means that you have a deep connection; if you don't have a deep connection with your customer through your product, then it's all just marketing. When you have that deep meaning with product, the marketing is just a way to communicate what that is.

Generative AI can help you to visualize it for others. And it can help you explain your solution more quickly to people in the early days without spending lots of time and money on trying to see if there's a there, and before getting other people involved. For example, I'm designing a house in Paris, and I'm using it to create storyboards and visualizations for each room and general ideas that it then assembles into something. I'm not taking those things anywhere literally, but they give me a rough visual and the inspiration to explore more of the solution space. And it happens more quickly because typically, with design, you start with an exact idea in mind and go for it. But sometimes you want to consider other people's opinions to help you better form your opinions. And that's what you can do with generative AI tools.

2. **You have said, "Embrace constraints." How do constraints provide a helpful framework for problem-solving that fosters creativity?**

They are an absolute asset, because they force you to put a positive pressure on the situation. As long as they're reasonable constraints. If they're unreasonable constraints, you're not going to get anywhere. But reasonable constraints push you to get to an idea that becomes a thing. Great artists have to ship. Great artists have to show the world what they do.

That means you have to go through each step of the process. Maybe you focus on some steps in the process, and you realize this isn't the right time, or this isn't the right problem to solve. Maybe I'm not asking the right question?

(continued)

Or maybe the technology is not right? That's okay. But you've got to get to that answer. And you've got to get to it in the context of the customer's needs and the state of the world, what the state of the world will be, or at least what the customer's environment will be when the product is ready to ship. That's why you need to continue to put constraints on yourself so that you evolve your assumptions into some qualitative or quantitative answers, so that you can get to the next step. Sometimes that means you just shelf something for a while, because you see where it's at and you also see things aren't right yet.

We didn't do that at General Magic because the environment was bright. You have to be able to constrain yourself, even if you have all the time and money in the world. Then you're never going to get anything done. And you're going to be solving problems for years from now. But who knows? The world changes so dramatically. The next thing we have is AI. That's changing everything. If you think you know the world and what it'll look like years from now and have the time and money, it might be great for you. But good luck getting the team motivated on that.

Teams like to make progress because anything you do is usually about making progress. And so, teams need constraints too, because if they're working on something that is open-ended, the team and their focus wanders over time. People aren't motivated to work together on something customers will get around to sometime. And then, before you know it, it all unravels into mush. You need to have some positive forcing functions to get you to the next answers to be able to make progress, whatever that looks like.

3. How do you get into a state of flow? And what does peak performance look and feel like to you?

There are different states to flow that I have: when I am alone working on the problem, when I am alone, not working on the problem, and when I am working with others. When I am working on the problem, I'm just draw-ing on the basic resources I have, throwing out all kinds of things, being really exploratory, and sitting down with even the craziest ideas I have. Whether that's pencil and paper, or a browser to do research, a printer to print out things and cut them up and paste them down. And it's using a whole set of different tools—even glue, and tape, and cardboard, and tearing apart products, too. The idea is to get your mind around all the variables that could go into something and try to build something. I always say, you have to make the intangible tangible. Try to get to that as fast as possible. And then you wake up, and it's hours later, and you realize the time passed because you're just so curious. You're curious as to all the bits and things.

There are other times when I'm just riding my bike, or I'm running, when I'm so focused on the task at hand, which has nothing to do with the design itself, where these solutions or ideas pop out of my brain because I'm in a state of flow. I hit a wall when I'm just working on the problem, I don't know how to resolve it. I can't see it. So, I have to step away from the problem. And whether that's sleeping, doing my workouts, in yoga, or whatever. Suddenly, when I least expect it, the solution just appears in my brain. It's the weirdest thing. You crack something, and then you think, "Oh, that's the way to solve it," and then you start going into that state of flow in your mind wondering if we could solve it that way. That means we could fix this, and we could change this. And you start pulling on that thread.

There's a time when you know your problem could be resolved because you're not thinking about it. Your brain is just trying to make sense of it while you're not focused on it, so it's a different state of flow.

Then the third state is when you're with a team of people, and everyone's throwing ideas out whether that's

(continued)

to solve a problem or generate something new. And you're just like, what do you have? Let's put this on the board, and you can feel the energy of the room and people being truly engaged and wanting to find incredible solutions. I'm doing this now in the house I am designing here in Paris, and I just have an incredible team of people who are willing to throw out any kind of crazy ideas. And I just let them. "Yeah, more of that. Wait, let's do this. Let's look at this." We might even be using generative AI. "Are you trying to say this?" We have generative AI visualize something for us very quickly. And when a meeting can turn into that, and you feel like it was only thirty minutes, but it was hours, that's a state of group flow.

4. **You have said, "Don't be afraid to fail and embrace failure as a step towards success." How important is failure or the acceptance of failure and cultivating creativity?**

Failure is only if you give up, otherwise it's called learning. I use this analogy all the time: if we gave up on learning to walk after the first time, no one would ever walk in this world. We had to fail a thousand times at learning to walk before we actually walked. You have to have an environment around you that encourages you that you're making even the slightest progress without saying, "Oh, it's never going to happen."

Too many times in our educational institutions, you pass or fail. That's it-you get the grade, and it's over. Instead of thinking, "I learned something, even though maybe I didn't get this right. But I'm going to go back and learn it and understand where I do need to improve." Or I maybe need to change the way I'm thinking about the situation. We get trained when we get into school, that failure is not an option, whereas when we were growing up before we got into school, failure is the only way we learned.

5. **How do you recommend cultivating one's creative abilities to build creative confidence?**

Everybody can be creative. It just depends on what they want to be creative doing. When you write an email, you can be creative with it. And when you pick out your clothes in the morning for the day. You can be creative there, and you can ask questions like "Who's my audience?" just like you would if you were building a product. "Who's my audience? What's the story I'm trying to tell? What is the impression I'm trying to give? What are the things I want to attract or repel?" All these different things are stories.

You need to get into a storytelling mindset to understand that the world—and everything we do every day—is about a story. You could be working at a corporation. How do you tell your boss about what you've done that day? And it has to be nonfictional, of course. How do you frame it? If you start with storytelling, then you start to get curious and you get creative about the storytelling, and then you might dive into more facets of the creative process. Should I tell a story visually or auditorily? It's really about the ability to tell a story. This skill can help with anything you do in life, and you can apply it to things you're curious about. How can you take the ideas to the next level? What aspects of it can make the story much richer?

Exercises

COMBINATIONAL CREATIVITY SPEED ROUND

Objective: Generate as many novel solutions or ideas as possible by combining elements from different domains or disciplines in a fixed time period, usually three to five minutes is best, *without using any digital tools.*

Instructions: Set a time limit for generating these compound products and a target for the number of random combinations to create.

Limiting the time and defining the target outcome assures focus on the exercise by not leaving room for distractions. Start small by targeting three products in three minutes to get the hang of the exercise, and then increase the output volume before increasing the time to invent them. The important thing is to proceed undaunted by the absurdity of anything that emerges, maintain an open mindset, and keep pushing forward without editing.

- ◆ Select two unrelated domains. Here are some category ideas to get things started.
  1. Personal-care items
  2. Jewelry
  3. Health aids
  4. Office supplies
  5. Tools and utensils
  6. Exercise/sports equipment
  7. Toys and games
  8. Kitchen tools
- ◆ Make a list of ten items from each domain. Work on one domain at a time.
- ◆ Pair one item from each domain.
- ◆ Develop ideas for novel ways to combine those two things. As you consider the items you are mixing, consider the following:
  - What aspects can be combined?
  - What should be discarded when combined?
  - Can the individual uses be combined?
  - Does the combination deliver an entirely new purpose?
  Consider using the Generic Parts Technique to help you identify distinct elements of each item that might be useful in the mixture.
- ◆ Define the purpose of the newly created product in a sentence or two.

Continue this practice by choosing different categories and building new lists. Pair items from each new domain to form a novel product. Write a description of each compound object created.

In the next round of ideation, take several of the newly combined products and add a twist. Consider what happens if there is a change to the target user's age, an adjustment to the material composition or underlying technology, scaling the item up or down, or deploying it in a new environment to assess how this changes the product's utility.

GENERATIVE AI COMBINATORIAL CREATIVITY BRAINSTORM

Objective: Use generative AI to generate innovative solutions or ideas by combining elements from different domains or disciplines.

Materials Needed:

- ◆ Access to a generative AI tool or platform (like OpenAI's Chat-GPT or Microsoft's Copilot).
- ◆ A method for recording ideas and insights.

Instructions:

1. **Select a Challenge or Goal**: Define a clear challenge or goal you want to address. This could be anything from designing a new product to solving a social issue to creating unique artwork.

2. **Identify Two Disparate Domains**: Choose two distinct domains or disciplines that are not commonly associated with each other but are of interest or relevance to the challenge at hand. For example, if your goal is to design a new educational tool, you might choose "mountain climbing" and "gamification" as your domains because they represent levels of difficulty and engagement.

3. **Prepare Your Prompt**: Formulate a prompt for the generative AI that clearly states your challenge/goal and asks for ideas or solutions that combine elements from the two selected domains. Ensure your prompt encourages creative and unconventional combinations. For example, "Generate ideas for an educational tool that combines elements of mountain climbing with gamification techniques to enhance learning in middle school science."

4. **Engage with Generative AI**: Input your prompt into the generative AI tool and review the generated ideas. If the first set of ideas is less creative or diverse than you'd hoped, consider refining your prompt with additional details or constraints to guide the AI toward more innovative combinations. You can also change domains to see if that produces more interesting options.

5. **Iteration and Refinement**: Select one or two ideas that intrigue you and use them as a basis for a new prompt, asking generative AI to expand or refine these ideas further. This iterative process can help deepen creative exploration and fine-tune innovative concepts.

6. **Evaluation and Reflection**: Evaluate the generated ideas based on criteria relevant to your initial challenge or goal. Reflect on the process of using generative AI for combinatorial creativity. Consider the following questions: What insights did you gain? How did the selection of disparate domains influence the creativity of the solutions? What adjustments to the prompts led to more innovative ideas?

7. **Further Exploration**: (Optional) As an advanced step, add a twist to explore how this affects the creativity of the generative AI's responses. This can provide a deeper understanding of the potential for combinatorial creativity facilitated by generative AI.

Outcome: By the end of this exercise, participants should have a collection of innovative ideas or solutions generated through the combinatorial creativity process and an understanding of how to effectively use generative AI as a tool for creative brainstorming across diverse domains.

CHAPTER 3

The Same, Only Different

*"Analogy is our best guide in all philosophical investigations;
and all discoveries, which were not made by mere accident,
have been made by the help of it."*

—Joseph Priestley

Analogical reasoning allows us to find connections and similarities between seemingly disparate domains, generating new insights and solving problems. The eighteenth-century scientist and theologian Joseph Priestley used analogical thinking to bridge the known and unknown worlds, leading to discoveries such as carbon monoxide and nitrous oxide, and the invention of carbonated water. The goal of analogies is to explain an abstract idea by referring the audience to a more familiar one. Without realizing it, we all lean into analogic thinking to help us navigate unfamiliar situations. For instance, we may think about starting a new job by considering how we navigated going away to college. Or, we might have to learn a new skill on the job, so we use the memory of how we learned to drive as a way to accomplish this task. The key is to reduce the problem to its essential characteristics, separate it from its context, and use this as a starting point to look for similarities in other categories or industries. The exploration involves identifying who, or which discipline, has already solved a similar challenge. In what context would someone experience similar obstacles or situations?

For example, begin by assuming our target domain is an urgent-care facility with a visitor experience that needs improvement. Then, look at abstractions, such as "How can we improve the check-in process?" From there, identify other check-in experiences for inspiration: the airport, a doctor's office, a hair salon, and the DMV. Exclude the doctor's office because it is too near the target domain. In this case, the airport may offer multiple insights because there are many moments when passengers wait before they are seated on their flights for their journey. Both environments share an element of stress that helps the audience connect with them.

Analogies are close cousins to mixtures. Both approaches depend upon finding and evaluating two entities to find what might be leverageable in a new experience. Additionally, the nearness or distance between the two things being considered impacts the level of transformation that may result. The main difference, however, between a mixture and an analogy is that the analogy does not imply a combination of the two ideas. Instead, analogies borrow, not blend. Creative thinkers use analogies to improve a target product or service by applying a process, system, or method belonging to another product or service from an unrelated domain. Exploring what happens if these structural attributes are used in a different context can generate disruptive solutions.

Novel approaches can become apparent by looking beyond the domain of a person's or an organization's expertise, abstracting a problem to its essence, and then studying other domains that have faced a similar challenge or opportunity to find the parallels. Finding a suitable analogy requires the abstraction to be at a level that enables an effective comparison with other products, businesses, or industries. For instance, the digital shopping cart is one of the most valuable analogies consumers use daily. This analogy has become a fundamental aspect of the e-commerce user experience. Using the mental model of a physical shopping cart, online stores enable customers to gather goods in one place before making their purchases and checking out. The digital shopping cart provides an organizational rubric that offers customers a way to navigate the steps in the purchase path. The rubric provides a familiar vocabulary that consumers understand. The vocabulary has been adapted based on the kind of online store being shopped to paint the appropriate picture in the shopper's mind. As an even closer bridge between the tangible and the digital, luxury online boutiques prefer to present a "shopping bag" instead of a "shopping cart."

Analogies are also a foundational part of the Supermind Ideator mentioned in Chapter 1. "Analogize" is one of the basic design moves. This activity is part of the "Explore Problem" move set to help users reframe and better understand their problem. Analogies encourage expansive thinking and are intentionally included to broaden your perspective beyond the immediate context of the problem.

When analogies are used in comedy to create an absurd juxtaposition between two unrelated concepts, they guide you to look for the similarities that exist in these two disparate ideas. The television show *Seinfeld* leveraged this technique frequently to provide unorthodox perspectives on everyday life, allowing the audience to relate to the problem with greater empathy. For example, Seinfeld professed, "Elaine, breaking up is like knocking over a Coke machine. You can't do it in one push; you got to rock it back and forth a few times, and *then* it goes over."[1]

Seinfeld acknowledged his propensity for using analogies in a 2014 cover story for *Complex*. "When I did the TV series, there was a writer on the show named Larry Charles. He said that if I were a superhero, I'd be 'Analogy Lad.' If you had a problem, Analogy Lad would bust into the wall and say, 'You know what this is like?' He can't help you, but he'll tell you exactly what it's like."[2] These unexpected analogous constructs can make accepting and understanding a novel idea easier.

The Startup Pitch

Adam M. Grant, an author and professor at the Wharton School of Business at the University of Pennsylvania where he specializes in organizational psychology, says, "To generate creative ideas, it is important to start from an unusual place. However, to explain those ideas, they must be connected to something familiar. That is why so many startups are introducing themselves as the 'Uber for X.'"[3] In the case of the "Uber for X" example, the message is that the operating model of Uber, a company that revolutionized the way we think about transportation services, can be applied to any other service (X) in a different industry or sector. In the analogy, Uber provides a reference to quickly communicate that a new service or startup is leveraging the well-understood concept of an on-demand, peer-to-peer platform that enables customers to book services or products on mobile devices.

Zum is a startup that was launched in 2015. It is a company that provides electric buses for school transportation. Initially, it started as an "Uber for school kids," making carpooling easier for parents. With the Zum app, parents didn't have to coordinate with multiple families to manage their children's commuting needs, and tracking their whereabouts was easy. Zum provided the buses and drivers and managed the logistics. The company ultimately pivoted its focus toward serving school districts instead of parents, providing the company with a larger and more predictable revenue stream.[4] However, entering the market as they did initially enabled them to raise capital, identify the larger customer need, and ultimately modernize school transportation services at scale.

Sometimes, using an imperfect analogy can be risky. While there may be similarities between the two entities, the analogy may miss some key differences between the two services that might undermine the utility of the comparison when pitching a new idea. For example, if BarkBox was described as "Stitch Fix for dogs," it might convey a quick, high-level idea of BarkBox's service model, but it ignores some key structural differences, including the level of customization and the customers' active decision-making about what to keep or return from the box of products that is core to the Stitch Fix model.

In 2012, "Warby Parker for" became a popular analogy for start-up founders. This involved analyzing and reinventing an overpriced product's demand and supply chain to create a new brand. Following Warby Parker's success, several startups sought to replicate its direct-to-consumer model in other overpriced and underserved sectors. The mattress industry is a prime example of this trend, with companies like Purple, Avocado, and Casper emerging to disrupt the traditional mattress-buying experience. These companies identified the mattress market as ripe for disruption due to its high markups, complex supply chains, and the generally unpleasant shopping experience associated with mattress stores. Despite the apparent difference, it took a creative thinker to see the structural similarities in selling eyeglasses and mattresses.

Another reason entrepreneurs are drawn to analogies is that analogies align their pitch to the business models and success stories of companies that they want investors to believe they can emulate. In 2015, MarketWatch analyzed nearly half a million startups on AngelList. The top three comparisons that startups made were to Airbnb, Uber, and LinkedIn.[5] The analysis has shown these analogies help raise capital because they can quickly orient an investor. However, it is essential to keep in mind that when there are negatives associated with the more familiar reference being used, like safety or regulatory issues, those may also transfer to the new entity when advancing the analogy.

Startups often deal with innovative, complex ideas. Analogies help simplify these by relating them to something the audience already knows. A good analogy sticks in the listener's mind, offering a memorable takeaway that helps recall long after it's over. Investors hear numerous pitches, and an analogy can quickly clarify your business concept without the need for lengthy explanations.

How Analogies Work

It's common to underestimate the difficulty of crafting effective analogies because a truly useful analogy goes beyond pointing out a surface-level similarity. People might think an analogy is easy because they themselves understand both concepts well. They might forget that their audience might not have the same level of familiarity, and the chosen analogy might need additional explanation to be truly successful. Crafting analogies is a complex and multistep cognitive process that involves various mental activities. It requires the ability to retrieve information from memory, identify core similarities between subjects, apply knowledge from one domain to another, and transform the target domain based on insights gained from the source domain.

To create a meaningful analogy, one must first have a grasp of the details about the subjects being compared. Identifying the core similarities between the subjects is crucial and requires mapping the information retrieved from memory. Applying the knowledge from one domain to another is a process called *transfer*. Finally, transformation involves modifying the target domain based on insights gained from the source domain, leading to potentially innovative ideas or solutions.

While generative AI tools are good at this type of data mapping, creating impactful analogies requires a high level of emotional intelligence and empathy that humans must provide. A deep understanding of the emotional and experiential landscapes of both the source and target domains is necessary to draw meaningful parallels that resonate with others. This understanding allows for analogies that not only illuminate but also touch people on a deeper level, making the ideas more compelling and memorable.

History provides many examples of this type of cross-pollination of ideas. Military experts have observed the behavior of insect colonies, examining their various organizational, relational, and tactical approaches to defense.[6] Insects such as bees and ants use swarm tactics to overwhelm or deter predators. This approach involves many individuals performing simple actions in harmony and has influenced modern military concepts of drone swarming in warfare. The technique also aids in search and rescue operations.[7]

Likewise, successful military strategies to conquer enemies have been explored for medical applications. In an experiment on analogical thinking reported in 1980, participants were told a story about a plan to capture a fortress that required an "attack-dispersion" strategy instead of a large-scale, direct assault. Then, they were presented with Duncker's Radiation Problem, which sought a way to eradicate a tumor with radiation without damaging healthy tissue or jeopardizing the patient's life.[8] Even with little domain knowledge of military strategy, the study participants could recognize similarities in the story's conditions, desired outcomes, and target problems.[9]

An important benefit of using analogies is that they help overcome expert bias because they require you to fully evaluate other mental models or assumptions. Analogies naturally guide us to explore new domains for solutions where our expertise isn't as strong and dive deep to validate the value within their mechanisms and design. Creative problem solvers are open to relying on something other than experts close to the problem because they want to avoid the risk that existing known solutions will constrain their thinking. A 2014 paper published in the academic journal *Management Science* dispelled the notion that target market expertise is essential in product ideation. In fact, "solutions provided by problem solvers from analogous markets show substantially higher levels of novelty [and] increases the novelty of solutions provided for a given target market problem by almost two-thirds of the gains from asking lead users (LUs) instead of average problem solvers."[10] Inventiveness is not the sole purview of experts in the original domain. During this stage of ideation, only experts who can operate with a growth mindset will be helpful in exploring an analogy's value and assessing what from the new domain can be cross-pollinated with the target.

While all analogies can be considered metaphors because they draw comparisons, not all metaphors qualify as good analogies. Metaphors and analogies both serve to connect concepts in people's minds, but not all metaphors require structural correspondence. That said, metaphors can be helpful in ideation even without the full structural connection between the domains as they permit explorations of new associations and allow our brains to look more broadly at a problem. When a metaphor falls flat, it often signals a mismatch in relevance, structural similarity, or an unintended connotation, urging a pivot to more promising ideas. For instance, comparing a city's nightlife to a classroom is ineffective because a classroom and nightlife do not have relevant similarities, and the listener may find it difficult to understand the intended connection between the two. Another example is when a new connection creates an unintended or inappropriate association with a familiar idea, such as comparing viral user growth to spreading cancer cells, which links a positive concept with a negative connotation. Additionally, the attribute you expect people to associate with the metaphor may be overlooked or poorly understood.

The effectiveness of analogies and metaphors in generating new ideas depends on psychological distance. Psychological distance is the degree to which objects, events, or concepts are separated from an individual's direct experience. This includes not only physical distance but also historical, cultural, and social distances. By distancing yourself from the specifics of a problem or situation and considering it from an abstract and detached perspective, you can explore a broader range of possibilities. While AI can process and analyze large datasets to identify metaphorical patterns, it relies on predefined inputs, correlations, and linguistic structures rather than the experiential or emotional insights that humans use because it lacks personal experience, emotions, and subjective perspective, which are central to understanding and creating psychological distance.

Many metaphors, especially conventional ones, succeed when they evoke an emotional response through the connection. Abstract ideas can be made more poignant using metaphors. Like analogies, metaphors can create shared understanding around a vision, provide a common language for a novel idea, and evoke emotions that motivate action. Unlike analogies, they tend to be less dependent on structural similarities and more reliant on descriptive imagery.

Structure-mapping theory is a powerful framework that helps explain and deepen the impact of analogies. Developed by psychologist Dedre Gentner in the early 1980s, the structure-mapping process involves mapping the relational structure from the base domain onto the target domain, where the "base" domain is the source from which information is drawn, and the "target" domain is where this information is applied. The more complex and detailed this mapping, the richer the analogy. The greater the number of structural similarities between the objects of comparison, the more likely the analogy will be durable. New inferences can be made for the target domain, and new ideas, insights, or solutions emerge that were not evident before. This is the step where innovation or creative problem-solving typically emerges.

According to Gentner, who co-founded Northwestern University's Cognitive Sciences Program and is an expert in analogical reasoning, "The strength of an analogical match does not seem to depend on the overall degree of feature overlap; not all features are equally relevant to the interpretation."[11] Consider Figure 3.1. Finding an analogy in Figure 3.1a is not difficult because two of the pairs, Pair 1 and Pair 3, obviously contain elements that match each other, while Pair 2 does not. However, finding two shapes that are analogous among the six in Figure 3.1b might require a deeper examination. While Shape 1 and Shape 6 both are structured with curved lines, one of those objects is three-dimensional, and the other is not. Shape 2 and Shape 4 are both four-sided, but the sides are not of equal lengths. Both examples do not have deep structural similarities. However, Shape 4 and Shape 6 both share a deep structural similarity in that they are

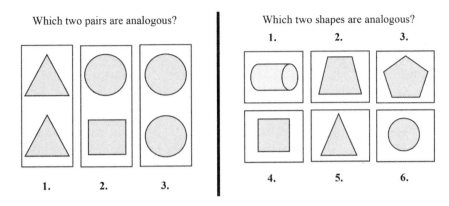

Figure 3.1 a. Pair 1 and Pair 3 are analogous. They both demonstrate the same relational matching. Each pair has a mirror image within it. In Figure 3.1 b. Shape 4 and Shape 6 are analogous structurally because the height and width of both shapes are the same within each shape and between each shape.

congruent dimensionally, with the width and height the same within each shape and across each shape. Identifying this type of similarity takes more effort than a cursory scan of the shapes. Even in the pair analogy, the individual shapes within each pair do not have the same attributes. However, the relationship between the shapes within each pair is the same, thus enabling the analogic relationship between Pair 1 and Pair 3.

By examining the elements being compared more closely, structure mapping can lead to various insights across different domains, including scientific discoveries, technological innovations, creative art and literature, and problem-solving in everyday life. In her interview in Chapter 7, Jules Pieri recalls working with Reebok on a shoe to help basketball players rebound higher. One of the engineers decided to study the chemicals in the legs of fleas because they can jump vertically up to 50–100 times their body length. Comparing the biomechanics and chemistry that enable fleas to jump remarkably high with the goal of applying similar principles to enhance human athletic performance in basketball is an example of structure mapping: systematically transferring knowledge from the study of fleas to the design of basketball shoes by aligning the functional and structural similarities between the two domains.

Types of Analogies

The Synectics method, a collaborative problem-solving approach enriched with analogies and metaphors, ignites creativity by leveraging these comparisons. Synectics was crafted more than 50 years ago by William J.J. Gordon and his team to democratize creativity. It operates on the principle that understanding emerges through the exploration of similarities between seemingly unrelated entities. While Synectics is about analogies, these analogies stem from action-oriented thinking. Verbs such as "isolate," "fragment," and "disguise" serve as trigger mechanisms that stimulate connections between abstract ideas and concrete concepts.

Within this framework, different types of analogies act as catalysts, propelling the exploration of various perspectives. These include *personal analogies*, inviting participants to embody the problem for more profound empathy; *direct analogies*, drawing from similar facts or experiences; and *symbolic analogies*, abstract representations akin to metaphors.[12]

The application of analogies, whether within the structured framework of Synectics or as a freestanding brainstorming exercise, liberates creative thought. The Stanford University d.school introduced the *POV analogy*, which frames design challenges through metaphorical lenses. *Biomimicry*—nature-inspired problem-solving—is another powerful form of analogical thinking that explores natural structures and forms to inspire innovative design solutions. Structural analogies are valuable tools in science and engineering, as they help clarify complex systems. For instance, likening the human circulatory system to a city's water supply simplifies understanding and proposes an innovation in urban planning by applying biological efficiency to infrastructure. Similarly, the Music Genome Project, which fuels Pandora Internet Radio, exemplifies a structural analogy by mirroring the meticulous classification of the Human Genome Project. This analogy doesn't just compare; it revolutionizes how we experience personalized music, demonstrating the power of applying genetic analysis principles to digital playlists.

Relational analogies, on the other hand, draw connections based on the dynamics between pairs. An analogy like "a tire is to a car as a ski is to a snowmobile" illustrates how objects complement and extend the functionality of others, providing insights into design and utility in engineering and product development. *Causal analogies* delve into cause and effect, elucidating the underlying mechanics of phenomena. An example of a causal analogy would be that adding more wood to a fire sustains its heat and fuels the flame, just as adding water to plants maintains health and fuels their growth. Both scenarios highlight the importance of a specific sustaining action or input (adding wood, adding water) to achieve a desired outcome (sustaining and promoting growth.) When creative problem-solving, using causal analogies can help identify similar cause-and-effect relationships that may occur in different situations.

On the other hand, *historical analogies* utilize past events to illustrate the importance and relevance of the current situation. Historical analogies compare events, conditions, or periods to provide insight into future outcomes. For example, connecting the invention of the Gutenberg printing press in the fifteenth century to the rise of social media platforms in the early twenty-first century links two groundbreaking advancements in communication technology that significantly lowered the barriers to content creation and distribution. *Symbolic analogies* can help to elicit emotions and create a sense of purpose to focus ideation by using familiar images, objects or concepts to represent the new idea. If a career coach used an image of a mountain on their business card, and the tagline "I help you reach your peak performance," the mountain peak would symbolize the elevation of one's potential. Each analogy type serves as a launchpad for devising solutions.

When choosing the type of analogy to explore, there are several important factors to consider. For instance, it is crucial to ensure that the intended audience comprehends the symbolism, scientific facts, or historical events that the comparison is based on. Additionally, it is essential to determine whether the comparison holds up in the context of different audiences. That's because things like age and group norms can bring different perspectives about how the two domains or ideas may relate, undermining the opportunity to find a novel solution.

Partnering with Generative AI

In the context of artificial intelligence (AI), analogies are particularly useful, as they help us explore the relationships between seemingly

unrelated things. Since one of generative AI's strengths is pattern recognition, we can use these tools to unlock new relational insights
that may not be immediately apparent to us, leading to even more
informed and innovative solutions. Researchers at Carnegie Mellon
University and the Hebrew University of Jerusalem hypothesized that
using a pre-trained language model (PLM) instead of a large language
model (LLM) could enable computational analogy at scale. The PLM
was focused on structural representations of products, specifically
their "purpose" and "mechanism." They found that the PLM allowed
for finding analogies with higher precision and recall than traditional
information retrieval methods, including LLMs. Additionally, they discovered the PLM model could successfully identify "far analogies"—
products with high purpose similarity but low mechanism similarity.[13]

Whether you use a PLM or an LLM, it is important to start by
listing the base problem schema's essential characteristics, functions,
properties, or processes. Understand its architecture, both business
and technical, and express the key elements that the analogy must
support. If you use a pre-trained data corpus, you will choose the
characteristics when you train the data that you wish to focus on as
the basis for comparison. If you have suggestions for distant domains
to explore, like nature or history, provide them as a starting point.
This can help guide AI and focus its ideation. Or you might prompt
your AI partner in this way: "I'm working on a new birdfeeder that
will appeal to birds while keeping out squirrels, rats, and other animals. Find three analogous products from different domains based
on similar purposes or mechanisms that could inspire novel features." When starting with a list of ideas generated by your AI partner, challenge the first set of outputs and delve deeper into specific
analogies that resonate.

It is also important to share the demographic and cultural differences that may affect the understanding and acceptance of certain
analogies that AI might propose. Because AI has a limited capacity to
understand a specific feeling or sensitivity, you might imagine its psychological distance is an advantage. The metaphors AI generates may
appear psychologically distant because it can access and recombine
data, but it doesn't "understand" psychological distance like humans
do. Prompts should, therefore, include any insights about experiences, values or brand attributes that will help AI align with your

business or personal goals. Giving your AI collaborator key insights to align the analogy more closely with your audience's interests or your personal preferences will be helpful since familiarity is key to making analogies work.

This type of collaboration produces the best output when it is approached iteratively. For example, you can ask your computational partner to evaluate or challenge your ideas. "I've generated 10 product ideas based on these analogies. Evaluate and rank them based on the novelty of their originality-feasibility combinations and the strength of their structural mapping." Test the factual and conceptual accuracy of the analogies provided. Explore the areas of dissimilarity to test the strength of the proposed analogy. Too many exceptions will undermine the durability of the analogy. You can also try different types of analogies—historical, relational, and symbolic—to find the most impactful comparison.

Test the analogy's usefulness in the real world to see if it communicates the same thing to each listener. The nuance may be too obscure to be recognized or convey a different meaning when shared conversationally with others. The analogy shouldn't be confusing or require a lengthy explanation to land. It can't be open to misinterpretation. Use this type of feedback to iterate the analogy again.

Don't be discouraged if the outcome of this collaboration doesn't immediately achieve your goals. If you remain open-minded, even the less inspiring comparisons may be a launchpad for a new line of investigation. Test the various ideas' durability. If the analogy works in one direction, does it also work in reverse? You might have a different perspective on what is important in the comparison when seeing it from both angles. This is because the first term in each pair is often seen as the standard or reference point and may present specific attributes that should be considered. The second term is compared to the first.

Collaborating with generative AI tools to come up with effective analogies for your ideas requires a joint effort to utilize AI's ability to access a broad range of information, patterns, and relationships across various fields. This process should be conducted iteratively, exploring different and distant domains. The advantage of this human-machine collaboration is that you can cover a lot of ground more quickly, which will help you exercise your creative muscle and enable you to achieve creative velocity.

Interview with Denny Post

I met Denny while we both worked at T-Mobile in 2008, when she was hired as the chief marketing officer. Denny began working at the wireless carrier after spending years as a senior vice president and a chief innovation officer in the food industry, working for brands such as Starbucks, Burger King, and Yum! Brands. In 2018, as chief executive officer of Red Robin, Denny invited me to join their Innovation Advisory Board, which she created to identify and discuss emerging trends in technology, culture, business, food production, and society that could disrupt Red Robin's business. Denny continues to influence the future of the food and hospitality industries, as a board member for companies like Travel+Leisure, Vital Farms, and Libbey.

1. **In this age of generative AI, what is the role of human creativity?**

    I see human creativity as the foundation for all great innovation. I'm fascinated by AI.

    And who knows what the capacity will be ultimately. But my belief is that there will always be the need for the core idea, the unique take, the forward-looking perspective, and an understanding of context. I see it as a tool to enhance, maximize, or broaden the possibilities. But I still believe that human creativity, that core idea, and, more importantly, that ability to actually take that idea through to true innovation will remain a human endeavor. I choose to see it as complementary, not competitive.

    The ability to derive insight from context clues, analogous situations, personal experience, and that sense of wisdom and gained experience requires the human mind and, to an extent, the heart to put it all together. It's not a purely data-driven endeavor. There is a huge amount of emotion in creativity. There's a huge amount of humanity. I don't know how else to explain it, but humanity is a big part of creativity. And I don't think that's ever going to be replaced. But the biggest thing for me is the ability to take the context and filter all that you have seen and what you know about what's needed with the information you can gather, and that will remain a human endeavor. Because creative ideas can also benefit from the ability to collaborate with people who have distinctively different strengths and sets of experiences, I see AI as another voice at the table.

2. **You said, "I like working within a set of constraints because that's sometimes where the smartest work gets done." How do constraints provide a helpful framework for problem-solving that fosters creativity?**

The constraints around you may require you to go deeper rather than shallower. So often, when people don't have constraints, ideas remain shallow, scattered, and lack the required true cohesion and collaboration. If you're simply brainstorming across a narrow domain, no idea is a bad idea. That's true. But if you are trying to play across the whole vista, it is really hard to take any idea and make it better, deeper, and stronger. The best thing you can do is know what's in and out right up front if you are working across a bigger business landscape. Constraints don't communicate that something is a bad idea; it just doesn't fit our current constraints. Constraints need not be negative. Some constraints are very positive in the sense they provide clarity about who my end user is, or where the work fits in. You know, some of those constraints are very clarifying and illuminating. I think about constraints shining a bright light on exactly where you should focus. And if you're willing to operate that way, the quality of what you deliver is much better.

Ideas are intellectual exercises. Innovation is the hard work of making the ideas real. That's why I think

(continued)

constraints are so important. They improve the quality of the ideas you have, making it more likely you'll be successful in innovating. Those realities come into play as you eventually try to go to market.

3. **How do you re-energize your creative spirit during periods of frustration or stagnation? How do you get yourself into a state of creative flow?**

I need to get out of myself and go someplace. For me it's a museum, anytime. Any kind of museum works. Just somewhere where I can completely become a consumer of great creativity. History museums are particularly great for me. I love art museums as well. Any kind, and every type. That is the best way to refresh my brain and my soul. Just get out of myself and go somewhere where there's a vast variety of amazing creativity to take in.

The second step is to get out of decision or assessing mode. Out of analytical mode and into open questioning. I broadly switch my mindset to asking why and why not. The more I can keep that in my head or speak it out loud, the more I start to knock down my own mental barriers and the barriers others are putting up. "Why" is one of my favorite words in the English language. And "Why not?" They are a great combination.

I grew up with a hypercritical mother, so life was about holding a mistake-finding point of view. That's why for me, it's the practice of completely flipping that script, particularly when I hear people being critical, negative, or dismissive of competition. An open mind comes from respecting, not criticizing. Even if it's something I look at on its surface and want to dismiss, I stop and don't dismiss it. I try to see and say what's right about it. I work hard to admire others' work even when it isn't necessarily what I would have done. That's why I like museums.

4. How important is failure or the acceptance of failure in cultivating creativity?

In some companies, there is a bias against failure because of past failure. That didn't work when we tried it in whatever year. Didn't you know that didn't work when somebody else tried to do it? So often, it is human nature to shy away from failure. That's why creativity favors the brave, for sure. I've never liked the fail-fast shorthand that everybody uses. My real belief is to learn from it. Understand it. Query it. You know. That's why context is important. What were the factors that created a failure? So often, failures become stories. It's like anything else in our life. We build up a story around it. But at the heart of it, there are facts. There is learning. Whenever I hear that something didn't work, I always say why. Then you have to ask why and why again. And then you say do some more digging and ask a few more people till you understand what happened. It's good to reflect, but don't ruminate. So often, it takes on its own story, and it is bigger than what really happened. I do think understanding past failures is critical to future successes. Creativity is about thinking around those barriers, not just running into them and backing off.

5. Can you share a moment in your life when you realized that thinking differently from others was a strength and not a weakness?

It was midcareer, and it was when I'd had a product failure. I'm a huge believer in Gallup StrengthsFinders. I was given the gift of doing the StrengthsFinders' process, and I learned that my strengths are being an ideator, strategic relator, maximizer, and positivist. I realized then that everyone's strengths are different, and I uniquely bring this set of strengths to the table. That was the most validating moment, and I wish I could create

(continued)

that moment for everybody at a much earlier stage in their careers because it creates agency, confidence, and clarity. What's great about this is that it helps you truly embrace your strengths and let go of defining your so-called weaknesses. That is the key; it was the most liberating moment of my life, aside from getting sober. It allowed me to declare who I was in a very positive way. It was like I finally knew who I was.

Not long after, I went to interview with Burger King and I sat across from the chief executive officer and looked at him and said, "Look, if the profile of the person you're looking at looks like this, I'm your person. If not, I'll help you find somebody else." I am not saying I'm not capable of other things. But when you lead with the things you're best at doing, it is a completely different experience. A completely new way of sitting at the table. If you show up and contribute what you uniquely bring to any organization, you will add that much more value. And you're going to be so much happier and more creative.

Exercises

BUILD AN ANALOGY

Developing effective analogies and leveraging them into new ideas is easier than you think. The following exercise not only helps in practicing the creation of analogies but also enhances lateral thinking, improves understanding of diverse domains, and fosters creativity. Repeating this exercise with different domains can further refine one's ability to draw meaningful and creative connections across various fields of knowledge. Try the exercise without the help of a generative AI partner. After the first round, partner with your favorite generative AI platform, using your selections as inputs in the prompt. At each subsequent stage, refine the output from the tool a few times by updating the prompt. Compare your effort with the machine.

Step 1: Select Two Unrelated Domains

Choose two domains (areas of knowledge or life) that are unrelated or only loosely related. For example, grocery shopping, washing a car, weeding a garden, or housekeeping.

Step 2: Identify Key Elements and Attributes

List key elements, characteristics, processes, or concepts for each domain. Try to be as diverse as possible in your listing to cover various aspects of each domain. Consider adjectives, reflect on mechanics, identify critical activities, and note senses and emotions.

Step 3: Identify Parallel Elements

Look for elements in each list that share a common function, purpose, characteristic, or underlying principle. Make abstractions to draw parallels between these elements, focusing on their relationships or roles within their respective domains.

Step 4: Create Analogies

Use a simple framework such as "A is to B as C is to D" to assist in organizing your thinking. Aim to make your analogies imaginative, highlighting an exciting or non-obvious connection. Do not edit any of the analogies you invent for reasonability. Just jot them down. Remember, even an absurd analogy can spark insight and allow you to look at the situation from a fresh perspective.

Step 5: Share

Sharing your analogies out loud with someone who was not part of the process will test the validity of the comparison. Listen to understand if the parallels you drew are not apparent to your audience and refine them. This step can reveal different perspectives and deepen the understanding of analogy-making and the method for comparing domains.

The answers to the following puzzles appear in the back of the book.

FIND CONNECTIONS

Instructions: Finding connections between unrelated things is not always obvious. The brain needs to consider many dimensions: context, utility, mechanics, materials, output, and users, to name a few. In this exercise, find the hidden connections to create four groups of connected words, using each word in the puzzle only once. Each group will not be connected in the same way. To exercise your creative muscle, try this one without the help of generative AI.

PUZZLE 1   PUZZLE 2

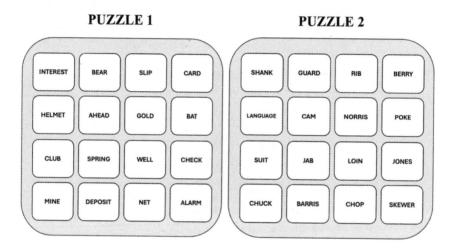

CREATE CONNECTIONS

In this exercise, you will create compound words after identifying the fourth word in the quartet and selecting the connecting element. For example, if "surf," "black," "bill," and _____ are given as the initial three members of the set, you could identify "cork" as the fourth word in the series and connect them all by adding the word "board" to each to make a compound word using each word in the set. To exercise your creative muscle, try this one without the help of generative AI.

1. door, gentle, sand, and _____ plus _____
2. battle, corn, play, and _____ plus _____
3. light, dog, green, and _____ plus _____
4. foot, hand, eye, and _____ plus _____
5. hump, play, out, and _____ plus _____

FILL IN THE ANALOGY

This exercise tests your ability to recognize relationships that include parts to a whole, creator to creation, function, opposites, groups, physical states, intensities, temporal relationships, characteristics, and roles. The key to successful analogies is to select a domain for the target that differs from the base domain that sets up the statement. After you have attempted this on your own, provide your answers to your generative AI partner to evaluate which are weak and which are strong. Ask for the rationale so you can learn where there may be a mismatch.

1. Petal is to Flower as _____ is to _____.
2. Chapter is to Book as _____ is to _____.
3. Heart is to Circulation as _____ is to _____.
4. Day is to Night as _____ is to _____.
5. Desk is to School as _____ is to _____.
6. Flame is to Candle as _____ is to _____.
7. Whisper is to Shout as _____ is to _____.
8. Cereal is to Supermarket as _____ is to _____.
9. Goose is to Swan as _____ is to _____.
10. Chef is to Kitchen as _____ is to _____.

CHAPTER 4

Change the Rules

*"Learn the rules like a pro so you can break them like
an artist."*

—Pablo Picasso

Creative velocity often involves a certain level of comfort with rule-breaking. A person's willingness to break the rules can indicate an openness to taking risks, which is a strength when exploring novel ideas and creative problem-solving. Researchers have found evidence that people who are comfortable with rule-breaking are also likely to demonstrate competence with creative thinking.[1] Individuals inclined to break the rules may be more willing to question conventional wisdom and explore uncharted territory, a hallmark of creative thinking. Indeed, empirical research suggests that individuals who are naturally rebellious (meaning that they feel less restrained by authorities) may also have a higher probability of being creative.[2]

Throughout our lives, we are taught that obeying rules and regulations brings rewards while breaking them carries negative consequences. This compliance helps to reduce risks and maintain order in society. However, blindly conforming to rules can also lead to an unwillingness to question authority or challenge the status quo. One of the common traits of the creative thinkers I interviewed for this book is their willingness to ask questions that test current assumptions, discover gaps in current beliefs, or disrupt business as usual.

63

Rules can sometimes take the form of organizational constraints, such as a bureaucratic approval process, a lack of executive support for pursuing a novel idea, or a scarcity of available resources. A 2018 *Journal of Creative Behavior* study suggests that these organizational conditions can "trigger the [rule-breaker's] 'rebellious' nature, leading them to look for other workarounds or alternatives to reach the inaccessible but desired level of creativity." This doesn't mean throwing tantrums. Instead, this behavior demonstrates a healthy desire to find pathways to alternative solutions. As Tony Fadell and Denny Post highlighted in their interviews in Chapters 2 and 3, limited resources can ironically force a higher level of resourcefulness and encourage ingenuity. You might have to improvise with new processes or combine existing tools in new ways. "When [employees are] expected by their organization to solve problems creatively, but at the same time they are not given the resources they need to achieve this," the researchers in the 2018 study said, "rule-breaking becomes a key attribute that fosters creativity" in this dissonant situation.[3]

The findings resonated with me when I first came across this research. As someone who is comfortable taking risks, questioning the status quo and accepting that disruption can be painful for some people, I enjoy leading my teams in a corporate setting, even under these conditions, to achieve a customer outcome. As the leader of Best Buy's Seattle Technology Development Center (STDC), I encountered processes, policies, and protocols that challenged our hiring capacity, inhibited our co-creation with frontline employees, and limited our ability to achieve our key business goals. When I encountered these hurdles, I improvised.

Prior to the STDC, Best Buy's retail operations team had an extremely time-consuming process for getting approval to conduct an in-store visit for employee or customer research. The process was put in place to diminish the impact caused by the constant flow of corporate employees into the stores in the Minneapolis area where Best Buy's corporate office is headquartered. However, since corporate technology teams rarely visited the stores in the Pacific Northwest, engagement with the STDC team in these stores was not seen at that time as a potential distraction by the local store leadership, and instead was viewed as an opportunity for frontline employees to be part of the discovery and ideation process to design innovative omnichannel experiences.

During an autumn weekend in 2015, I visited a North Seattle store to introduce myself to the store's general manager. The manager informed me that he wished he had more help supporting the massive volume of customers expected in-store during the madness of Black Friday. At the same time, product, design, and engineering leaders wanted access to customers and employees to do discovery work. We agreed to bypass the approval process for in-store visits, and in exchange for this accommodation, I agreed to provide extra temporary staffing for the holiday. We forged a partnership when we decided to "break the rules," energizing our teams to co-create and develop multiple in-store innovations for all Best Buy customers, including Blue Assist, Local Store Mode, and On My Way.[4]

Rule-breakers are focused on more than just subverting corporate policies or disrupting organizational norms. They are also attracted to opportunities to upend how customers get their tasks and jobs done. They are as delighted busting age-old business models as they are challenging traditional operating rules, disrupting the supply chain, or opening new channels to reach customers. As you will see in my interview with Scott Ehrlich at the end of this chapter, nothing is more fulfilling to rule-breakers than to disrupt an existing industry—in his case, traditional media—by deconstruction, modification, and reinvention.

When Apple launched the iPod in 2001, it was initially compatible only with Mac computers, which limited its market reach given the dominance of Windows PCs. The disruptive moment came in 2003 when Apple announced iTunes for Windows, effectively making the iPod accessible to everyone. This decision leveraged differing philosophies between Apple and Microsoft to define a new set of rules for streaming music. Up until that point, digital music was fragmented by device manufacturers, fraught with fear of piracy, and littered with unsuccessful monetization models.

Reed Hastings, the founder of Netflix, disrupted the home entertainment and film industries by shifting from a DVD rental business to streaming media, breaking the traditional cable subscription models. Netflix's approach to content distribution broke the rules of scheduled programming, allowing users to binge-watch series content on demand. This also changed availability windows, union contracts, and payment terms. But that wasn't the end of Netflix's rule-breaking. Its decision to invest in original programming expanded its role from content distributor to content creator and broadened its influence, competitors, and power in the entertainment industry.[5]

Creative Destruction

Creative destruction is an extreme form of rule-breaking in which a new set of policies, norms, business models, or technologies are required to achieve the benefit of an innovation. The term was popularized by Joseph Schumpeter, an Austrian economist who taught at Harvard in the 1930s and '40s. Schumpeter believed that the process by which innovation disrupts existing industries, businesses, and technologies is necessary to propel capitalism. Destruction is essential for revolutionary innovation to find the light. The idea that "there's got to be a better way" is central to his position, as are entrepreneurs whom he credited with sparking these revolutions.[6]

Creative destruction can give birth to entirely new industries that did not exist before. The more creative destruction that occurs, the faster the rate of creative velocity. For example, the rise of the Internet created new industries beyond streaming, such as e-commerce, cloud computing, mobile payments, and Bitcoin. The Internet fundamentally changed how we shop, manage our money, find work, access information, and communicate. Imagine we didn't have the Internet when the world went into lockdown. Not only did the Internet allow us to have our food delivered and track the Amazon trucks bringing all our essential antibacterial products and masks, but it also helped us stay connected to our friends and family on social platforms while we binge-watched every episode of *Parks and Recreation*. The Internet allowed thousands of disruptors to re-invent how things got done. While creative destruction creates novel opportunities for entrepreneurs to innovate, it also forces existing businesses to face extinction if they don't adapt, transform, and reinvent themselves.

Entrepreneurs tend to be comfortable with creative destruction because they focus on what needs to change when long-standing institutions or operating methods must be re-architected once they have become outdated, inefficient, or irrelevant. Creative destruction is much harder for existing enterprises to swallow, as breaking the standard ways of working inevitably creates a shift in business economics. (This explains why an economist popularized the term *creative destruction.*) Undertaking revolutionary innovations can be quite costly for companies; the labor mix may need to change, program or job cuts may need to be made to fund it, and there may be unexpected risks while making the transformation. Under these conditions, employees can get protective of their territory, letting their fears subvert their capacity to see opportunity when rules and processes change. Since rule breakers are biased toward choosing creativity over compliance, their behavior can cause them to encounter cultural antibodies that stifle innovation. The practical realities of the existing business make it difficult for some people in organizations to disconnect and explore the great unknown. This inevitably slows the organization's creative velocity.

Challenging established norms and conventions that hinder innovation is at the heart of creative destruction. Therefore, a deep understanding of the current landscape is essential to exploring a path toward disruption. Where are there inefficiencies in the current system? What if this step could be eliminated? These questions help explore the impact of different scenarios when the rules change. The process requires a willingness to break the rules that guide how customers, employees, and systems engage with each other. It can also involve finding loopholes in rules rather than breaking them. A great way to start breaking the rules is by using the "What if?" style of questioning. A few examples are "What if we stopped doing X?" and "What if we started using Y?" or "What if we added Z?"

Uber is a prime example of creative destruction. In many cities, the taxi industry was highly regulated, with rules and limits around how many licenses were issued, a schedule of fares and fees, and specific pickup locations. These regulations were implemented to protect the existing taxi and limousine industries. However, Uber found a loophole by positioning itself as a "technology platform" that connects riders with independent drivers. By connecting customers and drivers directly and circumventing cab companies, a new business model for transportation was launched. This positioned Uber to bypass many taxi regulations, offering a more accessible and potentially cheaper alternative for riders. Even though Uber launched in 2009, the impact of this act of creative destruction is still unfolding more than a decade and a half later, as demonstrated by a more recent legal debate about whether voters should have the power to allow app-based services such as Uber to classify drivers as independent contractors rather than as employees with greater benefits, such as minimum wage laws.

To succeed as a disruptor, one must be open-minded, resilient, adaptive, willing to take risks, and comfortable with the likelihood of significant change to business as usual. A commitment to maintaining the status quo and a belief that rules are immutable impede creative thinking and slow creative velocity.

The SCAMPER Method

While creative destruction works at the macro level, with the goal of transforming an entire system, the SCAMPER method of creative thinking works on a more micro level. Breaking mental limitations that might hinder creative exploration within the brainstorming process is a more personal form of breaking the rules. The SCAMPER method inherently encourages disruptive creative thinking by challenging assumptions and questioning how things are typically done. SCAMPER was derived from a seminal work on creative thinking by Alex F. Osborn called "Applied Imagination: Principles and Procedures of Creative Problem Solving."[7] Osborn was one of the founding partners of BBDO, a global advertising agency, at the beginning of the twentieth century and is known as the father of brainstorming. He created a 73-question checklist to guide the ideation process, which Bob Eberle expanded upon with the SCAMPER technique.[8] Since then, there have been further modifications to the activities, as represented by each of the acronym's letters. As shown in Figure 4.1,

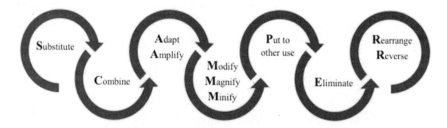

Figure 4.1 Bob Eberle introduced the SCAMPER mnemonic represented here in 1971 illustrating multiple perspectives on the meaning of the acronym.

the letters in some iterations may represent multiple words, and in others, the verbs that the letters represent change entirely.

Whichever variation you use, the goal is the same: ask questions to break your mental models, assumptions, and biases about how things are built, how they function, and what can be improved. The exercise is intended to spur divergent thinking by looking at a problem domain from different perspectives. Since divergent thinking aims to quickly generate many different ideas about a topic, it can help accelerate creative velocity.

SCAMPER inherently encourages rule-breaking in creative thinking by asking you to question how things are typically done and consider alternatives. The questions in this technique are targeted at disrupting an existing product, service, or business model to uncover opportunities to innovate. Completing the entire cycle of questions is optional, as you may find inspiration in one area of exploration and want to dwell there. The process is not linear, so you may start your journey anywhere. You can return to it any time and pick the next rabbit hole you want to investigate.

While the list of successful ideas that originated from using this method are not well documented, it is easy to find examples of products or businesses launched that exhibit the characteristics explored in SCAMPER. By examining the way these transformational activities can manifest in real product innovations, it is easier to see the value of this creative thinking technique.

Substitute, the "S" in SCAMPER, often involves replacing a component that has reached its maximum potential with a new, more advanced solution or a solution from an unrelated domain. Advancements in lithium-ion batteries have made it possible for auto manufacturers like Tesla to substitute internal combustion engines with battery-powered electric motors that drive the next generation of transportation. This substitution has resulted in a major disruption of the automotive industry, and it will ultimately spawn new businesses, affect energy demand, require new infrastructure, and drive new government regulations.

In Chapter 2, we stated that combinational creativity has been the source of centuries of innovation. This is the basis for the "C" in SCAMPER. The questions in this stage explore features, uses, or components that can be combined. This is when to imagine the possibilities of combining X and Y technologies. This creates the opportunity to envision that something greater can be achieved by the sum of two or more things than simply iterating an individual item. In a post on the *Smithsonian Magazine* website entitled "Combinatorial Creativity and the Myth of Originality," Maria Popova wrote, "To create is to combine existing bits of insight, knowledge, ideas, and memories into new material and new interpretations of the world, to connect the seemingly dissociated, to see patterns where others see chaos."[9]

Just like the smartphone and the all-in-one printer we highlighted earlier in the book, the Nest Learning Thermostat, the brainchild of Tony Fadell's Nest Labs, is a good example of a combinatorial consumer product. The device represents a ground-breaking blend of technologies that paved the way for further convergence and multifunctionality in upcoming devices. While other smart home devices existed before Nest, its success accelerated the development and adoption of various smart home categories, like smart lighting, smart appliances, and even the smart video doorbell.

Product, process, and service adaptations can solve problems by enhancing the existing system. This is what the "A" represents in SCAMPER. The scale of the adaptation itself is not as important as its impact on the value of the output. Adaptations can create an entirely new product category or change the audience for an existing one. A great example of an adaptation is the shipping container home, as shown in Figure 4.2. The primary function of shipping containers is transporting goods. Shipping containers are durable and built to withstand dramatic weather conditions. Their material, size, and shape make them easy to repurpose. They can be more cost-effective than conventional housing because they require fewer building materials and labor to construct.[10] Though adding electrical, plumbing, and windows can create special challenges, their durability, modular design, and transportability provide offsetting benefits.

Modify is the most common verb associated with the "M" in SCAMPER, although some practitioners may use "Magnify" or "Minify" as an alternative to focus the brainstorming process by suggesting specific modifications to be explored. Modifications can bring about significant changes to an existing idea, redefine a category, or

Figure 4.2 Photorealistic images of a luxury tiny house made from shipping containers nestled in a forest.

(images generated by OpenAI's DALL·E model, April 7, 2023.)

redesign an experience. Costco, a big-box retailer, made one of the most successful modifications that transformed the competitive retail landscape. Costco differentiates itself significantly from other big-box retailers like Walmart and Target by focusing on bulk buying and membership and embracing a warehouse environment. The shopping experience at Costco is more akin to pushing a large flatbed cart around the lumber section of Home Depot than a grocery store. The product selection is not always predictable, and you typically need to purchase large quantities of certain goods, though that's not the case for wine, clothing, or furnishings. Costco only takes one type of credit card to make payments. Despite all these modifications to the traditional grocery shopping experience, consumers flock to Costco to buy their office supplies, tires, and prime steaks.

The "P" in SCAMPER, which represents putting something to another use, is intended to help you envision products in new contexts or for unanticipated applications. This benefits from a "MacGyver" mindset, and is at the core of MacGyver's problem-solving techniques. The "P" explicitly encourages breaking the rule of intended use and letting go of biases fueled by preconceived notions of how a product should be used. It involves looking at the inherent properties and characteristics of an item and imagining how those qualities could be applied in new situations.

As an example, Play-Doh, now a popular children's toy, was originally created by a manufacturer of wallpaper cleaners, Kutol Products, in the early 1900s. It was initially designed to remove soot from wallpaper in homes that were heated with coal. However, as cleaner energy sources and vinyl wallpaper became more popular, Play-Doh lost its original purpose. A relative of a Kutol executive who was a nursery schoolteacher is credited with finding a new audience and purpose for the product as a moldable and pliable toy.[11]

The pharmaceutical industry provides great examples of repurposing. During initial drug testing, a medication developed for one purpose may be found to be effective for a completely different condition. Rogaine (minoxidil) and Viagra (sildenafil) both were initially developed to treat high blood pressure. During clinical trials, both drugs' side effects were so pronounced that researchers pivoted their attention and redesigned their testing to focus on these new uses. Rogaine became the first drug approved by the FDA for the treatment of baldness.[12] Viagra received FDA approval as the first oral medication for erectile dysfunction.[13]

Sometimes, the most innovative solutions address a fundamental need in a refreshingly simple way. As you evolve an existing idea, it is easy to get bogged down in the specific details or become attached to particular pieces of it, making it hard to let go of any of them. Eliminate, which represents the "E" in SCAMPER, prompts you to explore what the simplest version of a product could be. Simplification through elimination often involves the adoption of new technologies that eliminate manual steps. For example, the application of digital technologies to commercial banking eliminated the need for customers to enter the bank building to check balances, pay off loans, and make deposits to their personal accounts. The introduction of ATMs eliminated the need for a bank teller as a channel for receiving deposits and withdrawing cash for many bank customers. Then, using a smartphone camera, it became possible to deposit checks eliminating the need to find an ATM for that purpose.

Technology advancements have made elimination a popular form of rule-breaking. Dyson revolutionized the vacuum cleaner by eliminating the need for vacuum cleaner bags. They achieved this by using centrifugal force to separate dust and debris. This change addressed common consumer complaints about replacement bags, such as the lack of visibility when they are full, their tendency to clog, and the cost of purchasing them. This innovation also reduces waste and enhances the vacuum's suction efficiency.

The last letter in the acronym, "R," prompts thinking about what would happen if the process or product were rearranged or reversed. This technique breaks the rule of linear evolution, encouraging a backward or inside-out perspective to identify opportunities for innovation that wouldn't be apparent when following the normal way of delivering the experience. An example of this type of innovation is curbside pickup, also known as click-and-collect. The pandemic accelerated click-and-collect for grocery shopping, where store employees gather the groceries on behalf of customers, changing the role of a store employee in the item selection process. Customers select and pay for their shopping list online. Store employees do the work of picking and gathering the goods. By rearranging the order of activities, customers simply arrive at a designated pickup location, and their orders are ready for collection. This shift enhances convenience and increases efficiency, while reducing the time and physical contact involved in the shopping process during the pandemic. In Chapter 5, we will explore in depth the value of inversion, or reverse thinking, to accelerate novel solutions.

Rule-breaking in this context is about challenging assumptions. The SCAMPER technique may initiate a train of thought that leads to creative destruction, or it may help uncover the power of a simple change in mechanics, assumptions, or processes that can lead to an improvement, invention, or novel solution. Questioning current customer journeys or enterprise workflows, and reassessing the methods for acquiring, paying for, and using a product or service can lead to a revelation that drives larger-scale transformations that may affect not just a company but also the industry in which it operates.

Partnering with Generative AI

Generative AI can be a helpful collaborator when investigating opportunities that may be ripe for creative destruction. Prompting it to analyze historical data can assist in identifying industries that have stagnated, become inefficient, have high barriers to entry, are dominated by a few large players, or appear slow to adopt new technologies. This is the same kind of data analysis investors do when making bets to back or short a company. Generative AI can also evaluate sentiment, catalog user frustrations and trends in customer behavior, and analyze research reports and industry trends to assess current unmet needs or persistent pain points.

You can use this approach to analyze industries that have undergone successful transformations to identify the key disruptive elements of those models and apply them to the target industry you're exploring. Consider prompts that propose alternative technologies for AI to consider when assessing areas for redesign and reinvention. Ask your generative AI partner how resources currently used in the industry can be utilized differently or even eliminated, and what type of sustainable approach to materials or power could dramatically affect the effectiveness, pricing, accessibility, and utility of the industry's products and services.

Partnering with generative AI on a SCAMPER exercise is the perfect blend of human and computational creativity. Humans play an important role in guiding, constraining, and challenging the machine-made output to be useful, meaningful, and valuable. By providing specific goals for the exercise and offering relevant information and context in the prompts, you can launch an investigation of a specific product or service. AI has no emotional attachment to any ingredient, design, or audience and will only be limited by the constraints you represent. Refine and iterate by adding or removing constraints, or exploring ways to transform the sector's economic model.

It's always a good idea to engage in an iterative dialogue with the AI, providing feedback on the ideas generated so that the AI can adapt to the guidance provided. Including this refinement in your subsequent direction will improve the relevance and quality of the suggestions. When seeking ideas from your AI partner, inform it that you want to apply the SCAMPER methodology. Utilize specific and structured prompts that correspond with SCAMPER, and clearly state which element of SCAMPER you are concentrating on, for example, "Substitute," "Combine," "Adapt," and so on. As you review the responses you get, be prepared to dive into specifics, explore details, ask for the rationale, and challenge feasibility. Ask your AI partner to assess the costs and analyze the market opportunity for the new idea. As always, recognize the limitations of the data your partner was trained on and validate the output as part of your evaluation process.

It is important to iterate the output and provide feedback, details, and revisions to reframe the problem as insight emerges from customer research. A well-structured prompt should guide the AI toward identifying potential areas of disruption. Start by defining the domain and specify the subsector. Identify pain points and current challenges or inefficiencies in the chosen subsector. Suggest potential technologies that could disrupt the industry. Finally, offer specific details about the customer persona you are targeting. It is important to provide psychographic insights around relevant traits such as values, cultural norms, goals, priorities, and lifestyle choices.

As an example, imagine you might want to identify potential opportunities for creative destruction within the veterinary diagnostic services sector. Focus on pain points related to test accuracy, turnaround time, and cost. You could explore how advancements in digital twins and AI could disrupt traditional diagnostic methods. Emphasize the importance of aligning any potential solutions with the specific needs of both pet owners and veterinarians.

Interview with Scott Ehrlich

Scott Ehrlich is chief innovation officer and head of corporate strategy for Sinclair. Earlier in his career, Scott was senior vice president and executive producer of News America Digital Publishing at News Corporation and vice president of Media Acquisition and Distribution for RealNetworks, which is where I met Scott in 2000, at the start of the streaming media era. Scott and I, along with a handful of other colleagues at RealNetworks, co-authored a patent that was ultimately sold to Intel. Scott has built a successful career as a disruptor at the intersection

(continued)

of traditional broadcast and emerging media, working in both large media companies and startup environments. As founder and chief executive officer of Agility Studios, Scott led the development of Agility's International Emmy award-winning franchise, *The Legion of Extraordinary Dancers*, created by Jon M. Chu.

1. **In this age of generative AI, what is the role of human creativity?**

   I was asked this question on a panel for the first time at the *Variety* Entertainment Marketing Summit in 2023. And it was a pretty charged environment to be asked, "Is AI going to replace artists?"

   Humans must have the right expectations of what machines can produce; half the people I work with think AI can solve every problem for free tomorrow. If you've ever worked with an artist and seen their process and the way they think about how they're going to move an audience, you cannot believe that a machine will be able to do that. In my view, the more important part of this is the role AI will play in humans' creative process. Any artist who doesn't figure out how to harness AI will be at a significant disadvantage. And I mean a considerable disadvantage. The artists who figure out how to collaborate with AI usefully will be greatly advantaged over those who don't. They will be creating more impactful content at more velocity.

   Part of the problem with a hand-drawn storyboard is that by the time you realize you want to change that little component you are committed to that storyboard. You spent a month painting it. But with AI, you can switch it out. You can iterate so many times as part of the creative process, many more times than you can manually. So, the creative output will be better just because you can iterate on it more.

2. **Everyone knows a famous story about a eureka moment when innovation happened. Has that happened to you? Can we have intentional epiphanies?**

I believe there are inventors who get to have that, especially if you're trying to invent a piece of hard tech and you get to the point where you see it works. I think you have that moment when you are inventing. But I don't see myself as an inventor. That's not really what I do. I create businesses. When I create a business, that eureka moment is actually the minute that somebody writes you a check for the thing you're building. For example, if that's a startup when you get your first customer, you get your first investor, and that's the moment you know innovation happened. A flash or brilliance is only part of the equation. If it's an idea you've never heard before, it's a novel idea. The minute somebody else is interested, then it's novel *and* useful, and that is when you know your flash of brilliance is real.

I have bad ideas all day long. The way that I know that it's a good idea is when other people start to repeat it. When I can get people to pitch my idea back to me, that's when I know it's real. And that's the only bar I'm actually looking to meet—is this a real idea? By that, I mean, is this a useful idea that usually takes validation from other people? I've been around start-ups and businesses way too long to sort of overvalue an idea. Epiphanies only matter if they are useful, and there usually is some unpredictable amount of time between having the idea and validating the idea as having value. Time and time again, the world proves to us that execution is what makes a difference. I don't get that hyped on the idea. I get hyped when

(continued)

somebody says that is something I would buy because now we get a chance to execute. I have full confidence that if I get a chance to execute, I can execute.

3. **How do you re-energize your creative spirit during periods of frustration or stagnation? Where do you find inspiration?**

I get rid of as much noise as I can, and I give myself enough time to actually think through the problem. There are different ways of thinking through problems. There's a kind where you can say, "Let's look at the data. Let's talk through it. Let's put it up on a whiteboard." Then there are the ones where I have to come up with a solution to a challenge, and there is no precedent for this. It isn't like people have solved this problem before, so I can't learn from their efforts. I have to figure it out. So, I'll look at what is close and see if there is anything I can learn from what's close. I will consider who I should talk to that might help me think through the problem. Who's been through similar problems that can give you leads and information? Everybody does some version of those things. However, those activities don't actually do all that much for me in terms of solving a truly novel problem.

If I have to tackle a truly novel problem, I have to have music. I have to get away from the office and the things that will distract me there. I don't listen to a lot of music day to day. I listen to a lot of podcasts. But when I really need to come up with a breakthrough of sorts. There's only one way that has ever worked for me, and it's a headset with highly energetic music. I isolate myself from the world until I can figure it out. Sometimes, that's hours, and sometimes, it's a couple of days. I can't keep managing what's happening day to day if I need to come up with a breakthrough solution.

When I launched my last startup, we were stuck on the pitch and how to tell the story.

We were going round and round in circles, and I finally threw everybody out of the office for the day. It was just me and the dog. I cranked up the music and started doodling on a whiteboard. Four hours later, I had a pitch and the script, and we were off to the races.

4. How important is failure or the acceptance of failure in cultivating creativity?

True failure comes from two things. The first is that maybe you started with the wrong question; you see that all the time. The second is that you have convinced yourself that you have the right answer, but you find out you were asking the wrong question.

Personally, I don't think about failures. I think about failure as one of the steps on the way to success. Maybe the reason you failed is you found the answer to the question, and maybe it wasn't the answer you hoped for, or maybe it wasn't the right question. Either way, you are still mid-process. So, the work is only done when I have the answer. I have certainly had businesses where I felt like I got to the answer, so I moved on. A lot of times, I've been brought in to solve a specific problem or address a specific opportunity. And once you figure it out, then it's time to move on. Maybe you didn't really read the signals in the market. I see that all the time. But more often than not, what people think of as failure is really just about the fact that they started with a bad question.

5. Can you share a moment when you realized that thinking differently from others was a strength, not a weakness?

It was 1993, and I was at a small company, probably 10 of us in total, but it was built around a solo entrepreneur; he had created the political media consulting category. To pay the bills in non-political

(continued)

years, we'd offer the same kinds of media training and strategy that we would do for candidates, to corporations. Eventually, my boss was hired to help fix the cable network CNBC, and we moved together, doing the same thing at a media company. These were the early days of the Internet, and two things immediately occurred to me. The first was that the Internet was going to be a big thing; it was going to be our generation's opportunity to define a new media platform. And the second thing that was clear was that business news and stock quotes were well-positioned to be an early mover. Both things drove me to want to move CNBC into the Internet early.

I pitched this to a very senior group of executives at NBC, who told me not to screw up a very promising television career by talking about this Internet thing. Then, the most remarkable thing happened: I came away from that meeting and got all this negative feedback.

But I was still thinking I was right. And I think it was that moment when everybody in that room told me I was wrong, but I was still deeply convinced I was right, which encouraged me not to worry about being in or out of somebody else's box. Less than a year after that meeting, we all left NBC and joined Fox. So now I have worked for the same guy in three different companies, and he had this whole list of things he wanted me to do, and I told him I wanted to build our dotcom site. He literally rolled his eyes and looked at me and told me, "Alright, fine. But don't waste too much time on it." Then and there, I had a moment when I could make it happen. Everybody thought we were wasting our time, but ultimately, it proved to be the right thing to do, and we were way out in front online.

Exercises

PRACTICING SCAMPER

You can begin these exercises on your own and then partner with generative AI to explore them further. If you feel blocked on where to begin, skip to the next exercise. As you develop confidence in your ability to break the rules through collaboration, return to this exercise to continue to train your creative muscles.

1. **Substitute:** Pick a common object, such as something on your desk or in your kitchen.

   Write down the answer to the following questions as you evaluate the object:

   a. What are the most obvious things that can be substituted?

   b. How can I substitute the materials or ingredients used in the product to change its utility?

   c. What other power/energy source can be substituted?

   d. Can you use this product somewhere else or as a substitute for something else?

   e. What can be used instead of the object to fulfill the same function?

2. **Combine:** Choose a familiar service, like a car rental service or getting a haircut. Consider how this service could be combined with another existing service to create a more convenient or unique offering.

   a. How can I combine materials or ingredients to get better results?

   b. How can I combine any processes?

   c. How can I combine two or more features of each service?

   d. How can I combine technologies?

   e. How can I combine resources or staffing to find efficiencies?

3. **Adapt:** Select one of the following products or services and adapt it to another use. Choose from an ATM machine, a boxcar, a dog walking service, a car wash, or a roadside assistance service.

   a. How can it be adjusted to fit another purpose?

   b. How can it be adapted for a different audience?

    c. How can another process/technology/part be adapted to fit this purpose?

    d. Are there elements that can be amplified?

    e. Can I employ a known process to improve the speed or results?

4. **Modify:** Pick a common product or service you encounter frequently, like a parking meter, an icemaker, or a fitness app.

    a. Consider what aspects of this product or service could be frustrating or inconvenient. What could be improved?

    b. Identify the parts of the experience that you appreciate. How can you amplify them?

    c. What can be minimized, maximized, subtracted, or added to increase its utility?

    d. How can it be reshaped, redesigned, or revised to appeal to a different audience?

    e. What rules or policies should be changed to increase its value?

5. **Put to Another Use:** Take a common household item—such as a ladder, a dustpan, or an ice tray—and brainstorm all possible different uses for it outside its primary function.

    a. Identify five different uses for this product that are different from what it was originally designed for.

    b. What other unmet needs can this product fulfill?

    c. Can we recycle the waste or repurpose the parts from this product for another use?

    d. Can different groups of people use this product for purposes other than its intended use?

6. **Eliminate:** Pick a routine task, like washing your car or doing your laundry. Through the process of elimination, explore ways to improve the experience.

    a. What processes or steps can be removed or skipped?

    b. What rules or instructions can be ignored?

    c. What resources can be eliminated to execute the task?

    d. What tools or ingredients are not critical to complete the task?

7. **Rearrange and Reverse:** Look at a standard process or product and imagine reversing its order or layout. Examples might include renewing your driver's license, onboarding a new employee, or booking travel plans.

a. Can the order of any components or steps change?
b. Can the layout or pattern be changed?
c. Is it possible to redesign some parts for better results?
d. What can be transposed?

SCAMPERING WITH GENERATIVE AI

To be a good partner in this collaboration, remember that generative AI can access and process vast amounts of information to find relevant technologies and successful models. To focus the engagement, provide helpful context to frame the exploration—the more you can pinpoint specific parameters, the more efficiently you can generate, evaluate, and iterate.

- **Substitute core functions:** Evaluate completely new ways to achieve the core function of an industry. Ask generative AI what are the core functions of an industry that could be entirely replaced with new approaches to create a radically different industry experience.
  - Investigate functions related to production, distribution, or customer interaction.
- **Combine existing technologies:** Explore how existing technologies from seemingly unrelated fields could be combined to disrupt an industry. Ask generative AI to help identify frustrations or limitations users face in this industry.
  - Think about pain points, such as inefficiencies, costs, or unmet customer needs.
  - Brainstorm a list of rapidly developing technologies from completely different fields.
  - Now, creatively explore how these seemingly unrelated technologies could be combined to address the pain points identified earlier.
- **Adapt successful models:** Analyze industries that have undergone successful disruption. Ask generative AI to adapt the disruptive elements of those models to the target industry you're exploring.
  - Begin by breaking down an existing industry. What are its core functions, pain points, and current customer journey?
  - Identify areas where the industry struggles or could be significantly improved.

- Switch focus on an unrelated industry. What are the most successful models or processes used in this seemingly unrelated field?
  - o Think about subscription services, just-in-time delivery, mobile wallets, microtransactions, or anything else that revolutionized that industry.
- Explore how the successful model from the unrelated industry could be adapted to address the pain points and improve the customer journey in the industry.
- Translate the core principles of the borrowed model to function within this new context.
- Explore how this can create a more efficient, cost-effective, or user-friendly experience in the industry.

- ◆ **Eliminate unnecessary steps:** Explore elements of an industry that can be eliminated to improve efficiency, effectiveness, experience, or economics. Prompt generative AI to find candidates for elimination and evaluate the impact of this change.
  - Identify bottlenecks, redundancies, processes, rules, and policies that may affect productivity, access, execution, or revenue.
  - Examine the impact of excluding these factors on customers and the industry. What hurdles does this create? What changes for the better?

CHAPTER 5

Do the Opposite

"If every instinct you have is wrong, then the opposite would have to be right."

—Jerry Seinfeld

In the 1989 pilot episode of *Seinfeld*, George tells Jerry, "Never do what your instincts tell you. Always, always do the opposite." In Season 5, that advice became the centerpiece of Episode 22, called *The Opposite*. After George complains that every choice he makes has been wrong, Jerry encourages him to make a drastic change by repeating the same advice to George. All his dreams come true after George decides to do the opposite of everything he usually does. In an interview where he looks back on the episode, the actor who played George Costanza, Jason Alexander, recalled that he learned of several people who took the advice seriously and found themselves prospering.[1]

To be relatable, sitcom humor tends to exaggerate elements of the truth. *Seinfeld*, for example, used the concept of "opposite thinking." There is no single methodology that defines the way to execute opposite thinking. It has existed for centuries and has its roots in Eastern philosophy. In Taoism, the interplay of opposites, notably yin and yang, is the foundation of how we engage with the world. Over the centuries, scientists, psychologists, and artists have expanded upon the notion, and it is now widely considered a cognitive strategy for creative thinking.

Children learn the concepts of opposites between ages three and four.[2] Understanding opposites is a critical cognitive skill. It helps develop flexible thinking skills, process complex concepts, and encourage empathy. Opposite thinking stimulates innovative ideas by pushing the boundaries of conventional thinking and providing a different vantage point from which to view the problem. It encourages the exploration of new possibilities that question standard expectations, leading to breakthrough innovations and solutions.

To utilize opposite thinking, start with key assumptions about market dynamics, the target customer, and the business model, and then formulate the direct opposite or reverse statement. With these opposite statements in mind, explore potential solutions or approaches that would make sense in that flipped reality. Your purpose is to create alternate scenarios and see how and why they contradict more traditional approaches. Exploring contrary ideas can sometimes spark creativity because it allows you to consider an element that may provide new insight from something you'd otherwise dismiss.

Opposite thinking is a practical tool that can be applied in various industries and situations. It is particularly effective in highly competitive sectors where standing out is critical or in established markets where novel perspectives can result in game-changing innovations. This method is also helpful when standard methods have proven ineffective. Opposite thinking directly confronts conventional wisdom and the status quo by encouraging the pursuit of new possibilities and imaginative solutions. It challenges assumptions and evaluates patterns, potentially revealing unconscious bias or unintentional habits.

By actively seeking out opposing viewpoints, you can significantly boost your divergent thinking skills and generate a wealth of creative solutions. In fact, divergent thinking and opposite thinking thrive on cognitive flexibility, a willingness to consider other perspectives, and an openness to breaking existing patterns. Overall, divergent thinking benefits from opposite views because they introduce complexity and conflict, which are catalysts for creativity and deeper exploration. This approach to problem-solving may be overlooked in organizations that demonstrate expert bias and are quick to dismiss divergent perspectives.

While opposite thinking involves deliberately considering the opposite of a common assumption or belief related to the problem, inversion, on the other hand, flips the problem on its head. Instead of asking how to achieve a desired outcome, this technique prompts individuals to consider how to avoid failure or the worst possible outcome. This shift in focus can reveal vulnerabilities and lead to solutions that proactively prevent problems before they arise.

Janusian thinking involves the simultaneous consideration of conflicting ideas or concepts. Named for the Roman god Janus, who was famously described as having two heads facing in opposite directions, this approach to problem-solving allows for the synthesis of seemingly contradictory elements, leading to creative solutions that embrace that two opposing concepts can both be true.

Counterintuitive thinking is a unique and innovative approach to problem-solving that encourages individuals to look beyond conventional wisdom. Collectively, these creative thinking techniques challenge traditional thought processes and encourage novel solutions to complex problems. Living with the cognitive dissonance that usually accompanies a counterintuitive approach can be difficult for people without a creative mindset or the self-confidence to navigate the complexity.

Inversion Thinking

Billionaire Charles (Charlie) Munger, vice chairman of Berkshire Hathaway, recognized the value of inversion thinking, citing it as a key to his success in his wartime role as a meteorologist during World War II. And it was a philosophy he subscribed to as an investor. He regularly repeated the words of the brilliant nineteenth-century German mathematician Carl Gustav Jacob Jacobi, "Invert, always invert."[3] Munger added, "Many hard problems are best solved when addressed backward. This model is one of the most powerful thinking habits we can adopt."[4]

The origin of this type of creative problem-solving technique can be found long before the nineteenth century in the ancient philosophy of dialectics, which assumes the existence of something is dependent on the coexistence of two opposite conditions, such as up/down, love/hate, hot/cold, top/bottom, and happy/sad. By looking at the opposite outcome to the one you are targeting, you can explore the connections between the two states and better understand the triggers that can move an idea from one side of the coin to the other.

Imagine that rather than simplifying a problem, you thought about how to complexify it instead. You might ask, "How can I make this harder to use?" or "What if this was less efficient?" or "How might we make this less reliable?" Consider taking the answers to your questions and reversing them to see if they still make sense. This can help uncover any failure modes that you may not have previously considered or provide new insights into which problems are most important to solve. In Munger's telling of his initial success with inversion, he shares that he was tasked with providing weather reports to fighter pilots to ensure they didn't end up in unsafe conditions. His approach to solving this was to understand better what circumstances and conditions could risk a pilot's life. He would then focus on consciously avoiding those conditions, enabling him to predict best when they could fly safely. He could arrive at the most suitable solution by eliminating the undesirable options.[5]

Inversion thinking is not the same as planning for failure. While the technique does involve considering potential failures or negative outcomes, the ultimate goal is to avoid those pitfalls and increase the chances of success. This technique allows the problem solver to manage the conditions that might block success proactively. The objective is not to expect or ruminate over a bad outcome. It is to be mindful of what might derail the path to success. If you are worried that you can't retain employees, then you must consider why they would be inclined to leave and remove as many of those reasons for them to depart as possible to reduce the risk of attrition.

For anyone who may get enamored with a new idea, the inversion technique can help ensure you aren't missing possible pitfalls or potential barriers to realizing the vision. Working backward from an undesirable outcome can also create the opportunity to uncover a novel approach to avoid it. By challenging basic assumptions about a project, new product idea, or business and flipping the plan upside down, you can explore a range of solutions that may increase the odds of its success.

Klarna is a business that exemplifies inversion thinking. Traditionally, consumers had to pay for items before receiving them. Klarna flipped this approach with its "buy now, pay later" service, allowing consumers to receive goods without an upfront payment. Customers pay over time, but when shopping online, they can check out as if they were paying with a standard credit card. However, unlike credit cards, Klarna does not charge any interest or late fees on purchases paid in installments and does not set a total spending limit. Rather, Klarna evaluates each purchase individually. And the Klarna solution has no interest or late fees on the purchase.

In Chapter 4, we examined the SCAMPER acronym and said the "R" is intended to prompt thinking about what would happen if a process were rearranged. Some versions of this technique use the "R" to encourage an examination of the reverse of a process or workflow. The goal of this approach is to imagine what would make your idea worse by exploring if this reversal in perspective sparks unexpected improvements. In this version of the methodology, the "R" in SCAMPER and inversion thinking are very closely related. Inversion thinking is basically a broader concept that encompasses the "reverse" technique within SCAMPER.

Seneca, a Stoic philosopher of Ancient Rome, wrote, "What is quite unlooked for is more crushing in its effect, and unexpectedness adds to the weight of a disaster."[6] This counsel was not meant as a rationalization for endless rumination about possible negative outcomes. Instead, the Stoics believed that people who were the most unprepared for the negative forces that might block them from achieving their goals were the least equipped to avoid them. They used an exercise known as a "premeditation of evils," during which they took time to imagine things that could go wrong to prepare for, prevent, and avoid undesirable outcomes.

The key to making this approach constructive is consciously preventing it from becoming a forum for nurturing pessimism or a "woe is me" mindset. When you consider how your project could fail, you are forced to explore different angles and approaches. This kind of "what-if" scenario brainstorming can spark unexpected and novel ideas you might not have considered otherwise, but only if you stay positive and actively regulate any negative emotions that may arise by dwelling on the "evils." Thinking about potential shortcomings in your plan encourages you to think creatively about deploying available resources to address them.

Inversion thinking is helpful when you want to avoid mistakes and mitigate risks. It helps identify potential obstacles, risks, and failure points, which ensures a more robust solution and an awareness of pitfalls to avoid. If you are concerned about the sustainability of an idea, inversion thinking can help evaluate its long-term viability. Thinking about ways to fail in order to succeed requires comfort with the idea of failure. As Jules Pieri shares in her interview in Chapter 7, when she considers the choices she has to make, like whether she should start her own business, she says to herself, "What is the worst thing that could happen?"

Janusian Thinking

We often seek the simplest truth to quickly understand blossoming relationships, navigate new situations, and deal with our reactions to unexpected circumstances. Sometimes, however, the truth cannot be reduced to a single emotion or fact. For example, seeing your children leave the nest to start their next chapter on their own is often described as bittersweet, capturing both the sadness at their departure and the joy you feel for the new opportunity ahead. While these two sentiments are opposites, they coexist because both can be true.

American psychiatrist Albert Rothenberg introduced the concept of Janusian thinking in the 1970s. Rothenberg studied the world's most creative thinkers to understand what ignited their creativity. In his research, he noted that inventors and creators could accept firmly held propositions about everything from science to human behavior that were simultaneously true and not true, allowing both to coexist.[7] Rothenberg named this process after the Roman god of duality, Janus, whose two heads face opposite directions to symbolize change and the importance of dialectic thinking.

Rothenberg noted that the two opposites might converge over time because the goal is to design a singular state that combines and supports both truths. For example, an architect must design the outside and inside of a house simultaneously, though they serve different purposes.[8] Entrepreneurs may aim to make a business profitable and charitable, though these concepts may seem diametrically opposed. In fact, they can coexist and even complement each other effectively at the same time, as in the case of Bombas, Toms Shoes, and Warby Parker, demonstrating that the "Buy one, give one" model is good business.

The portmanteau "frenemies" is also an example of Janusian thinking that can be applied to business. Companies may compete as rivals on one front and collaborate as partners on another. For example, the consumer electronics and appliance retailer Best Buy sells Amazon's branded products, including Kindle and Alexa, in its stores. Similarly, Amazon sells Best Buy's Insignia-branded products in its online store, with Best Buy shipping the items directly to the consumer. At the same time, the two companies compete for customers who want to buy consumer electronics online. Best Buy also sells its own Insignia TVs in stores alongside TVs from other brands like Samsung and LG.

The act of holding two opposing ideas at the same time and merging them into a single solution is not intuitive. It goes against conventional thought patterns and instead values a both/and approach, which can be quite different from the usual logical processes. For example, consider the "good" bacteria found in probiotics to fight infections. The beneficial bacteria actively compete with harmful bacteria for space and nutrients, effectively pushing out the harmful microorganisms.

The practice of using these conceptual contradictions requires a willingness to look where your intuition won't naturally take you. It is easier for the mind to identify conceptual similarities and avoid the paradoxical solution because our brains are wired to use logic to find similar patterns, and, therefore, it is a less taxing cognitive process. Contradictions demand more effort to understand and manage the cognitive dissonance they create. Achieving creative velocity using this "both can be true" technique requires concentration, intention, and curiosity.

In his 1936 essay "The Crack-Up," F. Scott Fitzgerald observed that "the test of a first-rate intelligence is the ability to hold two opposed ideas in mind at the same time and still retain the ability to function." His observation has since been validated by researchers studying the connection between a "paradox mindset"[9] and creativity. The paradox mindset supports Janusian thinking by describing the ability to embrace and integrate seemingly contradictory or opposing ideas simultaneously. Research suggests that people with a paradox mindset are comfortable exploring the tension between conflicting ideas and see the opportunity to resolve opposing forces as energizing. The ability to focus on two ideas at once and not select just one to explore enables the generation of a broader set of novel ideas that pulls for the combined set of opposing ones.[10]

How does one embrace this type of mindset? Multiple behaviors enable it to thrive, some of which may feel unnatural to someone who is logically minded or avoids conflict. First, instead of running away from conflict or opposition, you must learn to accept it and address it. Incompatible concepts represent a tension that can be generative. Next, it is important to move from an either/or to a both/and mentality. Don't quickly seek the best idea among those in opposition; instead, explore if there is one that integrates the opposing concepts. Researchers describe this capacity as integrative complexity. "Individuals who are low on integrative complexity dislike ambiguity and dissonance, seek cognitive closure, and tend to form dichotomous (good-or-bad) impressions of other people. In contrast, individuals who score high on integrative complexity have a more flexible, open-minded, and multidimensional stance toward the world."[11] People with high integrative complexity are better poised to achieve creative velocity.

Integrative complexity also depends on comfort with the blending skills we discussed in Chapter 2. Understanding and being comfortable with divergent perspectives and conflicting demands makes it easier to integrate opposing ideas. Integrative complexity involves combining aspects of seemingly contradictory ideas with the expectation of finding a win-win solution rather than aiming for a compromise or middle ground. For example, when a product team is asked to be innovative and cost-effective at the same time, there is an inherent paradoxical nature to these two concepts. Innovation often requires time, experimentation, and failure, and when companies want to cut costs, their innovation labs are often the first to go. Research and development teams often complain that a focus on costs can stifle creativity and limit the team's ability to develop truly novel solutions. However, teams responsible for innovation can work in an agile manner, using rapid iteration, lean methodologies, open-source technologies, and scrappy experimentation tactics while also focusing on solutions that add customer value and simultaneously save the company money, effectively managing this paradox.

Partnering with Generative AI

Opposite thinking is an excellent exercise for engaging a generative AI partner. The large language models that power generative AI are free from personal biases, emotions, and attachments to specific ideas. This means they are not constrained by pre-existing mental ruts, or discomfort with radical ideas, which can sometimes hinder human creativity. Generative AI doesn't have an ego or a sense of the human experience, which can help propose surprising "opposite" solutions. Nicholas Thompson, chief executive officer of *the Atlantic*, recommends using generative AI tools "to point you to the obvious things [which will be the ideas you'll want] to avoid. Don't use them as part of the creative process; think of them as pointing out what is antithetical to the creative process."[12]

Maintain a healthy dose of skepticism when reviewing the opposite ideas suggested by generative AI. While writing this chapter in July 2024, I asked ChatGPT4 to provide additional portmanteau words like *frenemies* that describe the combination of opposites. Several, though not all, of the suggestions it returned, were portmanteau words that were a combination of similar words like *chillax* and *guesstimate*, and not opposites or antonyms as requested in the prompt. I pointed out these did not represent opposites, and Chat-GPT replied, "You're right; 'chillax' and 'guesstimate' blend similar rather than opposite ideas. They combine concepts that are related to each other and enhance or extend the meaning without necessarily being contradictory." I asked Gemini 2024.08.01 to do the same. It provided four replies: *bittersweet* (the only correct one), *splosh*, *oxymoron*, and *chummy*.

This is because large language models don't inherently understand opposites in entirely the same way a human might. While context helps both humans and machines, some words may appear in a sarcastic, metaphorical, or symbolic way, which can be challenging for generative AI tools to interpret. Because they use statistical associations to identify words that frequently appear together, the recognition of negation words like *not* or *no* or prefixes like *un* and *non*, can help identify an opposite. If *happy* appears with one of these in the same sentence, the LLM can infer there is an opposite context being presented. Sentiment analysis may help, but it requires an understanding of the context to recognize the opposite concepts being communicated. Words like *however* and *but* are helpful in identifying contrasting concepts. By just giving an LLM an antonym pair and asking for it to construct a portmanteau that represents the duality of the opposing concepts, there is not enough context for the model to be successful. This is especially true when words have multiple meanings, like the word *light*, which can mean "not heavy" or "not dark," the absence of context can undermine the accuracy of the response.

When creating prompts to work with generative AI during a brainstorming session that involves opposites, it is important to provide detailed context. This will help ensure that the AI understands the definition, situation, and objective that you are focused on. It is necessary to use specific language to identify the type of opposite you're seeking, such as physical, conceptual, or metaphorical opposites. The key is to frame the prompt explicitly so that it calls for conceiving two antithetical or contradictory notions simultaneously instead of just asking for general opposites. A prompt that is formatted in this way, where the opposite is not the antonym but rather the state of not being in the original state, can provide much better results. For instance, a prompt that starts with "imagine X and not X" will inform your AI partner that you're looking for the opposite without providing a different word to describe the opposite.

Interview with Jay Samit

Jay Samit is the former independent vice chairman of Deloitte Digital and a former executive vice president at Sony, where he was responsible for the creation and launch of their online music store, Sony Connect. I met Jay in the early 2000s when I was working in digital media at RealNetworks and was inspired by his commitment and approach to innovation. He is the bestselling author of *Disrupt You!* and *Future Proofing You*. He is a member of the Writers Guild of America, a member of the Academy of Television Arts & Sciences, and a performing member of the Magic Castle. In 2020, Jay launched his career as an artist with his first show, *America Disrupted*, at the Richard Taittinger Gallery in New York. Jay's art is heavily influenced by the impact disruption has on humans and our institutions.

1. **In this age of generative AI, what is the role of human creativity?**

    People don't understand what AI can't do. I'm chairman of an AI company. The large language models basically look for patterns and things. They don't actually read the words. They don't know anything. If you ask Gemini how many Ms are in the word Canada, it will reply, "One." However, if you told it "There were two," it would say you're right because it doesn't have any way to know.

Figure 5.1 Author's conversation with Google Gemini 2024.08.01.

(*continued*)

This made me think about a robot giving a TED talk in the future to an audience of robots, and they are saying that humans are stupid as one of his slides is, "Too err is human," but the word "To" is "Too," to highlight the blind spots of robots. It's still a fantasy that they will rule the world, and I put famous robots in the audience, which everyone would know from movies. I only paint half the painting. The other half happens in your mind. It is what you get from the painting. It's not me trying to dictate what your response is. It's me just trying to get you to pay attention. People will see something that wasn't what I was thinking about because their journey in life was different. They are connected with it because of something inside them. That experience is what will always differentiate people from machines.

When computers first came out, people said, "Computers are going to write stuff." When Photoshop was released, people were afraid we wouldn't need photographers. Now we understand that it makes it easier for somebody to create stuff. For instance, there are AI tools to create amazing music with lyrics in any genre and vocalist style; it is mind-blowing. But what makes a novel? What makes a piece of art? What makes a song is how it makes someone feel.

AI cannot feel and cannot relate to what feelings are. You can prompt it or instruct it for a certain feel or emotion, and what you realize when you take these large language models and large image libraries is that it will always give you a stereotype. It will also miss the Zeitgeist of the moment that we're experiencing, and that only comes from living in the current world.

2. What do you do to get into a state of flow?

I'm in a place where I am able to produce what I want in the time that I have allotted for it. However, when I was in college, I wrote for the school newspaper, and there was a press deadline. I did 300-plus stories in my undergrad years that were published. I learned that deadlines get me into a flow state for business. "Oh, my God! This meeting is tomorrow, so it's time to start the PowerPoint and stay up all night." That's never changed. What I found with painting is the physical process of painting doesn't require a flow state. It's not what your fantasy is of a painter where they stand with a blank canvas and do this, and it comes out. It's very much what I've mapped out or sketched. And then I am basically just coloring in the sketch.

The flow state for me happens when I usually wake up at two or three o'clock in the morning and work until dawn. I'm still in a dreamlike state, but I'm physically awake. I ruminate on my list of ideas that I don't seem to have right, and ideas seem to come to me during that time. Then I'll go back to bed for a couple of hours, and then I'll paint it. Your dreams are most vivid and most detailed in the later part of the evening and the early morning. So, if you can be awake during that window and you're not distracted by anything else, your body gets used to knowing this is the time when you do these things, and you can trigger flow.

3. How do you re-energize your creative spirit during periods of frustration or stagnation? Where do you find inspiration?

If I go a few days without being able to have a release for my creativity, I'm not a good person to be around. There are people I get energy from, like my friend, who has amazing charisma. His whole career is based on his ability to have charisma. He gets around people and then energizes them. I find people extremely draining. I've endless patience for children, and at this stage, I'm the old guy who says, "Get off the lawn." I don't have a lot of patience for annoying people, and

(continued)

that's probably the only luxury that success brings you is that you don't have to deal with anybody you don't want to deal with, which really helps protect your creative energy.

But if I'm in back-to-back meetings, flying around, and I don't have a way to do something creative, I am not happy. When I'm making creative things for my kids or my grandkids, that well will never run dry.

You have to find ways to make things fun, and I spend most of my life daydreaming. The world I can imagine is always better than the world I live in. I enjoy turning parts of my daydreams into reality so that others can share in the joy of whatever I am creating.

4. **You have said, "True success comes from failing repeatedly and as quickly as possible." How critical is failure or the acceptance of failure in cultivating creativity?**

What I realized after the first couple of things that I did is that it's really easy. The fear that people have of doing the unknown or that they will fail holds them back. But failure is part of the process. When you fail, you don't end up where you started. When you try something, you either earn or learn. But either way, you're propelling yourself forward. So, the more times you've failed, the more successful you actually are. Unless you learn how to innovate, how to take risks, and how to process failure, you're doomed. And society is doomed.

For a ton of my career, I would come out of meetings going, "Why don't they get it? Why don't they get it?" And then, one day, it dawned on me. It isn't their job to get it.

It's my job to communicate the future to people who are living in the past in a way that they can comprehend, and once I changed my way of thinking, that made it easy to keep moving forward. You must believe absolutely that you're right and pursue that.

A young Meryl Streep was called in to audition for Dino de Laurentis. In the meeting, he said in Italian, "She's ugly. Get her out of here." But he didn't know she spoke Italian. Imagine hearing that feedback as an actress, and you can't change your look. You're going to be rejected for 99% of the parts you go after. Think of the resilience that all those people have to conjure up every time they have been rejected. And then, if you think about anything that you've enjoyed in life—a painting, a movie, a book—that was the result of somebody who didn't give up, who didn't listen to all of that.

5. **Can you share a moment in your life when you realized that thinking differently from others was a strength and not a weakness?**

I'm dyslexic. As a kid, in first grade, they had three reading groups in Philadelphia public schools: the Eagles, the Hawks, and the Mud Hens. You don't need a lot of knowledge to know that you don't want to go through life being a mud hen. I mean, I was basically written off as being stupid, but it just turns out that I think differently, and I found that with many creative CEOs who are also dyslexic, like Richard Branson, John Chambers, and Charles Schwab, the way we're wired is an advantage. Divergent thinking is one of the hallmarks of successful dyslexic CEOs.

I think you realize as a kid that you can get more positive social action from getting people to laugh and being the class clown than being the smartest and brightest. I could disarm people with humor. Magic was my first passion, and it paid my way through college. What I took away from doing magic that helped me in the business world is that when people go see a magician,

(*continued*)

they want to see them fail. The audience is against you. They're trying to figure out what you're doing. When you go see Taylor Swift in a concert, you want her to be the best she can be. But with magic, you know, going in, the audience is trying to figure out what you did to execute the trick. If you can overcome a room full of people who want you to fail, then board meetings, pitch meetings, and sales meetings are nothing different. You've already figured out how to do that. My whole career, I have been looking at it that way.

Exercises

PRACTICE THE OPPOSITE THINKING PROCESS

- **Define the Problem**: Briefly describe a problem you're trying to solve. The more specific, the better! It can be as simple as "I want to save more money." "I want to lower my anxiety levels at work."
- **Identify the Desired Outcome:** What would success look like in this situation? What are you hoping to achieve?
- **Identify Key Assumptions:** What are the key assumptions about the outcome? Consider the environment, human behavior, market forces, competition, operations, etc.
- **Reverse the Assumptions:** Consider a world where the opposite of your key assumptions are true.
- **New Perspectives:** Look for hidden advantages within the "opposite" scenarios. Could they solve a different problem entirely? Can they fortify the original solutions?

PRACTICE THE INVERSION THINKING PROCESS

- **Pick a Goal:** Start by choosing a goal for which you want to brainstorm solutions. This could be anything from "Use my two-week vacation to take a road trip from coast to coast" to "I want to succeed in my career."

- **Standard Brainstorm:** Carve out no more than 15 minutes to focus on a regular brainstorming session. Freely generate ideas for achieving the goal. Write down all the ideas.
- **Enter the Opposite World:** Consider the goal is now the opposite of what was originally chosen. Generate ideas to ensure the new opposite goal will happen using no more than 30 minutes.
- **Devil's Advocate Time:** Now, considering all the ways you came up with to ensure the opposite goal from your original goal will happen, brainstorm ideas that will **prevent** you from achieving the originally chosen goal from happening. For example, what might block you from taking that two-week road trip across the United States?
- **Assess Learning:** Examine how to prevent the goal to reveal potential pitfalls of your initial plan.

PRACTICE THE JANUSIAN THINKING PROCESS

For each prompt, construct a single sentence without the help of generative AI that expresses two opposite or contradictory ideas simultaneously. For example, if you combine love and hate, you might write: "I love going out partying with my friends at clubs till late at night and hate how I feel in the morning after I do." The resulting sentence should present a paradox where both things can be true.

- Combine the opposites of rich and poor.
- Combine the opposites of near and far.
- Combine the opposites of high and low.
- Combine the opposites of life and death.
- Combine the opposites of long and short.
- Combine the opposites of fast and slow.
- Combine the opposites of easy and hard.

To partner with generative AI, reformulate the statements as follows: imagine X and not X and combine them into a single sentence in which both states are true. Compare those generated manually with those that were computer-generated.

CHAPTER 6

All the Feels

"Rational thoughts never drive people's creativity the way emotions do."

—Neil DeGrasse Tyson

While it may seem surprising, both positive and negative emotions can contribute to or distract from creative velocity. For most of us, it is not hard to imagine how positive emotions might open our minds to new possibilities. Positive emotions often lead to a more adventurous mindset, which is helpful for creative problem-solving. However, positive emotions can also limit our ability to make novel connections. Since positive emotions are transitory and the creative process may surface new emotions, it is possible that the motivation to switch between different mental frameworks or consider alternative perspectives won't be strong. The desire to stay in the positive emotion may eclipse the motivation to explore unexpected solutions or dampen the desire to enter a realm that may be uncomfortable or unsettling.[1]

Likewise, negative emotions can be constructive when identifying creative solutions. However, they can also be limiting when you attach negative emotions like fear to past or future events and ruminate over what could happen, you reduce your capacity to explore novel solutions. Worry consumes the imagination. That is why addressing negative emotions introspectively can prompt your mind to seek a new perspective and motivate you to adjust your behavior. This fosters cognitive flexibility and self-awareness, which can enhance integrative thinking, a crucial element of creativity. Integrative thinking, covered in Chapter 5, enables individuals to link seemingly unrelated ideas and concepts.[2]

Researchers and psychologists agree that both positive and negative emotions can be helpful or hurtful when it comes to fueling creativity. The key to balancing these emotions is self-awareness and self-regulation. Both types of emotions can be temporary, and since they are usually triggered by an interaction or event, they can be managed with conscious effort and pattern recognition. Once you're aware of your emotions, you can take steps to manage them. When you feel consumed by negative thoughts, triggering the activities that enable you to reach the flow state can be helpful.

Jason Silva, whose interview appears in Chapter 8, points out, "If you are able to mediate mood, then creativity will take care of itself. Because when you boost mood, you boost dopamine, and when you boost dopamine, you increase pattern recognition and lateral thinking."[3] Moods last longer than emotions and can be a more generalized state of mind without a particular event to trigger them. They can be sparked by a combination of things—physical wellness, lack of sleep, stress, for example—and can be defined by having a number of emotions at the same time.

In the past, psychologists believed that positive moods broaden our thinking while negative moods can have a narrowing impact. However, in 2012, psychologists Eddie Harmon-Jones, Philip A. Gable, and Tom F. Price introduced a new perspective. They suggested that a mood's motivational intensity impacts creativity, not the positive or negative nature of the emotions. Motivational intensity indicates the inclination to either magnetize to a positive situation or event or to avoid a negative situation or event.[4] Moods with low motivational intensity tend to expand cognitive processes and boost creativity regardless of whether they are positive or negative. On the other hand, moods with high motivational intensity, whether positive or negative, can have a narrowing impact on creativity. For example, when you're very excited about something, like a trip or a new job, you might find it hard to focus on other things. Your attention is drawn toward the source of excitement, potentially narrowing your focus to the exclusion of other opportunities. Curiosity is often considered a positive mental state with low motivational intensity. Curious people are willing to risk negative experiences to satisfy their need to learn. Scott Ehrlich, whose interview appears in Chapter 4, told me, "My motivation in my work is that I'm curious, and the process of figuring things out is what gets me out of bed each day."

High motivational intensity associated with an emotional state benefits from the use of distraction as an emotion regulation strategy. For example, if you're extremely angry about a work situation, you might choose to play a video game to take your mind off it. On the other hand, when our emotions are less intense (low motivational intensity), our mind is more open and flexible. This broader perspective allows us to use a strategy called *cognitive reappraisal* more effectively. Cognitive reappraisal involves looking at a situation differently to reframe how we feel about it. When you are mildly disappointed not to find a seat at your favorite café, you might consider getting your order to go and sit in a nearby park to enjoy it. Low-intensity states allow for a broader perspective, which helps people rethink and react to the emotional triggers in a different way.[5]

Emotion Regulation

Emotional regulation is essential for creative thinking. Emotions and mood can significantly influence the cognitive processes involved in imagining novel solutions and, consequently, achieving creative velocity. The results of a study published in January 2023 showed that "reappraisal of emotion-eliciting events is positively associated with creativity because both involve considering new approaches or perspectives. Cognitive reappraisal involves reframing the meaning of emotional events."[6] Researchers found this to be especially true for conventional thinkers, who tend to be lower on measures of openness.

Emotional regulation is a core aspect of emotional intelligence (EI) and one of the five components of psychologist Daniel Goleman's theory on the subject.[7] Emotional regulation is critical for creative thinking because it allows individuals to harness the benefits of various emotions while minimizing their negative impacts. The other four EI components—self-awareness, motivation, empathy, and social skills—are also vital to achieving creative velocity. Chapter 8 highlights that self-awareness can be helpful in achieving a flow state and, therefore, is a well-developed cognitive skill in successful creative thinkers. Understanding what can trigger a state of flow is as important as understanding what can trigger stress or frustration. Empathy facilitates understanding other people's emotions and supports cognitive flexibility, a key trait of creative thinkers. Social skills enable you to effectively interact with others, which is crucial for group brainstorming activities and customer discovery work.

Developing skills to regulate emotions helps you cope better with frustration, tension, and other negative emotions that can hinder your creative performance. In 2017, researchers in the Netherlands reported the results of a study to understand the impact of even a few minutes of meditation on creativity and discovered that "regularly doing it boosts your resilience, enabling you to mitigate stress, regulate emotions, and have a more positive outlook so that you can bounce back from setbacks."[8] Building resilience to navigate unexpected discomfort, challenges, and setbacks is crucial for maintaining creative momentum. Emotional regulation is also a fundamental aspect of Stoic philosophy. In Chapter 5, we discussed Stoicism in the context of preparing for the opposite of what you want through the "premeditation of evils." Additionally, in his interview in Chapter 9, Pat Copeland mentions that practicing stoicism helps him regulate his moods. Effective emotional regulation is rooted in the Stoic philosophy of understanding what is within our control and what is not.

Pat also highlights the good and bad aspects of mind wandering and the impact of negative rumination on creativity. Emotional resilience regulates the relationship between creativity and intrusive rumination. When you find yourself with free time to think and your habit is to obsess about and dissect things that have happened or could happen, you can easily trap your mind in a loop of negative thoughts. The cognitive resources that you could use to generate new ideas are instead consumed by unproductive thoughts. Rumination often exacerbates the fear of failure, which can block creative action. Resilient individuals perceive their failures as stepping stones to success. You can see this is a recurring theme across the creative thinkers interviewed for this book—failure should be embraced because it is a means to learn and grow.

After reviewing the research on emotional regulation, I created the graphic you can see in Figure 6.1 to help you manage your

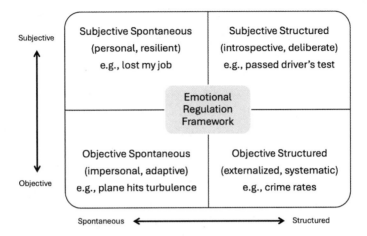

Figure 6.1 Emotion regulation assessment matrix, Leslie Grandy © 2024.

emotions. The premise of this framework provides four dimensions to help you recognize the main types of emotional experiences and their influences on creativity. The Y-axis considers experiences and emotions that are personal to you and that you can control, which is the **subjective** view, and the opposing dimension, the **objective** view, which represents events and experiences that are external and beyond your individual control. The X-axis goes from **spontaneous**, which categorizes those circumstances that are temporal and unexpected, to its opposing dimension, **structured,** and represents a systematic, ongoing set of behaviors and stimuli.

Since subjective-structured emotions are personal to you, they should be approached in an organized and deliberate way. An example of this might be the emotions that surround activities like passing a driver's test or planning a party. Subjective-spontaneous emotions refer to personal emotions that are triggered by unexpected circumstances, like losing your job or having a fender-bender. On the objective dimension, emotions arise from events beyond your control and affect a group or community. Objective-structured refers to those emotions that arise from external factors that affect us as a population, like the crime rate or climate change. At the same time, objective-spontaneous emotions are reactions to unexpected short-term events like sitting on a plane that unexpectedly hits heavy turbulence or a school closure due to a snowstorm.

The structured versus spontaneous axis aligns with the idea that both global conditions and unexpected, unplanned circumstances can trigger emotional responses. The subjective versus objective axis recognizes that emotions can arise from internal, personal situations as well as external, uncontrollable events. When you understand the quadrant you are operating within and can manage emotional reactions toward the things you can't control, you can deploy targeted tactics to manage the intensity and impact of your reactions. This will take practice, and the exercises at the end of this chapter can help you develop this skill.

Emotional management is the conscious ability to handle these states effectively. Regulating emotions to achieve a goal is imperative for fueling creative velocity. A 2015 Yale University study found that "emotion regulation ability plays a role in enabling individuals to move from a creative disposition, such as evident in trait openness to experience, (and) to creative behavior."[9] The research suggests that although people have control over their emotions, they often fail to take action to manage, direct, or mitigate them, thus hindering their creative capacity. Emotional regulation is critical to achieving creative velocity because the creative process can be fraught with emotional ups and downs.

The Empathy Gap

Even people who successfully regulate their emotions may struggle to relate to others in a different emotional state. For example, when you don't share a craving for an unhealthy habit you see in your friend, you may not understand their motivation or commitment to continue what you believe is bad behavior. Adjusting or understanding other people's perspectives can be difficult because we remain attached to the emotion tied to our current mental state. Sometimes, emotions are visceral, meaning they can be driven by primal forces deep within us, which makes them difficult for others to understand. These types of emotions are often challenging for our rational minds to control, making them even harder for people to predict or overcome. This also makes them trickier for other people to relate to.

Empathy can also be impacted by time and distance from an experience that created an emotion in the past. For example, the elation you feel in the present when you receive a job offer can make it hard to predict how you will feel after performing in the job a year from that moment. Emotional memories weaken over time, reframing our internalization of the events that caused them. For example, after a job layoff, you may feel embarrassed or angry to be among those chosen to lose their jobs, erasing the elation you may have felt when you landed it initially. The emotional intensity experienced when you accepted the job offer makes it hard to imagine how you'd react in the future, challenging you to prepare for how you might behave when these more recent emotions arise.[10]

In 2011, researchers explored the correlation between perspective-taking, a key component of empathy, and creativity. They found that "perspective-taking is an other-focused psychological process that strengthens the relationship between intrinsic motivation and creativity."[11] The research team references several previous studies that recognized that perspective-taking can directly enhance creativity by providing access to new ideas and increasing their usefulness. However, when there is an empathy gap, perspective-taking is a challenging process that involves two cognitive skills: self-awareness and flexibility. When this happens, having the capacity to recognize the bias and then adapt to perceived differences between yourself and others can help bridge the gap. In Figure 6.2, Jay Samit emphasizes that AI mirrors human input and does not possess the self-awareness humans have to recognize its limitations and biases. This self-awareness is a crucial characteristic that sets humans apart from machines, and this gap can hinder AI's ability to adapt its perspectives effectively.

The empathy gap can be caused by people assuming and overestimating their similarity to others. The strong urge to fit in can lead us to believe that others feel the same way we do, even when they don't. For example, you might be excited about a new project or strategic direction and assume that your colleagues feel the same, which can lead to problems with getting things done and create misunderstandings. Believing that everyone shares your views can also make you feel better about yourself and provide a sense of validation. It is important to recognize this is a type of bias known as the

Figure 6.2 When will you become self-aware? © 2022, Jay Samit.

"false consensus effect,"[12] because it can impact decision-making and create friction among team members who, conversely, feel their emotions are undervalued. This negative affective state will inevitably impact your team's creative capacity.

Naturally curious people are less susceptible to an empathy gap. They don't assume they should know how or why someone feels a certain way and are more likely to ask open-ended questions to understand another person's perspective and challenge the assumptions they may have. In the interview at the end of this chapter, you'll see how Scilla Andreen's natural curiosity about how others feel influenced how she handled being bullied as a child. Today, it is a vital part of her work as the founder and chief executive officer (CEO) of the Impactful Group. She firmly believes it is necessary to learn how to respond to different perspectives with curiosity to understand the root of why someone thinks differently than you do. Curious people are more aware of different perspectives, making them more empathetic because they typically seek out diverse experiences and are open to learning.

The first step in reappraisal is to notice and identify your emotions. To become aware of an empathy gap you might not know you have, you must engage in self-reflection, actively listen to other people's perspectives, and seek and internalize feedback. Using cognitive reappraisal can help you reframe your thoughts and perceptions about a situation or experience so you may be open to new approaches and notice previously unseen potential challenges. Reappraisal can help you detach from your own immediate emotions and see a situation more objectively. This allows you to consider the other person's perspective without the filter of your own feelings. Projecting your emotions onto others—positive or negative—can create an unwanted burden, especially for someone who does not share them. Inviting others to share their perspectives and feelings shows you are willing to regulate your reactions to hear them and that you are willing to imagine new solutions that could arise from these inputs.

Partnering with Generative AI

Generative AI's understanding of emotions is based on data, not personal experience. This means that partnering with generative AI to build emotional resilience, regulate emotions, and close an empathy gap will largely need to focus on data you provide about your goals, your known emotional triggers, and situational factors. You can develop a system for tracking your emotions throughout the day. After you describe a situation, generative AI can catalog the emotions you feel at the moment and how they may change over time. This will increase your self-awareness. Once you're better at identifying your emotions and the triggers, you can proactively manage how you react.

It is important to remember that, by design, machines operate without feelings or subjective experience and cannot relate to how experiences make you feel. Figure 6.3 reminds us that they are built from data, algorithms, and code. While AI can be programmed to mimic emotional responses or demonstrate behaviors that appear thoughtful or empathetic, it does not *feel* in the way humans or animals do because it lacks the biological underpinnings for emotion.

Figure 6.3 A dog and robot cartoon (image generated by OpenAI's DALL·E 3, June 22, 2024).

I provided ChatGPT4 with the framework in Figure 6.1 and created the Emotional Regulation Coach GPT, which you can use to manage your emotions. Using this GPT, I asked for assistance managing my frustrations with the hostility in the current political climate. In reply to my prompt, my AI partner identified this emotion as objective-structured, because political conflict is an external, ongoing issue that affects the broader population and it's beyond our immediate control. I pushed back and prompted, "Why is this not personal and therefore subjective?" ChatGPT replied, "While you experience frustration personally, the event triggering this emotion is not specific to your personal life. Political hostility is happening **outside of you** and impacts many people. Because it impacts society as a whole, it is **objective** rather than subjective."

Be careful not to consider your AI partner as your professional therapist when managing your emotional reactions to things. The lack of personal experience and context are major contributors to an empathy gap that will exist between AI and you, even with its capabilities to process information.

If you can keep a journal of your emotions and triggers, generative AI can help recognize patterns in them and find the emotions and triggers that appear most often in your log. This can be a good starting point for exploring further. Your AI partner can identify any trends related to the time of day, day of the week, or even external events (like deadlines or holidays) that correlate with your emotional state. If there are situations or people that frequently appear as triggers, AI can flag them for your attention. For this collaboration to be fruitful, provide the generative AI tool with sufficient details about the context and the emotions you experience.

Interview with Scilla Andreen

I met Scilla Andreen in Seattle after she founded IndieFlix in 2005. A DVD and later a subscription service focused on independent filmmakers, the company was acquired by Vancouver's Liquid Media Group in 2021, only to be reacquired by Scilla in 2023. In addition to being a successful entrepreneur, Scilla is an award-winning filmmaker, producer, director, and Emmy-nominated costume designer (*The Wonder Years*). She is also the founder and CEO of Impactful Group Inc., which creates award-winning, evidence-informed film programs for thousands of schools, businesses, and government agencies. Rooted in curiosity, empathy, and resilience, her Creative Coping Toolkit (CCT) fosters connection and positive action through storytelling, active listening, and conversation.

1. **In this age of generative AI, what is the role of human creativity?**

   Human creativity is necessary to keep producing the inputs for AI so that AI can iterate on itself and learn and teach itself more so it can eventually become more creative in its output. But human beings have what will always be the most essential piece of it: energy. We're all

   (*continued*)

just energy; everything is energy—it is a combination of emotion, empathy, and our ability to evolve. We bring that to the table, which fuels our uniquely human story-telling skills.

What I love about human beings is that we are unpredictable. And you still need that piece to feed into this whole AI machine. Nothing in the world has suddenly brought about the unknown. It has always been there, and how humans navigate it and deal with it is not easy to predict. I am a living, breathing example, like the poster girl for finding my way by not doing things the way you're supposed to do them.

2. **Why are empathy and perspective-taking essential to unlocking creativity and divergent thinking?**

In my job, it's the driving force. Some people look at perspective, and they take it as an insult, or they look at it like they're being judged. If someone says, I don't agree with that, I'll say, "Okay, can you talk about that a little bit more?" I'm so curious about the cause of that perspective that I want to know more. And then it brings about the richest conversations. I think it's probably the thing that inspires me the most. It's like a breadcrumb that I get to follow. Some people look at perspective, and they take it as an insult, or they look at it like they're being judged. I don't agree with that. I don't think that's true at all. I'll say, "Can you talk about that a little bit more?" I'm so curious because I want to know. And it brings about the richest conversations. To me, that is how we're going to evolve society.

We need to teach children about empathy and how to be open to other perspectives. And also need to practice and model it ourselves. We need to learn how to respond with curiosity when people open their mouths and say things that we don't necessarily agree with. If we can teach everyone to take it as a form of insight or let it be a creative force for improving our perspective, we will remove a lot of the negativity around thinking differently.

Ultimately, you want the people with you on the journey to know that's your way of operating so they can become more resilient when an unexpected incident or spontaneous event happens. They're ready to roll with it, accept that it happened, and move on. I have seen it go that way, which is so cool. If you can't learn to be flexible and shift with it, you're just not going to have a lot of fun.

3. **How do you re-energize your creative spirit during periods of frustration or stagnation? How do you get yourself into a state of creative flow?**

When I was younger, I used to say I need to go away on a retreat and it was always something expensive and big. Now, if I find myself sort of sinking or spiraling or stressing, I have the tools to hack my own brain, which then changes my whole being and my energy.

I'm not one who does breathing; breathing stresses me out. But I have learned all these cool tools, and so depending on what it is I might use a different tool from my Coping Toolkit.

For example, I love to challenge myself to flip the situation around, like, what's the worst that can happen? I am also a huge meditator, and I do Transcendental Meditation. I have been meditating since I was young, and I do different kinds of meditation every morning. Sometimes, I'll get in a few minutes in the afternoon, and that's instantly impactful. It's like flipping a switch. That is my number one go-to when I'm starting to feel like I need to reset.

(continued)

Also, it's always effective to just get a few minutes in the sunshine or walk around the block breathing fresh air. From the films I've made, I know for a fact that looking at nature or walking on the grass floods the brain with feel-good chemicals that boost one's sense of well-being and strengthen one's immune system.

Another thing I have added to my toolbox is finding something nice to say to at least one person each day. Because I used to be a stylist on TV shows, it's usually easy for me to find a way to compliment someone's style or shoes when you are standing in line for the bathroom. And then that opens a conversation with a stranger that may teach me something or help me make a human connection that usually energizes me.

4. How important is failure or the acceptance of failure in cultivating creativity?

I don't like the word failure. We need to rebrand failure. I'm not a fan of that word. I also don't even like the advice "be afraid to fail," or "what would you do if you knew you wouldn't fail." I have a hard time with that one. I've certainly failed plenty of times. But honestly, when you look at it, it's not a failure. I mean there are challenges, but that's where you have the most growth. That's where you learn the most. Maybe I was originally starting someplace and just ended up somewhere else. Is that a failure? Or when I evolve an idea from, "this is what we're going to do," to saying, "Now here we are doing this." After the pivot, it's totally different. Is that a failure? How do you even measure failure when you are learning how to change ideas for the better? Or when you are dealing with an unexpected opportunity or turn of events? Do we have to consider any idea you dropped or changed as a failure?

I just don't think failure exists. And if a company is thriving and then suddenly goes away after so much time, it may be that it is simply time for that company to be done. It doesn't mean it failed. I think of failure in terms of its role in building resilience, surviving challenging times, and learning from it. It can also help you be smarter, less afraid, more open, and not closed-minded or jaded. How could it be bad if it helps you to be more self-aware, awake, and connected? Everybody's got a different version of failure and success anyway. We've just got to keep changing and evolving and flowing. Failure can be one of the most inspiring things that can spur you to create even more awesome stuff.

Failure shakes us, right? It's not the failure itself. It's the shame associated with the failure. People are going to judge me because what I said I would do didn't work out for whatever reason. And it's the shame involved in it that makes you push through and get back out there and try again. You're going to be even stronger and more resilient.

5. **Can you share a moment in your life when you realized that thinking differently from others was a strength and not a weakness?**

When I was in third grade, I was really bullied. It was old-school bullying—kicked, spit on, and pushed. I lived in Breckenridge, Colorado, and I was the only Chinese kid or even a kid of color, in all of Summit County. I got locked in a cupboard in the classroom for the whole afternoon. I didn't knock and yell for someone to let me out, because it was so humiliating that I was even in there. I waited till the school bell rang and let the janitor know because I knew the janitor would come in at some point.

(continued)

I remember I had so much time to myself in that closet, and I just thought, "Gosh! If they could just get to know me a little bit, they wouldn't hate me so much." And I made a promise to myself that I am going to do everything in my power not to let anyone feel this way. That was such a defining moment for me when I felt like maybe I was just wired differently because I actually didn't hate these people who hated me; I think they just didn't understand me. I thought to myself, "I don't know why they don't like me, because I didn't do anything to them except exist." I really wanted to understand why they didn't like me for existing. That was when I was aware and cognizant of my curiosity about the human race.

When I would share that story with people, they'd say, "Is that even healthy? Did you learn to stand up for yourself? Shouldn't you fight back?" And I thought, no, because I started to recognize at a young age that I am what I would call sort of a different thinker—someone who is wired differently. I simply don't meet people like that with the same energy. I am a dyed-in-the-wool empath, and I need to listen to learn where their energy is coming from. And if it's something that I did or something that has to do with us, let's address it because I promise we can do something to address it.

I choose to understand why the other person is coming at me that way or why other people are projecting their hostility or emotion on me rather than absorbing it. That perspective is part of why I tell the stories that I choose. I like exploring these emotions to understand them, help people cope with them, recognize those emotional triggers, and share the cost of carrying them.

Exercises

AUTOMATIC THOUGHT CHALLENGE

By questioning and challenging negative automatic thoughts, you can prevent them from spiraling into negativity and impacting your mood and you can gain more control over your emotional response to situations.

- ◆ **Step 1—Identify the automatic thought:** When faced with a situation that triggers an emotional response, notice and document the first thought that pops into your head. This is your "automatic thought."
- ◆ **Step 2— Challenge the thought:** Ask yourself questions to appraise the thought's accuracy and helpfulness.
  - Is there evidence to support this thought?
  - Is this thought helping me or making me feel worse?
  - Is there a more realistic or helpful way to think about this situation?
- ◆ **Step 3—Replace the thought:** Based on your challenge, develop a more balanced and realistic thought to replace the automatic one. Write down several alternative thoughts.

PATTERN RECOGNITION CHALLENGE

Becoming aware of the situations or cues that trigger your automatic thoughts and emotional responses is helpful in cognitive reappraisal and reframing.

- ◆ **Step 1—Group your emotions:** Using the emotional regulation framework, track the triggers and associated emotions you feel over the course of a few weeks. Place them within each quadrant. Feel free to use Generative AI to help you tag them properly. You can access the Emotional Regulation Coach here: https://chatgpt.com/g/g-FrnKi3gJ9-emotion-regulation-coach.
- ◆ **Step 2—Rate motivation intensity:** On a scale of 1–3, with 1 equal to low and 3 equal to high, rate the vigor or strength of the motivational intensity that defines your mood state when you experience the emotion.

◆ **Step 3—Identify patterns:** Looking dispassionately at the data, observe the distribution, type, and intensity of the emotions you documented.

◆ **Step 4—Develop an action plan:** Based on the following suggestions, practice the behaviors when these emotional patterns arise. Repeat over time till the pattern becomes easier to recognize and mediate.

Subjective Spontaneous

◆ **Tasks:**

- **Doodling:** Draw spontaneously without pre-planning. Use visual expression to diffuse the emotional intensity.

- **Spontaneous journaling:** Write in a journal whenever you feel the surge of emotions, capturing thoughts that you can revisit when you feel emotional distance from the experience.

- **Meditation and breathing:** When unexpected, out-of-your-control, spontaneous events happen suddenly, meditation and breathing exercises can activate your parasympathetic nervous system, reducing your heart rate and blood pressure.

◆ **Why it helps:** Fosters immediate self-expression and the ability to tap into raw emotions quickly, enhancing creativity through spontaneity.

Objective Spontaneous

◆ **Tasks:**

- **Meditation and breathing:** When unexpected, out-of-your-control, spontaneous events happen suddenly, whether you caused them or not, meditation and breathing exercises can activate your parasympathetic nervous system, reducing your heart rate and blood pressure.

- **Progressive muscle relaxation:** To release tension, focus your attention on different muscle groups in your body. Moving from your toes to your head, focus on a singular muscle group—your toes, calves, thighs, glutes, etc. Squeeze that specific group only and hold muscle tension for a count of five. Release.

- **Reframe your thoughts:** Look at the situation from another person's perspective in the same situation. For example, if you are on a plane that experiences unexpected turbulence, consider trusting the pilot's perspective and preparedness, including their experience and training. Or consider how panic might interfere with the flight attendants' ability to execute their safety duties.

- **Why it helps:** You might confront unexpected events at any time that you do not control. Allowing them to unconsciously redirect your mental state means you might just as easily and regularly be pushed to a negative mood from a positive one, and vice versa. Taking a pause can help you recognize the emotion and decide how to manage it calmly.

Subjective Structured

- **Tasks:**
  - **Understand the components of the issue:** Break down the architecture of the problem, which will allow you to take control of how you tackle it and, in turn, allow you to focus on your progress over your emotions.
  - **Personal goal setting:** Create detailed plans and timelines for achieving personal goals. You can partner with generative AI to establish a plan and track progress.
- **Why it helps:** Enhances self-awareness and emotional regulation through organized self-reflection and accountability to measurable goals.

Objective Structured

- **Tasks:**
  - **Understand the components of the issue:** Break down the architecture of the problem, which will allow you to identify what you can impact and what you can't. Use journaling or self-reflection to identify common emotional triggers.
  - **Recognize what you can control:** Consider what parts of the issue you can personally control to solve the problem. And control how much of your attention you give to the problem.

- **Develop a structured plan:** Create a detailed list of tasks and actions you can take for those aspects of the issue.
- **Be patient:** Given the scale of these issues, it can take time to tackle them and completely remove the triggers.
- **Seek professional help:** The scale of these issues has the potential to make them seem unmanageable. Consider working with a therapist or counselor who can provide guidance and tools to help you regulate your emotions.

◆ **Why it helps:** Develops critical thinking and systematic problem-solving skills, enhancing creativity through structured analysis and planning.

COGNITIVE REAPPRAISAL CHALLENGE

Reinterpreting situations or events can change your emotional response.

1. **Identify your triggers and negative thoughts:**
   - Pay attention to situations that evoke strong negative emotions or trigger automatic thoughts.
   - Once you're calmer, reflect on the automatic thoughts that popped into your head during the situation. Were you catastrophizing? Mind-reading? Projecting?
2. **Challenge your negative thoughts:**
   - Ask yourself if your initial thoughts are entirely realistic. Are there any alternative explanations for the situation? Are there elements that can be seen in a positive light?
   - Look for evidence that contradicts your negative thoughts.
   - Evaluate any benefit this negative thinking is offering.
3. **Reframe the situation:**
   - Try to view the situation from a different perspective. How might someone else interpret it?
   - Can you find a positive aspect or opportunity within the challenge?
   - Evaluate how this problem compares to other problems you may face. Placing this situation into a greater perspective can diffuse the emotions associated with it.

4. Identify and recapture moments of "waking sleep:"

- Notice the times you complete a task without memory, and you are less attentive to your surroundings. This is when your muscle memory dominates and your body performs actions without conscious thought.
- Alter your routine to introduce novelty or slightly modify how you perform routine activities.
- Focus on different senses during autopilot-prone activities. Consider verbalizing your thoughts and narrating your experience of these tasks to yourself.
- Designate specific autopilot periods for creative reflection.

PRACTICE EMOTIONAL REAPPRAISAL WITH GENERATIVE AI

1. **Identify the Emotion:** Using the Emotional Regulation Coach GPT craft a prompt that describes the feeling and the situation that triggered the emotion. Start with a prompt such as "I'm feeling really frustrated because my ideas keep getting rejected in meetings."

2. **Understand the Impact:** Add detail to the prompt describing how the type of emotion impacts your goals. For example, "As a result of this feeling, I don't feel respected in my role."

3. **Consider Consequences:** Communicate what results when you feel that way. Do you shut down or act out? You could add this to the prompt: "When feeling this way, I tend to communicate my frustration with my body language rather than words. People can see I am tense."

4. **Identify Patterns:** Provide insight as to whether this is a recurring issue that occurs under specific conditions. This will help identify relevant triggers. You might say, "This is most likely to happen when my manager's manager is present."

5. **Alternative Perspectives:** Ask for different ways to interpret the situation that might help reframe your point of view. Using a prompt like this "Can you help me see this situation in a different light?"

6. **Challenge:** Dive into the responses to better understand them.

Sample Prompt: I'm feeling really frustrated because my ideas keep getting rejected in meetings with my manager and her manager. I don't feel respected because no one wants to take the time to hear me out or explore my ideas. When this happens, I don't argue, but I do tend to cross my arms and legs, and my body tenses. Help me reframe this so I feel less irritated in meetings with my leadership team when this happens.

CHAPTER 7

Conscious Mind, Unconscious Behaviors

"Creativity is a habit, and the best creativity is the result of good work habits."

—Twyla Tharp

By deliberately challenging our unconscious behaviors, we can identify and cultivate habits that enhance our creativity while being mindful of those that might block it. It's important to recognize that our habits can create routines that enable unconscious bias, which can significantly influence our creative expression. Therefore, it's crucial to acknowledge that some habits can unlock our creative potential while others can obstruct it. To identify these habits, we need to develop a level of introspection and self-awareness to recognize the habits that are holding us back and those that are helping us achieve creative velocity.

The challenge of aligning intentional thoughts with automatic actions is a central theme in both psychological study and self-improvement disciplines. We enjoy the freedom that comes with not dwelling on every one of hundreds of minor decisions we make during the day. This makes us appreciate that some actions are automatic. We often act automatically on routine tasks freeing up brain power to multitask and think ahead. Unless you have a toothache, you probably don't spend time deciding how you chew your food;

and you may not spend much time deciding where you set your keys down when you come home. In his book *The Psychology of Habit*, psychologist Bas Verplanken described the "automacity" of habits this way: "We experience habits as a natural flow of events, whereas in fact, we are making thousands of small choices and decisions all the time, such as where to sit, how to move, where to go, what to take, where to look, or what to say."[1]

This challenge arises because much of our daily behavior is governed by habits and reflexes that operate below the level of conscious awareness. Our brains develop these automatic behaviors because they are efficient; they allow us to perform many tasks, like making coffee each morning and folding laundry, without expending much mental energy. However, this efficiency comes with a downside: we can continue behaviors that are no longer beneficial or even harmful simply because they have become ingrained. Pulitzer Prize–winning reporter Charles Duhigg writes in his bestselling book *The Power of Habit* that habits emerge because the brain is constantly looking for ways to save effort. "Left to its own devices, the brain will try to make almost any routine into a habit because habits allow our minds to ramp down more often."[2]

While psychologists and social scientists don't all agree on whether the "habit loop" is a three or four-step process, the core premise for all researchers is that this feedback loop helps our brains create habits to reduce cognitive load and find comfort or reward in their predictability. Duhigg proposes a three-stage model, illustrated in Figure 7.1, that includes cue, routine, and reward, while James Clear, author of *Atomic Habits*, suggests there are four stages—cue, craving, response, and reward.[3] In Clear's model, craving is the motivation that drives the need to respond to the cue. For instance, what drives your need to respond to a notification you receive on your phone? The answer may not be the same for different segments of the population. Maybe it depends on the type of notification—do you pick up your phone and read any message you receive right away? And if so, why? By understanding the root cause of the "craving," you can more easily manage the behavior. Clear maintains that cravings are powerful drivers of habit creation because they are the motivational force that propels us to achieve the benefit or reward of the habit. Duhigg agrees, he merely believes cravings are why there

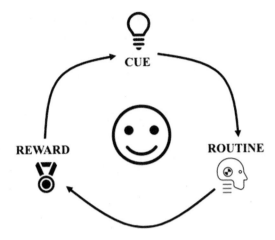

Figure 7.1 The habit loop.

is a habit loop at all. He writes, "This is how new habits are created: by putting together a cue, a routine, and a reward, and then cultivating a craving that drives the loop."

Therefore, it follows that awareness is the first critical step in aligning conscious thoughts with unconscious behaviors. It involves monitoring one's own actions and reflecting on their implications and origins. This can be as simple as noticing when you reach for your phone out of boredom or as complex as recognizing the unconscious biases affecting your decision-making. Awareness requires self-reflection and mindfulness and is often cultivated through practices like meditation, reflective journaling, or therapy. In the interview at the end of Chapter 8, Jason Silva observes that these behaviors are also associated with achieving a flow state. "Many of us get trapped in routines and habits that don't serve our personal development. We become imprisoned by expectations and obligations, and before we know it, our world has shrunk, and we can't see beyond the trivial and stressful." He points out that "we can harness the power of flow to shake the snow globe and find something more visceral and beautiful."[4]

Examination of your unconscious behaviors comes next and involves a deeper exploration once they have been brought into the conscious realm. Here, you ask why these behaviors exist. For example, you might find that your habit of procrastination is tied to anxiety about failure or that your reaction to certain social situations stems from past experiences. This stage often requires confronting uncomfortable truths about oneself and one's past.

Modification is perhaps the most challenging step, as it involves actual change. Once a behavior is recognized and understood, altering it requires deliberate effort. This might involve setting up new routines that override the old, using techniques like positive reinforcement, self-talk, or cue-based strategies. For example, if you are trying to change a habit of negative self-talk, you might practice immediately replacing a negative thought with a positive one each time you catch yourself.

This process is inherently difficult because it not only requires substantial mental effort but also encounters resistance from the brain's preference for energy-efficient routines. Change can also trigger psychological discomfort, as familiar patterns are disrupted in favor of new, untested ones. Despite these challenges, aligning one's intentional thoughts with one's actions is the key to overcoming inertia and habitual patterns, developing cognitive flexibility, and enabling a more adaptable and resilient mindset. All of which are essential to achieving creative velocity.

Children of military families often develop these traits due to frequent relocations. Change itself becomes a habit. This aids in building cognitive flexibility and enhanced personal and social skills like empathy and self-reliance, both traits of a creative mindset. Exposure to different communities and social norms can also aid in building self-confidence as family members adapt to new schools, neighbors, and experiences. Regular changes in routines and environments can stimulate neural plasticity, keeping the brain adaptable and receptive to new ideas. This increased flexibility supports the formation of new neural connections, which is essential for creative thinking.

Personally, change has been a constant in my career. In a way, change became a habit. For 13 years as a second assistant director in the Directors Guild of America, I worked on scores of different projects; each new television commercial or film production I worked on brought a new set of challenges, colleagues, locations, and expectations. The frequency of these changes gave me constant insights into which behaviors were effective and which weren't, allowing me to quickly adjust my approach, adapt to new dynamics, and put unproductive habits behind me. When change is a habit, you're more likely to be open to exploring new perspectives, taking risks, and stepping outside of your comfort zone—all key ingredients for innovation and creative problem-solving.

If change is something you naturally embrace, you're likely better equipped to generate original ideas and experiment with different solutions. Whether organizing the cast and crew to film a Kleenex commercial on a decommissioned aircraft carrier in South Carolina or moving a multinational crew around Mexico for two weeks to film a Coca-Cola® commercial, I discovered that the brain has a remarkable capacity to adapt and transform in response to novel stimuli and dynamic situations.

Bad Habits

William Wordsworth wrote in "The Excursion," published in 1814, "Habit rules the unreflecting herd." Many people do not actively choose their actions based on careful thought or a deliberate decision-making process. Instead, they are governed by the inertia of habitual behaviors and societal expectations, seeing conformity as an expedient way to accept others' leadership and follow without critical reflection. This is why awareness is the first critical step in aligning conscious thoughts with unconscious behaviors. It is also an essential part of breaking bad habits. Breaking bad habits can be a challenge because the routine is deeply ingrained and the craving for the outcome is strong. Problem gambling, for instance, can be driven by an intense craving to make fast money.

In the context of creativity, bad habits are those that limit our exposure to new experiences and hinder mental flexibility. They include behaviors that make us less adaptable to change and show an overreliance on our biases to guide us. Avoidance is one of the most common habits that can obstruct creativity. A tendency to dodge difficult thoughts, feelings, and situations undermines the creative process, which, by definition, includes periods of discomfort. Procrastination can also negatively impact creativity. It can reduce the time to explore solutions and iterate and refine them. Waiting until the last minute to begin tackling a problem can cause increased stress and anxiety. When pressure ratchets up our stress levels it can inhibit the brain's ability to think divergently and make creative connections. Likewise, giving into the compulsive need to attend to whatever is in front of us can create a pattern of precipitous decision-making and anxiousness. This is why in his interview in Chapter 8, Jason Silva shares that he intentionally focuses on task-based thinking in the morning, so his mind is free to wander and come up with counterintuitive solutions to challenges in the afternoon.

Sometimes, fear can stop us from exploring new opportunities and experiences. This can lead to unhealthy thinking patterns that can cause excessive worry and negative thoughts. These negative thoughts can turn into a habit loop, making it hard for us to think creatively and take risks. When we encounter change, make mistakes, or face ambiguity, we may be triggered to avoid them and seek comfort in what we know. To overcome this habit, we need to recognize the situations or thoughts that trigger this fear and block our creative problem-solving ability. As Jules Pieri explains in her interview later in this chapter, the fear of making mistakes can limit our willingness to explore new ideas and prevent us from playing an active role in improving a flawed system.

Sleep is a domain that can be plagued with bad habits. Since sleep is so important to emotional regulation and mental health, it should come as no surprise that habits that disrupt a healthy sleep cycle are likely to suppress our ability to think creatively. Until I found sleep meditation, I would read in bed or stay up in the den working because I wasn't tired enough to go to sleep until I reached a state of exhaustion around 2 a.m. After all, I said to myself, some of us are night owls. After reading a 2019 research study titled "Sleep and Entrepreneurs' Abilities to Imagine and Form Initial Beliefs about New Venture Ideas," I learned that "short-changing sleep is associated with less-effective abilities to imagine new venture ideas, to attend to and process the kind of structural similarities known to foster opportunity identification, and with less-effective abilities to form congruent third-person confidence beliefs about the perceived attractiveness of new venture ideas."[5]

I further learned that our bodies naturally produce melatonin, a hormone that signals sleepiness when it gets dark. Bright light suppresses melatonin production, making it harder to fall asleep and potentially lowering the quality of sleep. It occurred to me that I had made myself a night owl by keeping the lights on. "Compared with dim light, exposure to room light before bedtime suppressed melatonin, resulting in a later melatonin onset in 99.0% of individuals and shortening melatonin duration by about 90 minutes. Also, exposure to room light during the usual hours of sleep suppressed melatonin by greater than 50% in most (85%) trials."[6] Said simply, when it's bright, your brain receives signals that it's daytime and time to be alert.

Another poor sleep habit that can greatly reduce creative velocity is maintaining an inconsistent sleep schedule. If you travel frequently across time zones for business, you are likely confusing your body about when to go to sleep, when to be awake, and when to eat. When your body is confused about sleep, it makes you vulnerable to illness, it can promote inflammation and introduce digestive issues. Researchers have determined that a shift of 90 minutes or more in one's sleep schedule can interfere with emotional self-regulation as well as cognitive functions like memory and analysis.[7]

While we can't always control our travel schedules, it is possible to limit the impact of this habit. First, when it is time to go to sleep in your new time zone, even if you are not tired, you should still turn off the lights and close your eyes. Then, lay flat on your back with your hands resting by your sides, and release your muscles from any responsibility to maintain a position. Avoid consuming food or drinks that can confuse your metabolism, like alcohol, sugar, and caffeine. Utilize breathing exercises to shift your focus from tasks and activities that keep your brain alert to activate your parasympathetic nervous system which calms your body.

Companies, like individuals, can fall prey to bad habits that squash creativity. They can rely on standard procedures to sustain the present situation or resort to formulaic approaches to tackle problems. The intention is often to preserve the existing business, achieve predictable outcomes, and reduce risk. This creates an environment that can stifle experimentation and block exploring novel ideas. Companies can also have a habit of rewarding conformity and consensus. Anticipating friction from management to divergent approaches, employees habitually steer clear of ideas that might create exponential, not incremental, change. Research demonstrates that when a corporate environment encourages learning, diverse perspectives, and owner-ship, employees are likelier to demonstrate innovation behaviors that include curiosity, experimentation, adaptability, and agility.[8]

Good Habits

Habits are built with repetition and positive reinforcement. Even bad habits can satisfy cravings in a way that makes us believe we'll feel better, even if only for a short while. A 2023 Forbes Health/One Poll survey found that the average New Year's resolution lasts just 3.74 months. "Action-oriented goals are more likely to result in suc-cess after a year than avoidance-oriented goals (58.9% versus 47.1% in this specific data set)."[9] Why is this true? There is a lack of moti-vational power and measurability associated with avoidance goals that makes them less effective in the long run than action-oriented ones. Habits that are measurable allow us to see progress, which fuels motivation.

A good habit is typically considered "good" if the value it adds to one's life is wholly positive. What defines a good habit is heavily dependent on a person's goals, context, and values. It makes sense that a habit contributes to your personal or professional well-being, it is likely to be a good, healthy habit. However, while habits can save time, if you habitually cut corners to save time you may not always be rewarded with a positive outcome.

Good habits often have long-term rewards, like good health or mood improvement, bolstering one's capacity for creative problem-solving. However, our brains are wired to prioritize immediate rewards, even if there are negative consequences in the long run. Even with the awareness of a good habit, people might not have the willpower or the self-discipline to be patient for the long-term reward. Researchers at four universities discovered that two compet-ing areas of the brain vie for control when individuals attempt to balance short-term rewards with long-term goals.[10]

You need to look no further than TikTok's 75-day trends for evidence of the value of repetition and reinforcement. This trend advances self-improvement or self-care challenges that last for 75 days straight. They offer a structured plan with daily tasks designed to achieve specific goals. There is measurability and accountability, a community of people taking the challenge with you, and a sense you will get a positive outcome from a commitment to make these adjustments for two-and-half-months. On average, research on how long it takes to form a habit indicates it takes more than two months before a new behavior becomes automatic—66 days, to be specific.[11] So if you stick with any of the TikTok plans for 75 days, you are more than likely to develop the habit. The breadth of these 75-day trends indicates this behavior modification technique can be used to train oneself to be more creative, more productive, more grateful, cozier, and healthier.

While I have never taken one of these TikTok 75-day challenges, I did make a commitment to address my poor sleeping habits and decided to go to bed at the same time as my husband did, listening to a sleep meditation each night when the lights were out, laying still and relaxed on my back. Previously, I could never fall asleep on my back, but I was all in on this New Year's resolution, and the soothing voice coming through my headsets instructed me to lie that way. I followed all the instructions, like concentrating on my breathing with my eyes closed, methodically releasing muscle tension, and allowing my mind to let go of the day that passed as well as ignore the day to come. The apps I tried had several different methods to achieve deep rest, so I varied my approach and used multiple tools, which admittedly helped keep this routine interesting. Some advocated nighttime gratitude, others concentrated on muscle relaxation techniques. They were 25–35 minutes long, and in the beginning, I listened to the whole meditation. I even listened to a few "sleep stories" that let me visualize myself on a slow train, walking along a beach, or sitting by a campfire in the woods. When it ended, I would remove my earbuds and continue the breathing exercises, falling asleep only a few minutes after the meditation ended. Over time, I could train my brain to drift off in half the time because I anticipated the state of relaxation that would take hold as soon as I heard the guide's voice.

This is the one and only New Year's resolution I have kept over multiple years, and it is because it was measurable (time to fall asleep, hours of restful sleep), and it was a routine loop I could activate even when I traveled to new time zones. The craving for a good night's sleep was a consistent trigger for me to maintain this habit. I became even more motivated to maintain the habit when I saw the many rewards of a restful night of sleep. Sleep helps regulate the stress hormones and helps to maintain a healthy nervous system. Good sleep supports higher heart rate variability, which in turn promotes recovery, resilience, and lower stress. All of which are core to achieving creative velocity.

New habits can be created by attaching them to existing habits. This process is known as "habit stacking."[12] Habit stacking simplifies the process of building new habits by integrating them into the routines you already perform daily, making the addition of new behaviors less daunting, more manageable, and easier to remember. For example, you might decide that you are motivated to learn a new language during your commute before your vacation or business trip to a foreign country. Every time you get into the car, you can remind yourself to listen to another lesson. You can also develop the habit of using a meditation app to recharge your brain or reset your mood whenever you find yourself waiting in a room. Progress can be measured, and the routine is built upon a predictable, recurring activity that regularly presents the cue.

New habits need to be created to replace the bad ones that have burrowed their way into our self-conscious minds. In his book *The Power of Habit*, Charles Duhigg writes that to "change a habit, you must keep the old cue and deliver the old reward but insert a new routine."[13] Habit tracker apps for your phone are designed to assist you on this journey. Some of these apps use gamification to help reinforce the reward component of the habit loop and motivate repetition. Research suggests that app-based habit-building predicts behavior's automaticity through repetition.[14] By prompting consistent check-ins and keeping your goals top of mind, these apps may make it easier for some people to progress on developing a new habit than using a personal journal to record and analyze the entries. Regardless of the app you might choose, you can learn to be more present in your decisions and actions through thoughtful self-reflection. This will help with aligning intentional thoughts and automatic actions.

Partnering with Generative AI

There are a number of generative pre-trained transformers (GPTs) on the market to help manage habits. "Habit GPTs" are focused on behavioral modification and can offer advice, provide planning tools and motivational messages, and track progress. While it can be helpful to have a "partner" to encourage and guide you on your path to developing healthy habits, there are a few things to consider when partnering with a habit GPT. For example, it is most important to remember that the resources that GPTs might use to offer advice are not always scholarly articles or vetted scientific research.

To begin, you will want a partner who can maintain and recall past interactions to provide consistent and personalized support. Since habits take a few months to become routine, it will help if the GPT can retain your inputs to identify patterns and potential roadblocks based on past entries. It can then offer proactive suggestions or reminders to help you stay on track.

Not all GPTs can maintain context over longer conversations, which is vital for tracking progress over time and continuous feedback. Also, if integrating your plan into your schedule is helpful, look for those GPTs that enable integration with Outlook, Google Calendar, or iCal.

Searching "habit" on ChatGPT, reveals dozens of options, several of which have the same generic name "Habit Helper." (Keep in mind that some habit GPTs require the premium version of ChatGPT. And cost may also be a factor in your decision.) You can view the number of conversations each GPT has engaged in, which can give you a sense of its experience and exposure to different types of interactions. It could suggest that the model has encountered a diverse range of questions, prompts, and conversations, contributing to its ability to generate more relevant and accurate responses.

You will also want to read reviews to assess their strengths and relevance to your needs. For example, if you are a commuter, you might want to use the Habit Stacker GPT to build a new habit. Or you can access insights culled from James Clear's book *Atomic Habits* through a GPT of the same name, which sources answers to prompts from the book and provides tips for habit management. This GPT also comes with a habit tracker tool to help monitor progress.

Interview with Jules Pieri

Jules Pieri is an investor, founder, chief executive officer, and author of the book *How We Make Stuff Now*. She was previously an industrial designer for three big computer and telecom equipment companies and an executive for several well-known consumer products brands. She has built three startups, the most recent being The Grommet, an online marketplace and product discovery platform for consumer products from makers, inventors, entrepreneurs, and small businesses. In October 2017, Ace Hardware acquired a majority stake in The Grommet, and in 2022 The Grommet was acquired by GiddyUp. I met Jules in 2009 on Twitter. We found a shared connection over design and common ground as two people who combined dissimilar threads in their careers.

1. **You said that "human creativity is a very good bet" at the Adobe Imagine 2019 conference. In this age of generative AI, what is the role of human creativity?**

    One of the most obvious things about generative AI is that it is only as good as its input. So, humans have to be there to guide it and provide appropriate and inspiring input to get quality output. The output still needs a lot of human intervention. I recently worked with a young entrepreneur on an application that uses AI to create images of people's spirit animals to personalize sweatshirts. I really like the red-crowned crane, which is a Japanese crane, and it took many rounds to get it right. It struggled with the proportions of the animal. If an actual human had been asked to re-create it, I am sure they'd understand the intent was to mimic what was in the picture they found in a Google search, not create a different bird. What I don't know yet is if it is a today problem that AI has these limitations or if the human brain can understand subtleties that AI never will.

    I believe there will be a schism in the market. Generative AI will produce a wealth of useful output that may not be super high quality, custom, or bespoke. But for different uses, we will have different ways of getting what we want. Look, nobody is claiming that AI is creative. That's not the promise of AI. The word generative tells you everything—it is generating from what already exists. Right around the corner, there is some art expression that doesn't exist today, or some trend in pop culture that doesn't exist today, and therefore AI will always be a little bit behind. We still need humans to create the edge.

2. **In a 2014 article in *Inc.*, you recommended several tips to boost creativity. One of those tips was to "Think Irrationally." If you generate a lot of "irrational" ideas and want to explore them, how do you decide which ideas to pursue and which to set aside?**

At the start of any ideation process, your job is to be super expansive and push against any boundaries without second-guessing or evaluating ideas prematurely. This helps get more extreme ideas that may lead to more doable ideas. Let me give you an example. I worked at a consultant firm, and our client was Reebok. We had engineered the pump shoe in my firm, and then they were interested in the shoe that helped basketball players rebound higher, and one of the engineers studied the chemicals in the legs of fleas because they have the most extreme capacity. Fleas can jump vertically up to 50–100 times their body length. It would be like a man of average height could jump over the Statue of Liberty in one leap. Well, that's irrational. You're not literally going to perform surgery on a whole bunch of fleas and pull-out chemicals in their legs. But what can we learn from nature? There might be something in there that might be a synthetic thing you can actually re-create in a component material. But if you don't study fleas, you don't ever get to the idea of studying the existing technologies or possible technologies that can do that or that can lead you to something that does.

(continued)

You just can't live in an "irrational land" forever. You must combine feasibility and novelty.

3. **What is the biggest myth about creativity you confront when mentoring young entrepreneurs? What advice do you give them to help them build their creative confidence?**

People are mostly afraid of making mistakes, and I think they somehow think that creative people can't or don't make mistakes. I try to help with this, giving them permission and unlocking a bit of freedom in themselves to make mistakes, and that seems to help them access their creative skills.

One of my favorite things was when a new employee came in. It was an operationally intense business. There was a lot of room for error in how somebody operated, and visible errors were made by all of us. But when a new employee surfaced their own error, it was like they got the unofficial company award that day for being the best performer because it said things to me. I would always tell them if they made a mistake and they're a new employee, chances are it's not because they're being sloppy or careless. It's because they didn't know something, or systems don't work very well, and they thought one way, and it went the other way. That's not on them. That's on us.

If I could have, I would have publicly celebrated the error. Privately, I actually would have a conversation with the person to let them know I was grateful it happened, and they surfaced it. I would tell them I have so much more trust in them to do the right thing when no one's looking because they have the confidence to surface their own errors. So, it's a gift, and it helps unlock their creativity by diminishing their fear of mistakes.

4. **How important is failure or the acceptance of failure in cultivating creativity?**

I have been studying people who are happy in their older age, and I find very few people regret things they did, but many people regret things they didn't do. And so, I have always tried to solve for that, and often, that means picking the riskier choice—the unconventional choice. There are accessible choices, like picking a school to attend or a sport to try, and then there are riskier choices, like choosing a job you never did before. I think about these choices and say, "What is the worst thing that could happen?"

When I started my company, my brother, who loves me, was worried about my decision because it was a pretty crazy idea for a business. He said, "What will you do if it fails?" And I knew he was thinking, "What will you do when it fails?" I couldn't describe it very well in the early days. I told him that I didn't think I'd be black-balled in the business world—I have relationships and a reputation, and I'll just pick myself up and get a job. That's not so bad. I told him I'd make sure I didn't lose my house over it and that I would protect my core assets. I am not saying there wasn't some financial risk for me and my family, but it didn't seem that bad to me. It seemed recoverable.

I would much rather invest in somebody who has had a failure than only success. Ideally, a person pitching me would have one success and one failure, but if all they had was a failure, I prefer it in some ways. They are going to be much more curious and likely more open to help so I can coach them. Things like that make someone richer to me.

5. **How do you get into a state of creative flow? What does it look and feel like to you to operate at peak performance?**

You can't force it, but you can set conditions. When I was writing my book [*How We Make Stuff Now: Turn Ideas into Products That Build Successful Businesses*], I had to write 21 chapters in less than five months. So I

(continued)

allocated all day Wednesday to write a chapter. I needed uninterrupted time, like sanctioned time to do this. I would reward myself with the noon yoga if I was pretty far along by then, so rewards work for me. I would say that I was only able to get into flow about half of those weeks. I've never had this in other parts of my life. But I would know I had achieved a flow state because I'd be sitting at the desk, and I would forget where I was. I was in my own home. But I'd pick my head up after, say, a straight hour and go, where's the bathroom in this place? I didn't know if I was in a Starbucks or someone else's home. It is such a joy, but it's just not easy. I can't get there by forcing it.

Exercises

CHANGING HABITS SOLO

Even if you are not actively looking to change your habits, you will benefit by documenting habits that you have to ensure you can reflect on their value and contribution to your creative output.

HABIT 1	
Identify a habit you currently practice that you want to evaluate.	
CRAVING Describe the emotional or physical sensations you feel when the cue occurs.	
CUE What triggers your current habit?	
ROUTINE Describe the actions you typically perform after encountering the cue.	
REWARD What benefit do you derive from engaging in this habit?	

Address the change you want to make using any combination of the following techniques that resonate with you:

1. *Mindfulness and Meditation*—Once you recognize the cue, you can break the routine and introduce a pause into the cycle through breathing exercises that focus your thoughts inward and raise your consciousness to the next action you take. You can use any of several apps to aid in this process: **Calm, Headspace, Insight Timer** are my go-to apps to reset my emotions and pause unwanted, unconscious behaviors.

2. *Journaling*—Focus on what triggers your automatic behaviors and how you respond. This can help you understand the underlying causes of these habits. This is a great way to use Habit GPTs to manage progress. You will want to use those that can maintain and recall past interactions to provide consistent and personalized support.

3. *Sharing*—Identifying or adjusting your patterns does not have to be a solo activity. Consider engaging the support of a friend, family member, or trusted therapist who can help you recognize triggers and intervene with suggestions of alternative actions you can take.

4. *Change your routine*—Sometimes, even a small change to your daily routine can trigger new pathways for your brain by disrupting automatic behaviors and making you more conscious of their existence.

CHANGING HABITS WITH A GPT

You don't need to use a habit management GPT to partner with generative AI to develop desired habits. The key to a strong partnership is to be specific in the goal, consistent in the engagement, clear about the parameters you need to execute, and clarity on how you will measure progress.

1. **Identify key current parameters in your prompt:** Provide demographic and relevant physical attributes to give the GPT context on who you are. For example, "I am a 34-year-old working mother of two pre-teen girls. I am up at 6 a.m. and I go to bed by 11 p.m., after I help my daughters with their

homework and return some work emails. I feel like I am busy from the minute I wake up till I go to bed. I used to be a painter before I had children, but now, I don't have time for any creative outlets I can enjoy by myself."

2. **Establish a reasonable, attainable goal:** Define clear and specific habits you want to develop. For example, "work out 45 minutes every day before work" or "create space for my mind to relax before bed."

3. **Create a schedule:** Identify with your generative AI partner the best times and triggers that fit your existing schedule. Creating a routine will require dedicated time, either by not doing something else or changing how you prioritize your time.

4. **Report in regularly:** Log your daily or weekly progress in your GPT conversation, and identify unexpected hurdles in the plan so you can adjust to maintain momentum. This is why it is important to choose a model that can maintain context over longer conversations to track progress over time and provide personalized responses based on past interactions.

5. **Motivational and Educational Support:** Define the kind of support that works for you. You can request signals like badges or gold stars, or maybe you respond well to motivational statements or stories of people who overcame obstacles. Identify the kind of educational content that appeals to you (e.g. how-to videos, self-help books) so the GPT can surface the type of material you are more likely to consume.

CHAPTER 8

Go with the Flow

"Flow lives beyond boredom and anxiety and at the inter-section of discipline and surrender."

—Jason Silva

Creative velocity thrives on focused immersion. The lack of noise—both figuratively and literally—produces an environment that allows the mind to relax and expand. By eliminating mental chatter, you can direct all your brain power and creative energy to ideation. Being "in the zone" represents a pinnacle of human performance across various fields, from athletics to artistic endeavors and professional activities. This state, characterized by profound immersion and undivided focus, was termed *flow* by psychologist Mihály Csíkszentmihályi in the 1970s.[1] Flow is not just about peak productivity; it's a state of mind for experiencing unparalleled creativity. In this state, barriers between disparate ideas dissolve, fostering an environment where original solutions emerge naturally. Flow enhances the ability to make connections between seemingly unrelated ideas. This happens because flow promotes a mental state of deep focus and engagement in the task at hand, allowing ideas to cross-pollinate freely.

Csíkszentmihályi and his research partners identified ways to improve the odds of achieving a flow state. They identified several preconditions necessary to support one's ability to experience flow. The first is the need to balance the level of challenge and one's exist-ing skills. Frustrations that arise from taking on an impossible task or tackling a problem that is outside one's competency inevitably block flow. Second, it is important to have a sense of purpose or an end goal for the effort. Knowing where the effort is intended to go will help measure progress, encouraging deeper engagement. An interest in the topic of exploration and the potential outcome of the effort reduces the risk of apathy that is counterproductive to flow. By its nature, flow creates a sense of fulfillment, enjoyment, and purpose that can't be achieved in the face of neuroticism, anxiety, and listlessness. The positive nature of flow makes it a natural playground for creative thinking.

Research, including a notable study by McKinsey involving 5,000 business leaders, underscores the critical role of meaningful engagement in reaching flow. This study introduced the concept of the *meaning quotient* (MQ), a measure of how meaning in work fuels peak performance, suggesting that a high MQ in organizations correlates with increased energy, purpose, and, consequently, enhanced creativity and productivity.[2]

When employees are moved out of the flow state, attending meetings and dealing with distractions like email and group chats, less time is spent on research and development. In that state, motivation is impaired, and creativity is stifled.[3] In 2004, Google's founders created the 20% Project to encourage employees to spend up to 20% of their paid work time pursuing personal projects. Sergey Brin and Larry Page wrote in their initial public offering (IPO) letter. "This empowers them to be more creative and innovative. Many of our significant advances [like AdSense and Google News] have happened in this manner."[4] The recognition that employees' imaginations may be more fertile if they aren't booked wall-to-wall in meetings each day has also prompted innovative companies like Facebook, Asana, and Atlassian to implement meeting-free days, acknowledging that uninterrupted time is essential for deep, creative thinking.

Flow transcends mere productivity, freeing the mind from linear constraints and enabling a dynamic exchange of ideas. It fosters a deep, intrinsic connection to thoughts and a sense of being fully present, nurturing the conditions under which innovative solutions thrive. Echoing this sentiment, former Patagonia chief executive officer (CEO) and ex–Navy Seal Michael Crooke pointed to the alignment of personal and organizational values as the cornerstone of organizational flow.[5] By embodying their authentic selves at work, employees unlock a level of intrinsic motivation and creative capacity that benefits them personally and drives forward-thinking solutions for customers.

Similarly, REI consistently ranks on the best place to work lists because of its overt purpose, which gives meaning to employees who share the same values. The co-op offers employees "Yay Days" to enjoy their favorite outdoor activity, learn a new skill, or help to maintain outdoor spaces through a stewardship project.[6] These activities support the co-op's mission and create distraction-free days that clear the mind and inspire employees to explore new experiences.

Humans tend to come up with creative ideas while not actively trying to think of them. The "Shower Effect," a term coined by researchers in 2022,[7] describes this phenomenon they found in their research. This insight underscores the importance of environments that blend relaxation with sensory engagement, promoting mental conditions where original ideas flourish. This is why many people, like me, report having their best ideas or solving complex problems during this seemingly simple daily activity. Taking a shower can relax your body and mind and lead to greater clarity, creativity, and introspection. The sensory experience of showering—the sound of water, the feel of warm water on the skin, and the visual solitude of the shower space—can also stimulate the brain in ways that contribute to creative thinking. The routine nature of a shower requires less of your brain power to execute it, leaving space for your mind to wander or to circle a topic and explore options without distractions, judgment, or consequences.

The researchers proposed one explanation for why this is true— generating original ideas requires a balance between focused, logical thinking and free, random associations. Usually, these two ways of thinking directly conflict with each other. However, activities such as showering, walking, and riding a train can allow our minds to wander and strike a balance between these two modes of thinking. This is why many people, including several of the people interviewed for this book, say they come up with their best ideas while hiking in nature or going for a run. These are times when the mind can wander freely. However, as the cartoon in Figure 8.1 illustrates, not everyone enjoys hiking, and not all experiences you might have

Figure 8.1 Image generated by DALL-E for the input "Line-drawn image of a person walking in the woods using the style of a New Yorker cartoon" (June 2024).

while hiking in nature may be calming; the most important thing is to find the place and activities during which your mind relaxes, allowing your negative or stressful thoughts to peacefully drift by.

People who have experienced the benefits of a flow state are motivated to learn how to activate it when necessary, and, as a result, they understand the conditions that help them achieve it. Many of the people interviewed for this book can describe what flow feels like and how they can activate the state to experience peak creativity. On the *Fly on the Wall* podcast, Jerry Seinfeld described the feeling of flow when he is onstage doing standup. "You walk into someone's house, and you've got your coat on, and your job is to take your coat off and just be comfortable in their house. That's the state that you seek in writing, or performing, or socializing. Flow has movement, and that's what you are always trying to find."[8]

Self-Reflection, Mindfulness, and Meditation

It may be a challenge for the average person to find these opportunities. High stress undermines abstract thinking. In our busy, jammed-packed lives, it seems that just when you are ready to take a break, your to-do list bubbles to the top of your conscious mind, suppressing any creative thoughts you might have had in favor of the list of things you still have to do that would be a better use of your time. The enemy of creativity is the thought suppression that happens when you ruminate over your unfinished business instead of allowing yourself to reach a flow state. For people like me, the guilt of an unfinished task or a delayed responsibility can fill the space where creativity would otherwise flourish.

Navigating the tightrope of thought suppression requires finesse. Thought suppression is related to creativity both positively and negatively. While blocking distractions is crucial for reaching flow, indiscriminate thought suppression can stifle creativity. The art lies in selectively silencing the noise of pending tasks to immerse oneself in calm reflection, perhaps through music, a warm bath, a breathing exercise, or a leisurely walk. Thought suppression can hinder and help creativity, depending on your ability to choose which thoughts to push aside.

Self-reflection, like thought suppression, walks this fine line between fostering insight and spiraling into counterproductive rumination. Negative thought patterns can trigger feelings of sadness, depression, and other unpleasant emotions. Creative thinkers must cultivate optimism and a belief in future possibilities, momentarily sidelining negative thoughts that obstruct the creative flow. A person who suffers from chronic anxiety or self-doubt can struggle to create a safe space in their conscious mind to ideate freely because the negative thoughts are too overwhelming. Strategies to manage stress and anxiety—such as mindfulness practices, physical activity, or engaging in creative pursuits—can support this delicate balance, enhancing our capacity for innovation and creative thought. This is an opportunity to leverage the Emotional Regulation Coach mentioned in Chapter 6.

Meditation and mindfulness, which create a calmer, more aware, and more peaceful state of mind, activate the flow state because they train the mind to focus on being present, which mitigates rumination. The deep concentration and singular focus characteristics of flow allow individuals to abstractly ponder concepts, principles, and theories without the distractions that typically hinder deep thought.

People can better grasp overarching themes, see beyond the tangible, and understand complex relationships and patterns in this state. The immersive nature of flow promotes abstract and associative thinking by allowing for sustained contemplation of ideas beyond immediate sensory experiences, creating a seamless current of connected thoughts.

A flow state can also be a double-edged sword. While someone can achieve flow and be deeply present in the moment, enjoying a singularity of focus, unaware of time passage, there can be risks that this leads to self-indulgent behavior. In a recent study investigating the flow states experienced when using Instagram and TikTok, researchers found that TikTok's algorithm reinforces the behavior of scrolling and consuming so effectively it creates a higher level of flow state than Instagram.[9] "Watching videos doesn't require skill the way that many flow-inducing activities do, yet the app is able to induce the same feelings of enjoyment, concentration and time distortion that are characteristic of flow—possibly because of the algorithm's immersive quality."[10] However, while this feeling of flow may be enjoyable, this behavior may not be conducive to creative thinking because it lacks purpose and intention. The passive nature of this endeavor undermines the mental activities that encourage associative thinking.

Abstract and Associative Thinking

The relationship between flow and abstract or associative thinking is synergistic. Flow creates an optimal psychological environment for deep, creative thought processes, enhancing the capacity for abstract and associative thinking. Conversely, engaging in abstract and associative thinking can help individuals achieve flow by presenting them with challenging and rewarding tasks that align with their skills and interests. Together, these elements foster a cycle of engagement, learning, and creativity that can lead to significant achievements and personal fulfillment.

Abstract thinkers are adept at thinking big. They enjoy allowing their mind to wander because they are open to where it may take them. They recognize patterns and trends and are unwilling to be blocked by details during ideation. Recent research shows that abstract thinkers are comfortable spending time reflecting on their thoughts, feelings, and interactions with their environment.[11] The Chapter 1 exploration of the MacGyver mindset highlighted how these capabilities enable abstract thinkers to make connections between seemingly unrelated things, which is essential to support creative velocity.

In problem-solving, abstract thinking helps to understand the problem's core principles or to envision the problem in a generalized form. Associative thinking then aids in linking these abstract understandings with specific knowledge, examples, or techniques that might offer a solution, even if those solutions come from seemingly unrelated fields. Abstract thinking allows individuals to conceptualize broad, overarching themes and principles, while associative thinking connects these abstract concepts with disparate ideas and experiences. The ability to think abstractly about future possibilities, combined with the ability to associate these possibilities with existing technologies, theories, or practices, is at the heart of innovation. Abstract thinking expands the breadth of what we can consider, while associative thinking explores the depth of connections between these considerations.

Associative thinking and flow complement each other, with associative thinking serving both as a catalyst for entering the flow state and as a characteristic of the flow state itself. In associative thinking, the mind seamlessly transitions between ideas; resistance softens, and immersion increases, which can help maintain a state of flow.

It is possible to cultivate abstract and associative thinking by engaging in activities that can unlock new creative pathways and achieve a state of peak creative velocity. Doodling and coloring are two examples. Unstructured activities like these encourage daydreaming, which, in turn, can unlock creative connections. Engaging in thought experiments where you explore hypothetical scenarios and their outcomes can also be helpful. One of my favorite exercises is to imagine renovating our home and envisioning different options for the layout. This type of "What if?" activity triggers the imagination and opens the mind to new possibilities.

The flow state is characterized by a perfect balance between the challenge of the task and the skill level of the person performing it. Consequently, certain types of puzzles are particularly effective at inducing flow due to their design, complexity, and the level of engagement they require. For a puzzle to be conducive to a state of flow, it must be appropriately challenging for the individual's skill level—not too easy to be boring, but not so complex as to cause frustration. The puzzle should also have clear goals and provide immediate feedback to the solver, allowing for adjustments and the satisfaction of progress. Puzzles require an open mindset, generally associated with a good mood or positive attitude, to navigate through the initial chaos and balance sudden insight with analytical thought processes.

Sleep Fuels Creative Flow

Sleep is the opportunity for your subconscious mind to rule your thoughts. Unconstrained by the rules of appropriateness, logic, and pragmatism, the mind can wander freely while you sleep. Ideas can surface, leading to creative breakthroughs. Sleep enables the unexpected association of memories and experiences, allowing you to access and integrate them more effectively. During sleep, you have permission to stop sorting and organizing the mental clutter that builds during the day. This helps to restore emotional balance and reset your mood, which enables a mindset that is more conducive to creative thinking.

On the flip side, lack of sleep, unsurprisingly, has the opposite effect. As shared in Chapter 7, research studies confirm that "sleep deprivation has a strong impact on mental and behavioral states associated with the maintenance of flow, namely subjective well-being."[12] There exists a body of research that highlights the detrimental effects of poor sleep habits on emotional regulation, productivity, creativity, and happiness. Sleep disruption undermines the ability to think through complex challenges and inhibits the formation of new connections.

When studying the effects of poor sleep habits on creativity and productivity, researchers also discovered that, not surprisingly, problem-solving and task performance improve with quality sleep. The brain's ability to recharge and refresh itself is evidenced by the speed at which people who slept could complete a task relative to those who were sleep-deprived.[13] This period is known as Stage 1 sleep. Scientists have discovered that this period before falling asleep can be a prime time for the onset of dreams that can enhance our cognitive abilities. Thoughts and ideas drift by like clouds moving along with a summer breeze, releasing us of the responsibility to address negative thoughts or unpleasant recollections. Specifically, the fluidity of this state enables novel connections and unconstrained exploration, which promotes creative thinking and facilitates our ability to solve complex problems.

By providing a break from logic and conscious thought, sleep facilitates the incubation of ideas, allowing the subconscious to explore and recombine information in novel ways, permitting it to ignore the realities of the waking world. Harvard University psychologist Deirdre Barrett, author of *The Committee of Sleep*, notes, "Conscious awareness is able to focus on only one thing at a time," while the subconscious mind is free to randomly explore connections and relationships between ideas during sleep.[14]

Research suggests "there is a creative sleep sweet spot during which individuals are asleep enough to access otherwise inaccessible elements but not so far gone that the material is lost," according to Jonathan Schooler, a psychologist at the University of California, Santa Barbara.[15] Dream exploration fuels creativity in interesting ways. Researchers have found that by incubating participants' dreams, "they were able to boost post-sleep creativity on tasks related to the incubated theme."[16] This notion that you can plant a seed of an idea before falling asleep to enhance creativity is itself a novel idea. It suggests that we can prompt our brains to explore a topic when they are in an optimal state to integrate it with other knowledge, memories, and experiences.

Jay Samit shares in his interview at the end of Chapter 5, "The flow state for me happens when I usually wake up at two or three o'clock in the morning and work until dawn. I'm still in a dreamlike state, but I'm physically awake." He says his sweet spot is in the later part of the evening and the early morning. Likewise, Salvador Dali and Thomas Edison both recognized the value of Stage 1 sleep in revitalizing their creative energy. They both employed a technique to leverage this state of cognitive flow to enhance their capacity for divergent thinking. While holding a small object—a key or a spoon—in their hands, they would drift off to sleep, usually seated in a chair. When the item fell to the floor, it hit a metal bowl or plate and woke them up just as they started to doze off. They'd resume their work, mentally refreshed by the free flow of images and ideas that accompanied this state.

Director James Cameron claims several of his ideas for films, like *The Terminator* and *Avatar*, came to him in dreams. In a 2022 interview with *GQ* magazine, Cameron said, "I have my own private streaming service that's better than any of that s**t out there. And it runs every night for free."[17] Like Cameron, inventors have leveraged insights from their dreams to solve problems. A legendary story about the invention of the sewing machine by Elias Howe recounts a vivid and somewhat violent dream Howe had during which he was chased by spear-wielding warriors. He observed the spears had holes near the heads, which re-oriented his perspective on how the sewing machine needle had to be designed to thread it near the point and not on the head as it was traditionally placed.[18]

Even though we don't always remember our dreams after we sleep, our brains have made a subconscious connection between disparate ideas that can help us make the association at another time. Actively taking a moment in the morning to reflect on your dreams can boost creativity. A 2017 study published in the *Journal of Creative Behavior* indicates that demonstrating curiosity about the spaces your brain occupies during sleep, a time when you are not in control of your thoughts and more likely to associate unrelated ideas freely, can aid in dream recall. Dream recall is associated with well-developed cognitive processes, including perception, learning, and memory, enabling people to remember dreams.[19] Our dreams are often nonsensical and nonlinear, making them harder to remember; our conscious mind can easily dismiss their irrationality when faced with the practicality of our morning routine.

Adequate sleep is critical for achieving peak creative velocity. It helps reinforce the cognitive skills needed for divergent thinking. When your mind is well-rested, it is better equipped to handle emotions, reach a state of flow, and be more receptive to new ideas and possibilities. The connections that our brains form between concepts, topics, and ideas while we sleep are a valuable resource for generating ideas.

Partnering with Generative AI

Several conditions need to be met for a human to achieve flow while working with generative AI. The task at hand should neither be too easy nor too difficult relative to your capabilities. Ongoing engagement is necessary, and your concentration, which is essential for flow, will decline if the challenge makes you feel frustrated, overwhelmed, or bored. Flow state also requires an environment free of distractions, whether collaborating with generative AI or working alone. Since you'll be using your computer to engage with these generative AI tools, turn off all notifications and close all messaging applications to help you achieve flow. Given that AI can sometimes produce unexpected results, comfort with experimentation and uncertainty is crucial. Being open to surprises and learning from them can enhance the flow experience.

Create a comfortable physical environment to encourage relaxation. Ergonomics plays a crucial role in facilitating a state of flow. An ergonomically designed workspace minimizes physical discomfort, allowing users to concentrate fully on their tasks without being distracted by pain or fatigue. Music may be helpful or distracting, depending on the individual. Each person is different; there is no perfect formula. For some people, jazz unlocks mind wandering and open-mindedness that is conducive to achieving flow. For others, jazz feels like auditory chaos. Flow requires not only psychological but also physical comfort.

Establish an amount of time you can commit to the collaboration. Flow can affect your perception of time. Hours spent immersed in the creative process can fly by, allowing you to accomplish a significant amount of creative work in a compressed timeframe. The deeper the connection you can make to the partnership, the more likely you are to reach a flow state. Iteration is a common way to get into flow. By continuously adjusting the idea's components or redefining the constraints or boundaries set for the solution or idea, you can immerse yourself in the partnership and allow your mind to achieve a state of flow. As your AI co-creator refines the output with your ongoing guidance and priorities, the rhythm created by this back-and-forth ideation is naturally conducive to flow.

In a July 2024 LinkedIn post, Steven Kotler, the executive director of the Flow Research Collective, noted, "It's the combination of human-based creativity, intuition, and emotional intelligence (three categories where humans seriously outperform machines) with AI's data processing speed and pattern recognition capabilities (things humans can't compete with) that offers business the biggest advantage." He concludes, "AI systems need to be designed for user empowerment. The ability to control interactions, the ability to explore and experiment, the ability to amplify skill development—these are critical flow-driving categories."[20]

Interview with Jason Silva

Jason Silva is an Emmy-nominated and world renown TV personality, storyteller, filmmaker, keynote speaker, and futurist. Jason is known for hosting five seasons of the global hit TV series *Brain Games*, on the National Geographic Channel, which was broadcasted in more than 171 countries. His YouTube series, *Shots of Awe*, has received more than 100 million views. The videos explore topics such as futurism, technology, creativity, the science of awe, disruptive innovation, relationships, and mental health. I came across Jason's work in 2013 while I was a senior vice president of Digital Product at Discovery Communications, and Shots of Awe anchored the launch of Discovery's new *TestTube* subnetwork. His willingness to share his passion for exploring the human need for meaning, connection, emotion, and inspiration has been a gift for me personally.

1. **In your journey, what has been the most profound personal experience of flow that altered your understanding of creativity?**

    You know that line that says the only thing standing in your way is you? Before I discovered flow, my own excessive self-consciousness was always a creative block. When it came to expressing myself performatively, I was always in my head imagining how I looked in the eyes of others, and doing those cognitive gymnastics was doing everything except allowing me to be a vessel for creativity or extemporaneousness of any kind. And so there was a stiffness.

I was always the kid that just didn't like to dance at parties. I couldn't get out of my own way. I was a shy kid, a timid kid, very self-aware, but consequentially very self-conscious and insecure. And the point is that I just couldn't stop the monkey mind, the inner chatter. So, I just preferred never to really take that many creative risks when the possibility of being exposed in one way or another was there.

So, arriving at a flow state was an exhilarating surprise. It started to happen in high school. I started to host these salons with some of my close friends. We were very inspired by the movie *The Dead Poets Society*, and the idea was that thoughtful, passionate friends would get together and talk about the things that matter.

I was never comfortable with lighthearted or superficial conversation. I wanted to get to the depth of things with my close friends. You could also say that these get-togethers were inspired by Baudelaire's hashish parties in Paris, in the twenties, when artists and painters and creatives would come together and enter a kind of fever dream of intoxication, where they could get out of their own way and tap into this emotional synchrony, or this fluidity or this flow state where to paraphrase Khalil Gibran, "it comes through you, but not from you and though it is with you, It belongs not to you." I was able to get past my inhibitions, past that self-consciousness and I got into a flow state, and it was, and it was exhilarating.

Of course, I was afraid of how it would come across to the more scrutinous eyes of my waking self the next day. But what I found, surprisingly, was that I was super lucid, super eloquent, super coherent—and that my fears

(continued)

were unwarranted. I didn't need that hypervigilance or the second-guessing mind that is so concerned about how I come across that it ends up becoming this block. You know that chatter is trying to protect you, but it ends up neutering you. And so it was about learning to self-trust. Without that inhibition, I was actually a much freer person, much more playful, much more present, much more alive.

It's just that the overthinking, over-vigilant part doesn't need to be there for you to be safe. In fact, it's impeding your capacity for flourishing. It was self-acceptance. It was like what happens when I get the superego out of the way, and even part of the ego out of the way and allow more of my Id, more of my raw, visceral, impulsive qualities, to manifest themselves.

I could watch the way that I was taken over by inspiration or ideas, and it was the first time that I started to record myself. Before that, I used to make home movies and videos. And I was creative growing up. But it was always filming other people. I didn't put myself on camera, didn't record my own stream of consciousness until I started to host those kinds of ritualized gatherings. The collective high or the reverie that we entered into was really sacred space. And it was in that fever dream that flow happened, and when flow happened, suddenly, the creativity was boundless. And so, I realized that it was only me in my own way. For me at least, it became a prerequisite for creativity. Creativity couldn't happen without flow, and flow couldn't happen till I got out of my own way.

2. **How do emotions and self-awareness factor into your creative capacity?**

The relationship between creativity and mood regulation is an important one for me. It's context engineering. If I control the environment, my sleep, and the people I'm with, that's a pretty reliable recipe.

My favorite zone from which to bring forth my creativity is from a place of ecstasy and exaltation. I'm really big on nature, on novelty, on the aesthetic sublime. I'm a very sensitive person, and so I'm very resonant with my immediate environment. If I'm on a subway in New York at rush hour, I'm anxious. I'm sort of depressed. But if I'm staring at a gorgeous mountain, the sun is shining, and I'm listening to some music, it doesn't take much until I get into a trance state. I am very susceptible to what you might call the aesthetic trance, and when I'm in the aesthetic trance then I'm euphoric. I have a euphoric response to it, and it's from that place that I like to record.

3. **How do you re-energize your creative spirit during periods of frustration or stagnation? Where do you find inspiration?**

Sleep is so crucial just to get myself to the biggest spot from where I can leap. Assuming that I'm able to get the sleep under control, I split my day between left-brain thinking and right-brain thinking. I wake up in the morning. And I say to myself let's do like the left-brain checklist consciousness. Let's have some espresso. Let's do some exercise immediately. Let's go through the list of whatever I have to do that requires convergent thinking and focusing. And let's get this all out of the way, like a checklist of consciousness for the left brain.

And then the second half of the day is more for divergent thinking or creative thinking, or out of the box thinking. Getting things done happens in the morning, and solving problems or coming up with counterintuitive solutions to creative challenges happens in the afternoon. That usually will involve a walk in nature or finding someplace where I can sit in solitude or silence where I can stare at trees or at something beautiful that will evoke a more pensive, re-associational kind of consciousness.

(continued)

So that has to do with how I structure my day. Left brain in the morning, right brain in the afternoon. I can't have anything that's due. Otherwise, I can't be creative. Creativity only happens when there's a sense of like everything's taken care of. And now I have an open horizon in front of me for an extended period of time.

4. **How do you deal with failure when you are trying to enable a state of flow? How important is failure or the acceptance of failure in cultivating creativity?**

What might happen is I go too far on a tangent, and then I can't bring it back to land. That is more of an art than a science when you are improvising and, at the same time, tracking what you're saying, where you're going, and whether or not you can land the throughline at the end. Once in a while, I feel like I lost it. You know that it does happen. I don't get angry because I've been doing this for so many years, and I've never had the issue of being creatively blocked. That's never happened to me, at least for this particular genre that I'm known for, which is a kind of improvised verbal poetry.

When I create my recordings, one of the things that I take great pleasure in is that all of my monologues coming out of those flow states are single takes. It's not like I say I am going to make a video on this topic, and then I'm doing it 10 times until I get it right or mixing different takes to create something edited. It's not that, although there is room for that. My stuff is born from extemporaneous thoughts, similar to freestyle rap. And it's very important to me to cultivate the mindset, the mood, the setting for that to emerge. The vast majority of the time, I get what I want in a single take.

If I only got one or two things I'm happy about, that is still a good session; there are other days I might get eight things I'm happy with. It's not a failure if something doesn't produce what I'd hope to. I'm not upset because I know tomorrow's another day, and it'll come through. I've never had a situation where for months nothing came out; that's never happened to me.

5. Why is flow so important to you?

My creative practice is coupled with my creative output, which is coupled with my art making and it is indistinguishable to me from a meditation practice. It's a sport in a way. It just so happens that it's also rapturous for me—a very devotional, sacred practice. Probably a musician would say that when they're making music, it's rapturous. You get taken possession of, and it's exalting and redemptive. The state of flow, when the sense of self vanishes and the sense of time vanishes, is experienced as liberation.

Exercises

The best puzzles for creating flow can be scaled in difficulty, allowing individuals to challenge themselves as their skills improve continuously.

- **Jigsaw Puzzles**—At Best Buy's Seattle Technology Development Center, there was always a jigsaw puzzle waiting to be completed in the break room, and anyone could take a few minutes to study the pieces and clear their minds while grabbing lunch or a coffee break. Finding, sorting, and matching pieces to complete a picture gradually can be incredibly absorbing, providing a clear goal and immediate feedback, which are critical components of the flow state.
- **Crossword Puzzles**—I start my day with *the New York Times* Mini Crossword (and the Connections puzzle from Chapter 3). It is as much about speed as accuracy, as it tracks time statistics, not successful completions. The short time it takes to complete these puzzles makes them a palate cleanser for the mind. Longer crossword puzzles, thanks to the variety of clues and the need for a broad knowledge base to solve them, are also helpful in creating a state of flow.

- **Sudoku, Wordle, and Spelling Bee**—I enjoy letters more than numbers, so Wordle, Connections from Chapter 3, and *The New York Times* Spelling Bee are also part of my morning routine. At night, I usually play a card game on my phone. The pause before my day begins and the focused activity right before bedtime help create a distance that allows for self-reflection and helps to separate those thoughts from the day's demands. Sudoku may work better for people who love numbers, though either type of puzzle requires concentration and pattern recognition skills, which help achieve flow.
- **Logic Puzzles**—App stores are a great place to find logic puzzles. Logic games typically refer to those that require players to use deductive reasoning, problem-solving skills, and strategic planning without the influence of chance. An escape room is a logic puzzle that I have used as a team-building activity because the essence of escape rooms is to solve a series of puzzles and riddles, often under a time constraint. These puzzles frequently require deductive reasoning, pattern recognition, problem-solving skills, and sometimes physical dexterity or coordination. Some apps create virtual escape rooms for individuals to solve.

Here is an example of a logic puzzle that requires concentration, relational analysis, and the power of deduction. You can access the answer to this puzzle and the Magic Square puzzle that follows it, at the back of this book.

THE THREE HOUSES PUZZLE

The Scenario
There are three houses on the street. Each house is painted a different color and has a homeowner with a unique profession. Your task is to determine who owns the fish and in which color house the fish lives.

The Clues
1. There are three houses: yellow, blue, and red.
2. The doctor lives in the yellow house.
3. The blue house is home to a dog.

4. The house next to the lawyer is red.
5. Parrot doesn't live with the fish.
6. The tea drinker lives in the red house.
7. The lawyer lives next to the music lover.
8. The teacher doesn't like music.
9. The teacher lives to the right of the parrot.
10. The music lover drinks coffee.
11. The doctor lives next to the dog.
12. The dog lives to the left of the tea drinker.
13. The house with the fish is not home to a coffee drinker.
14. The coffee drinker does not own the parrot.

The Question

Who owns the fish?

To solve this, you need to use the process of elimination and logical deduction based on the clues provided. By carefully analyzing the clues and the logical relationships between them, you can deduce the correct arrangement of houses, their colors, the homeowners' professions, their pets, and, finally, who owns the fish.

(It is interesting to note that I provided this puzzle to ChatGPT multiple times to solve it, and each time, it failed to get the answer correctly. The reason was that each time, it seemed to randomly neglect a fact presented. I would then prompt it with "Why can't the X live in the Y house?" and it would reformulate the answer, often dropping a clue again.)

THE MAGIC SQUARE PUZZLE

A magic square is a grid of numbers where the sums of each row, column, and diagonal are all the same. This value is called the "magic sum."

15	16			9
		20	21	2
1		13	19	25
24	5			18
17			10	11

CHAPTER 9

Go Play

"If you want creative workers, give them enough time to play."

—John Cleese

Playtime during childhood provides more than just a break from routine. It is a gateway to unexplored realms and a way to indulge in activities purely for the enjoyment they bring. Children at play feel free to imagine themselves in new roles, experiment with materials, and explore new relationships. The lack of pressure to achieve a finite outcome from play provides much of the joy that comes with playtime. However, as we move from adolescence to adulthood, the meaning and purpose of play change.

As adults, play takes on a different role. It becomes a means to release pent-up energy, like the exhaustion that comes from the repetition of hitting balls in a batting cage, or a way to recharge, such as the euphoria that comes from endorphins after a brisk run. Play can also become competitive with age, introducing a stress factor that might diminish its positive impact on creative thinking. Adding more play to your life can boost creativity and productivity and improve cognitive skills like problem-solving, flexibility, and emotional intelligence. This naturally leads to an increase in creative velocity.

Play is often what we forego in our busy adult lives. Between a meeting-packed day, managing childcare, sitting in traffic, and tackling our to-do lists, play is not always afforded the time it deserves.

163

Pretend play is typically ignored in adulthood and often ridiculed as a childish pursuit. Although it's easy to mock adults who participate in cosplay, those involved in this community appreciate the freedom to express themselves and their imagination through improvisation, storytelling, and character design. Cosplayers not only create and explore characters, they also develop their creative abilities in a supportive community environment.

Much of our play as adults has a purpose or a reward associated with it. We want to achieve the top score playing a video game, win a race, a championship, or a contest. This is why adults respond to and are motivated by gamified experiences. As adults, we value the sense of achievement and accomplishment and are motivated by extrinsic factors like badges, medals, and praise, even when we play. However, children enjoy an intrinsic motivation to play and do it for the sheer fun of it.[1] Open-ended play, such as building structures in the sand, finger painting, or splashing in the kiddie pool, helps children develop curiosity, autonomy, and master skills. However, as adults, we often engage in less open-ended play due to self-consciousness, decreased spontaneity, and a focus on end results rather than the joy of the journey, which limits our creative capacity.

Play is one of the reasons some researchers suggest that children are more creative than adults, even with fewer experiences to draw on. Children do not readily censor their imagination, and they have more naturally open minds than adults, who tend toward being pragmatic as well as having more fixed beliefs and biases. Since children are more likely to participate in pretend play, they tend toward divergent thinking and demonstrate strong cognitive flexibility, in part due to the lack of prior experience providing any constraints on their imagination.[2]

In a highly popular 1991 speech titled "Creativity in Management," John Cleese discusses the importance of cultivating an open mind, like a child, when playing with ideas. He cited Donald MacKinnon's research into creativity in the 1970s at the University of California, Berkeley, which showed that creative people "simply acquired a facility for getting themselves in a particular mood—a way of operating—which allowed their natural creativity to function."[3] Cleese goes on to describe this mindset as relaxed and less goal-oriented. It is open to humor and a wider range of perspectives, and it permits curiosity to operate without a specific goal to achieve besides discovery. Scott Ehrlich, whose interview appears in Chapter 4, described how he spent his downtime during working trips in Europe walking toward something that interested him until he figured out what it was, and then he'd move on to the next thing to explore. When free time is spent in pursuit of curiosity's sole purpose of discovery and learning, creative thinking can flourish.

This ability to get into a particular mindset to spark creative thinking is a common trait shared by the people I interviewed for this book. While no two people follow the same playbook to get into that state, they all know precisely what they need to do to activate it. With an awareness of these triggers, once in that state, their child-like comfort with their irrational thoughts, their willingness to be self-reflective without judgment, explore without purpose, and a lack of expectation about the outcome empower them to achieve creative velocity. They find a way to be okay in this "messy" state and release the compulsion to judge the good ideas versus the bad ones, approximating this child-like open mindset. As Pat Copeland shares in his interview later in this chapter, when in this state, it is important to catch and release an idea, not ruminate too long, and try not to control the chaos.

Serious Play

Play in the workplace has recently become a topic of research for social scientists. Previously, play had mainly been analyzed in the context of childhood development and the role it serves in building cognitive and social skills. By the 2000s, the normalization of ping-pong and billiard tables in the workplace brought play to the forefront of corporate culture, making it a much more interesting subject for researchers. Under the banner of "work hard, and play hard," companies tried to create fun, engaging, and employee-friendly work environments to attract top talent. Recruits soon learned that just seeing these game tables on premises wasn't as important as understanding whether the company culture—and their specific hiring manager—actually supported their playtime.

Author Michael Strage, a research associate at MIT Media Lab and columnist for Fortune, popularized the term *serious play* in 2000[4].

Researchers have since expanded upon it to describe when employees deliberately engage in playful behaviors with the specific intention of tackling important work-related goals. This type of adult play is distinct in its purposefully paradoxical, goal-oriented nature, setting it apart from children's play. This juxtaposition of intrinsic motivation (play) with extrinsic motivation (work objectives) creates what researchers have called a "paradox of intentionality."[5] The marriage of creative activities and work-related agendas requires a balance to ensure that attempts to control play do not undermine creativity and unstructured play doesn't wander aimlessly without producing relevant and useful novel ideas.

Not to be confused with "work fun," which is typically intended to cultivate an environment where people socialize and relate to co-workers through planned events, serious play is focused on using playful activities to solve business challenges and encourage ideation toward a focused objective. The two concepts do share the benefit of building camaraderie in an enjoyable manner. However, serious play distinguishes itself in its methodological and intentional pursuit of a business outcome.

In 1996, before Schrage generalized the concept, two visionary professors at the Institute for Management Development in Switzerland and the owner of The LEGO® Group, Kjeld Kirk Kristiansen, explored different tools and systems for strategic planning. Through their partnership, an innovative concept emerged that involved using LEGO® elements to create three-dimensional models to help teams represent and tackle complex business issues and challenges. This revolutionary approach to strategy was branded LEGO® Serious Play®.[6] This technique for serious play has been sustained over multiple decades because it leverages several proven principles for effective creative problem-solving, including metaphorical thinking, nonjudgmental exploration, visual and spatial thinking, storytelling, and playfulness.

The LEGO Serious Play (LSP) methodology is an open-source creative thinking technique that has continuously expanded and evolved through an active community of innovation facilitators. Facilitators provide everyone with access to LEGO bricks and ask them to build a model with them to address a specific challenge or issue. People work individually to build their models. The LSP methodology guides the participants to use the bricks to communicate their personal perspectives as metaphors. Because LEGO bricks can't directly represent business concepts, metaphors help explain the approach taken when building the model. Metaphors are an essential component of LEGO Serious Play. As described in Chapter 3, metaphors help reframe a problem or idea and unlock creative thinking.

Building with LEGO bricks does not require technical or artistic skills, making it accessible to everyone. The process of physically constructing the model while trying to express your thoughts through metaphors is meant to be introspective and thought-provoking. Once the models are finished, each participant shares their model and discusses their thoughts about it with the group. Everyone is expected to present their ideas and listen to others' thoughts without passing judgment. Participants may choose to combine their models and collaborate on a new shared one (an example of combinational creativity from two), or individuals can continue to refine their own model by incorporating different perspectives and insights gained from reviewing others' models.

Doodling

Doodling can be considered a form of unstructured serious play, especially when it occurs during work hours. The benefit of doodling is that it allows the unconscious mind to surface. In addition to providing a potential path to achieve flow, doodling has also been shown to increase concentration on primary tasks. The lack of any expected outcome from spontaneously drawing or scribbling prevents it from competing with other more intentional activities like listening to a presenter or getting a business update in a meeting. Doodling can be seen as a playful, exploratory activity that reduces anxiety and slows impulsive reactions to the primary focus of your brain. Like brainstorming, doodling provides a way to allow ideas to evolve naturally without censorship or judgment. Unlike LEGO Serious Play, doodling is a solitary activity that doesn't need to represent a specific issue or metaphor. The abstract nature of doodling allows for more spontaneous, open-ended, and unconstrained exploration.

Although it may seem counterintuitive, researchers believe that doodling is, in fact, helpful to concentration and memory because it uses none of the verbal processing skills required to continue listening.[7] The act of spontaneously drawing without specific goals to accomplish invites the brain to connect previously unrelated ideas, including the ones being verbally processed at the same time.

In 2009, psychologist Jackie Andrade researched the impact of doodling on memory and learned that those subjects who doodled while listening to a rambling voicemail message were better at paying attention to the message and recalling the details than those who did not. How is this possible? Researchers believe "brain activity in this default system seems to be inversely related to activity in another intrinsic network, the 'attention system,' which is activated during goal-directed cognition."[8]

Doodling stimulates the brain in a way that improves focus and reduces stress. It consumes just enough effort to keep you from fully drifting away when someone is speaking. And, by choosing to riff off a word or an object related to the speaker's topic, doodling may actually aid in recall and fuel associations between what's being said and what lies in your subconscious mind.

In the interview at the end of this chapter, Pat Copeland shares how he uses doodling as a tool to tap into his unconscious mind and surface unexpected connections. He recognizes that the act of doodling creates a channel that bridges one's rational and uncategorized thoughts. This is because doodling is normally accompanied by a relaxed state of mind that can allow cognitive processes to function more fluidly. And the lack of mental rules associated with doodling makes it easier to visualize abstract thoughts.

Playfulness, Improvisation, and Creativity

While play describes an activity, playfulness represents a set of human behaviors. There is a lot of evidence correlating playful behaviors in adults and creativity. Patrick Bateson, a biologist at the University of Cambridge, studied the relationship between playfulness and creativity and connected the two in this way: "Playful play is associated with a positive mood and when it occurs is taken as an indicator of well-being. Playfulness encourages humor, and humor encourages playfulness, and the result is greater creativity."[9] In a survey he conducted, he noted a high correlation between one's ability to act playfully and the capacity to come up with new ideas.[10] Individuals who show a playful attitude tend to think in an unstructured and flexible manner, which opens them up to associate seemingly unrelated concepts in new ways.

Not everyone feels comfortable showing their playful side, especially at work. It may take some conscious effort to reconnect with that carefree mindset from childhood. Stress and a lack of autonomy can naturally stifle a playful spirit at work. In our interview, Pat Copeland pointed out that feeling judged or frequently dismissed in your job inevitably makes it difficult to find the motivation to explore one's curiosity freely. This blocks the capacity for playful behaviors and divergent thinking, both important contributors to the generation of novel ideas.

Pretend play and improvisation share the concept of "yes and" thinking. This type of exercise depends upon an open mindset to encourage the expansion of an idea by accepting its premise and adding a new insight or connecting it to another idea. Improvisation can be done individually or as a group. When engaging in improvisation as a group, the core tenets—accepting and expanding on ideas, withholding judgment, and spontaneous reactions—must be understood and internalized by everyone in the group for the exercise to be productive. In both scenarios, maintaining a sense of humor can help ensure a relaxed, playful environment and an open mindset, which will be most conducive to creative velocity.

Successful improvisation requires skillfully responding to unexpected circumstances. It enables individuals to effectively address sudden challenges and quickly devise creative solutions in the face of uncertainty. The writers of MacGyver said in their interview in Chapter 1 that "to think like MacGyver means thinking improvisationally." Appropriately incorporating elements of playfulness and improvisation into professional settings can accelerate creative velocity. For example, Zappos' customer service employees are empowered to deliver a great customer experience. They are more likely to improvise to achieve the intended outcome when normal processes fail to deliver. The company's playful culture encourages thinking on the spot and acting immediately, hallmarks of improvisational behavior. When faced with a customer issue, the customer service agent responds instinctively. "Yes, I accept your problem exists, ***and*** I will fix it by doing X and Y."[11] The power to creatively solve problems this way is borne from a mixture of curiosity, imagination, and divergent thinking, all traits of playful people.

Effective improvisation requires practice, whether on your own or in a group. Researchers in 2020 at the London Business School studying the development of improvisational skills suggest there are three types of improvisation: imitative, reactive, and generative.[12] If you are just starting out and want to test your capacity for improvisation, begin with imitative improvisation. Imitative improvisation is a foundational skill that teaches you to react by mimicking others' actions while operating within established rules, roles, and frameworks. Imitative behavior is about observing and learning from the improvisational actions of others within your team, community, or social groups and adopting those behaviors that align with the group's culture. Your observations should prompt you to ask yourself when faced with an unexpected problem, "What would they do?"

Imitative improvisation can also involve mimicking objects. In this exercise, you use a variety of materials to replicate the function of the original object. The key is to use common items found around the house or in nature, rather than store-bought crafting supplies. Imagine items like straws, leaves, toothpicks, rubber bands, old containers, office supplies, and so on. The aim is to recreate the purpose of an existing tool. Instead of trying to create an exact copy, focus on making something that can achieve a similar result.

The next level of improvisational skills, reactive improvisation, requires spontaneously responding to unexpected situations by combining resources and knowledge to find a novel solution, like MacGyver. People who feel empowered in their roles rely on this technique to manage around constraints and focus on what can be done with what is immediately available to them. Reactive improvisation requires the capacity to be open-minded, curious, imaginative, and willing to take risks.

Generative improvisation, which involves creating completely new actions and narratives without relying on existing cues or structures, is understandably the most challenging to master. An example of generative improvisation is the popular team-building activity known as the spaghetti tower challenge. In this activity, teams are required to proactively try new ideas and approaches to build the tallest possible tower using 20 pieces of spaghetti, a yard of string, and a yard of tape to support a marshmallow placed on top of the structure. Working with unconventional resources and building on others' ideas to create a unique design that meets the goals of height and stability is at the core of generative improvisation.

Practicing improvisation enhances creative thinking skills. Creative thinkers know how to access and activate their playful spirit and are unafraid to look or act in unexpected ways. They are more likely to break habitual thought patterns and more willing to take risks to explore new perspectives. Being comfortable with the spontaneous nature of improvisation also builds resilience, adaptability, and confidence.

Partnering with Generative AI

When using generative AI to improve your improvisational skills, it's important to follow some best practices. Training an AI partner to recognize and appropriately react to playful elements will yield better results. You'll need to feed the AI with a dataset of responses that showcase different types of playfulness since many AI partners do not understand all types of humor. For example, sarcasm, situational humor, and self-deprecating humor are difficult for AI to interpret and reproduce because of nuanced elements like context, emotion, and self-esteem. Humor that heavily relies on human experience, social understanding, and cultural context, which informs improvisational play, poses a challenge for AI, so it is essential that you acknowledge these limitations and find creative ways to work within or around them.

You can guide the AI by providing a specific persona for it to use, and the more details you give, the more relevant its responses will be. You can also prompt the AI to take on different personas or improvise dialogue, which allows you to practice perspective shifting and thinking on your feet while interacting with the AI character you've created. Not every idea that comes from this exercise will be worth pursuing, so it's essential to avoid being judgmental with your computational collaborator, just as you would with a human partner.

Instead, give the AI a starting sentence or situation and let it generate unexpected, funny, or completely new continuations. This can help you practice "yes and" thinking, a crucial aspect of improvisation.

You can prompt your AI partner, "I want to task you with creating an entirely new improv game, scene, and exercise that you and I can play and is tailored to developing specific skills like active listening, spontaneous decision-making, or 'yes and' storytelling." In this playful, solo environment, allow AI to push you out of your comfort zone. It's worth noting that while GenAI can simulate playful behaviors, it doesn't have genuine emotions or consciousness. Playful behavior in artificial intelligence results from pattern recognition and generation based on training data. The level of playfulness and its appropriateness can be managed through careful prompt engineering and model fine-tuning. When integrating playful behaviors in AI systems, it is important to consider the context and ensure that the level of playfulness is in line with user expectations and the overall purpose of the interaction.

While a serious play session with a team will benefit from a facilitator trained in the Lego Serious Play methodology, you can still work with an AI partner to practice your visual thinking skills and build confidence in using metaphors to communicate an idea. You can look to AI to generate build challenges for you to practice modeling an emotion or an experience, and specify you wish to use the LEGO Serious Play technique. You can provide AI with an objective or domain you'd like to explore; the more specific, the better. For example, you might prompt, "Provide me three good examples of build challenges for the Lego Serious Play workshop that I can do with my team of three people to help us tackle X problem." AI can then provide you with relevant build challenges to practice the basic skills of modeling abstract concepts using physical pieces. Move from building representations of objects that AI proposes to ideas and emotions and then to more dimensional scenarios that communicate an activity or event. You can then share your model with a trusted friend or colleague to practice communicating your approach to the challenge as you would in a group session. You can also share with members of communities of LSP advocates online. Explain the ideas and stories behind your model. Get feedback on how effectively you communicated your thoughts.

Interview with Pat Copeland

I met Pat Copeland in 2020 after I joined Amazon where Pat was a vice president with Amazon Ads. Most recently, Pat served as the chief engineering and product officer at Zendesk. For more than two decades, Pat has led global engineering and product teams as an executive at Autodesk, Microsoft, and Google. In addition to being a member of the Board of Trustees at Harvey Mudd College, Pat is an aspiring astrophotographer, artist, and author of Codex Dnal Epoc, a book of more than 250 of Pat's drawings. Pat's LinkedIn profile tagline is "Software Innovator and Aspiring Runway Model," which should give you a sense of his playfulness.

1. **In this age of generative AI, what is the role of human creativity?**

   I was listening to somebody talk about this, and they were saying that no child born today will ever be smarter than AI. I thought that was an interesting and provocative statement. I started thinking about, "How do I interpret this?" I thought that it meant AI could be better than humans in problem-solving, data processing, and maybe even some decision-making at scale.

   Then I thought about a second interpretation of this statement—what if we think of AI as a tool? Maybe it's not a challenge to our intelligence or our creativity, but a tool that could help us move society forward in some way. The next generation will be able to use these tools in ways that we can't even imagine. Right now, these are baby tools.

   My last interpretation was what if we step back and rethought what it means to really be smart or intelligent? And that might take you down the path where it suggests that intelligence is about emotions, creativity, ethical judgment, and expressing ourselves to each other. This means doing many things that machines can't do for us or each other. So maybe intelligence is a lot more

   (continued)

than about summarizing information or data. It's really about our connection with each other. I think that's a more positive way to think about it.

2. **You have said, "Doodling serves as a stress reliever and gives us a view of our unconscious thoughts." Why is that important for enhancing one's creative capacity? How can someone leverage this action of bringing ideas from the unconscious to the conscious mind?**

I tend to do art because it helps me stay sane. I have to do it. It's an obsessive, compulsive behavior. It's an immersive activity that allows me to stay laser-focused on something that is not required in my critical decision-making. It's a way of wandering. I am allowing my mind just to go free. When I'm in a lucid mindset, I feel more creative and less judge-y of my ideas. And so that creative period where I'm not trying to edit myself, I'm not trying to come to a closure on something, I can let ideas ruminate and be okay to exist. When I do art, I try to suppress that judge-y part of my brain and just let myself go and let things be okay. It doesn't matter if it's a good idea or a bad idea; it just exists. It's just a thing. And what I try to do is not to be too attached to reaching a conclusion.

If you're in a lucid state, it's as if you are allowing those ideas to pour in. There are times when I will doodle on a pad or draw in meetings sometimes. I blend that together with work. I'll actively doodle or draw, and I'll be hyper-focusing my attention on what's happening in the room. Having my hand doing something and drawing simultaneously while listening is helpful. This somehow taps into a different creative part of my mind. That helps me think about what's being said, whereas if I'm taking notes, I'm actively taking the information, processing it, trying to decide what's been said, categorizing it into things, deciding what's right and what's wrong, and then regurgitating it back onto a thing which requires me to type into a computer and think about how I'm typing.

Taking a more lucid approach allows me to wander with the conversation that's happening, be very curious, and explore the other person's thought process on a deeper level. I don't feel pressured to react while taking it all in. Brain theorists have the perspective that there's a part of your brain that decides what's important and sticks it into your memory somehow or processes it differently. And if you're actively judging those ideas, it doesn't work the same way. But if you're in a lucid state, you're open to allow those ideas in.

3. **How do you re-energize your creative spirit during periods of frustration or stagnation? Where do you find inspiration?**

When I left Google, I experienced incredible stress. It wasn't necessarily about Google or the situation at all. It was more about my reaction to things and how I felt about what I wanted to do. I also realized I had just been running on this treadmill of wanting to be successful, and it was like kryptonite for me. And I asked myself what in the world I was trying to prove.

I wanted to change my mood, so I started taking these long walks. The exercise was really a walking meditation. I would listen to podcasts, and the light bulb went on for me. I remember walking up in the hills above our house, and suddenly, I could smell tomatoes in the distance and tomatoes on the vine. They were just in the sun. I could smell the soil. I also could smell the body odor of someone, with a slight tinge of aftershave, which was strange because I couldn't see anyone, but I could smell this. Suddenly, I realized my senses were lit up. I was feeling the world in a way that I had not in a long, long time, and I realized what stopping and smelling the roses meant. That's a good go-to for me. I expect to use it like a tool. I don't know if it always works, but if I practice it regularly, sometimes I'll have one of those epiphanies.

(continued)

When I am in this state, it's kind of catch-and-release. Catch an idea, try to put it into perspective, and then release it so I don't ruminate on it and fall into a negative spiral or force it to a conclusion.

4. **How important is failure or the acceptance of failure in cultivating creativity?**

The easy answer is you just have to accept failure as a major possibility; you're almost guaranteed that most things will probably fail. I try to stay optimistic, but I also try to integrate the religion of being okay with early failure and not falling in love with my idea.

This is congruent with creating artwork, too; if you step up to a canvas and think, "I'm going to create a masterpiece today that's going to be perfect," what do you think will come from that? You are going to be self-editing. You're going to be thinking about achieving perfection. You're going to be doing all of these things that are contrary to improvisation, and that's going to make it hard to explore the idea. You need to ask yourself, "What am I really trying to solve? And how do I not fall in love with the project midway through?" Because if you are locked into an idea and you can't break away or find objectivity from that idea, you can pursue the wrong path for too long. You must kill off things that you are really, really interested in solving. And that's hard. I don't think anybody is good at that. It is painful because it feels like you've messed up or wasted time. It's very difficult to break from an idea. But you can do that by doing it earlier and smaller and being okay with walking away from a path that's not working.

You must remove your ego from it, say the market will help identify the right answer here, and tell yourself, "I need to be open to what I'm observing." You cannot fall in love too much with what's going on because you might be on the wrong path. You need the courage to pull out or change course early enough that it doesn't damage a bunch of things, but sometimes it is better not to do something.

Forgiving yourself for your own failings is part of it, too, because you don't want it to feel negative. You must have the confidence to say, "I'm okay with being flawed in some way because creativity isn't about being perfect." It's about taking risks and being okay with mistakes, and if you are trying to shoot for perfection, you will fail anyway. It's okay not to be great at certain things. And I'm not good at all situations. I'm not good at all the things I try to do. I will try something and not give up on it knowing I am not perfect at it, because I want to at least feel like I'm learning something from the effort.

5. **You created a work of art called "Real Thought Crimes" (Figure 9.1) that highlights the importance of regulating your thoughts and feelings, especially the negative ones. How do you recommend people manage these emotions so as not to impede their creative capacity? Are there behaviors or habits that can be employed to vanquish these sentiments when they encroach on your daily life?**

As a manager of a group of people and multiple teams, the issue of getting into a downward spiral comes up frequently. When you are in a crisis, you must recognize the first step in the spiral. When you see you are in the spiral, it's crucial to intervene and break out of it. In that comic you referenced, I depicted myself intervening in my thoughts and likened it to being pulled over by a cop. This intervention is a way of disrupting and correcting my negative thought patterns.

Being pulled over by a cop is shocking and frightening, similar to the feeling of embarrassment and self-criticism when you realize you've made a mistake. These feelings are a result of our genetic responses to failure,

(continued)

which have been amplified over time. Recognizing this, I try to intervene in my thought process by questioning its effectiveness, redirecting my focus to finding solutions, and identifying what I have control over.

It's difficult to catch myself in a downward spiral early on. I have learned you just have to accept those painful feelings. You don't get over sadness. You just accept that sadness exists and that it's okay to have these emotions as long as they exist in the right perspective. When I see that people are beating themselves up, I tell them, "You're beating yourself up. Is this working for you? Is this downward spiral really helping you solve the problem? You're focusing on what happened before. Why not focus on what we need to do next?" Just observe it and just let it exist. And look forward.

Figure 9.1 *Real Thought Crimes*, ©2023, Pat Copeland.

Exercises

LEGO SERIOUS PLAY

This exercise builds on LEGO® SERIOUS PLAY® Open-source guideline, which the LEGO® Group makes available under a Creative Commons license. This is a variation of a traditional facilitated workshop.

Define the Challenge

You can follow the exact instructions that follow the description of the build challenge for each round.

> *Round 1:* Start with a challenge that expresses an emotion or feeling. For example, "Build a model that communicates how you feel when you don't get a good night's sleep." Or, "Build a model that represents a feeling of exhilaration."
>
> *Round 2:* After you have practiced this type of challenge, build a model of an object of your own invention that doesn't exist today and repeat the following exercises. For example, "Build a model of a toaster that spreads butter on the bread when it is finished toasting."
>
> *Round 3:* Finally, practice this exercise with a build challenge focusing on a time period or event and repeat the following exercises. For example, "Build a model that describes your daily commute."

You can collaborate with a friend and take turns providing the build challenges or ask generative AI to propose them for you. For each round of build challenges, follow these instructions:

Gather Materials

Compile a colorful assortment of LEGO bricks to help unlock endless possibilities for expressing your innovative ideas.

Build

Set aside some dedicated, uninterrupted time, put on your favorite music, and dive into building a unique model that encapsulates your vision. Let your imagination run wild as you use various LEGO elements to bring your solution to life.

Reflect

After crafting your model, take a moment to ponder:

- What does each part of your model symbolize?
- How does your model ingeniously solve the problem?
- What are the unique features and benefits of your solution?
- Are there any opportunities for enhancement?
- What challenges did you face when visualizing your model?

Document

Write a description of your model that effectively captures your creative inspiration. Bring the model to life through words. Then, take multiple photos from different angles to showcase your novel solution.

Iterate

Review your creation and reflections. Embrace the freedom to refine and rebuild parts of your model to align perfectly with your grand vision. Share the model with a friend or colleague and get feedback. Iterate again.

IMPROVISATION

Imitative Improvisation

Objective: To practice imitative improvisation, replicate an existing solution with unrelated materials and then create a unique solution to a new challenge.

Round 1
1. **Select a Tool:** Choose an existing tool you want to mimic (e.g. a set of salad tongs).
2. **Gather Materials:** Collect found items around your house or environment that could potentially replicate the tool's function.
3. **Imitate:** Use the found items to create a functional version of the tool.
4. **Analyze:** Examine how well your improvised tool performs compared to the original.

Round 2

1. Innovate: Use the found items to create a unique tool that serves the same purpose but with an entirely different design or added features.

2. Reflect: Evaluate the effectiveness of your new tool, what improvements could be made, and how the process enhanced your creative thinking.

Reactive Improvisation

- **Object Transformation:** Pick an object in your environment. Start by describing it realistically, then gradually transform it into something fantastical. How does it move? What sounds does it make? Does it have a new purpose?
- **Scene Improv with AI as a Partner:** Start a conversation with AI with this prompt:

    "I want to practice an improv scene with you. It starts with this line: [use a starter from the bullets below or create your own.] Now it's your turn."

    - Remember, each reaction must accept the premise of the AI partner and add to it. See how far you can take this scene in three minutes. Example conversation starters:
        o Is that a ghost?
        o You can't bring that animal on the plane!
        o What's that under your foot?
        o Where was the photograph taken?

Generative Improvisation

Objective: To practice generative improvisation by building a narrative solo from scratch.

- **Materials:** Collect five random objects you have in your house. Have a timer, notepad, and pencil. Assemble them all on the table in front of you.
- **Instructions:**
    - Set the timer for fifteen minutes.
    - Select three items from your collection
    - Create a basic scenario using these objects and write it in your notepad. For example, "The mug is the mom, the comb

is her male infant, and the spatula is her toddler daughter. They are walking down the dairy aisle at the grocery store."

- o Identify what each object represents in the scenario.
- o Identify the relationship between the objects in the scenario.
- o Identify the location of this scenario.

- Challenge the scenario by putting the three objects in some form of peril or facing a challenge. Describe this event in the notepad. Time is of the essence so keep the narrative brief and on point.

- Add the two remaining objects from your collection to the scenario to address the peril. Give each object an unexpected superpower that will remove or address the peril. Add that to your narrative.

- ◆ **Self-reflection:** How far did you let your imagination go? How literal or figurative were you in your narrative? Was the scenario you chose real, personal, or wholly invented? What guided your choices?

DOODLING EXERCISE
Copy the image provided here twice.

In both versions of this exercise, you may add shapes, extend the lines, and fill in spaces. However, you must incorporate the three lines in the that were provided.

Exercise 1: Using the three lines provided, expand upon the first set till you create something recognizable. Repeat the exercise this time with the second set of three lines.

Exercise 2: Do the same thing with a second copy of this image. Only this time, flip the paper upside down and create an entirely new representation of pattern or design.

CHAPTER 10

Spin a Story

"You're never going to kill storytelling because it's built in the human plan. We come with it."

—Margaret Atwood

Storytelling is a powerful tool that invigorates the imagination and challenges us to visualize various outcomes from different scenarios, characters, and settings. We can expand our creative capacity and cultivate a unique perspective by actively engaging with stories, whether by reading, listening to, or creating them. Storytelling leverages the human tendency to understand, relate to, and retain information best when it is structured as a story. Regardless of the type of story, characters, or environments involved, adding new elements can reveal unexpected challenges that stimulate our minds and push us to explore new possibilities. Storytelling is not a nice-to-have skill for creative thinkers; it's a core cognitive capability contributing to creative velocity. Scilla Andreen, whose interview appeared at the end of Chapter 6, maintains, "Storytelling is one of the most important things in the world." She believes it is the skill set everyone must develop to connect and relate to other people emotionally. Scilla believes that even as AI takes on some of the jobs that exist today over time, it will never supersede the human capacity to influence, connect, and resonate with others through stories.

Stories are foundational to product development methodologies. As Tony Fadell pointed out in Chapter 2, "The world and everything we do everyday is about a story." Designers and product managers often use stories to convey context, needs, purpose, motivation, and intent while creating empathy for their target customers, who should benefit from their deliverables. In this domain, stories enable development teams to engage in perspective-taking and provide a larger understanding of the problem space. The "what if" narrative is crucial in the design thinking process. By imagining different situations and user journeys, "what if" narratives can disrupt conventional thinking and inspire innovative solutions. For example, the founders of Airbnb may have wondered, "What if homeowners could easily rent out their unused spaces to travelers looking for affordable and unique lodging options?" As Scott Belsky, who is interviewed at the end of this chapter, writes in his blog Implications, "Airbnb was clearly an idea at the edge of reason, as most VCs couldn't even imagine opening up their homes to strangers."[1] The same can be said of the founders of Uber, who radically pondered, "What if we could connect drivers directly with passengers using technology?" By exploring different "what if" scenarios, entrepreneurs and innovators reframe problems to reveal new perspectives on standard ways of operating. Narratives are widely regarded as a valuable source of ideas for shaping system design, especially because they take a holistic view of the customer journey and account for the causes and effects of actions taken along a particular storyline.

Narrative intelligence (NI) describes the ability to interpret and create narratives successfully. NI involves recognizing patterns and structures in stories, identifying central themes and characters, and using this information to make better decisions and plan for future scenarios.[2] Two Netflix shows, *Black Mirror: Bandersnatch* and *Kaleidoscope*, expand the concept of narrative intelligence. Both introduce nonlinear narratives driven by audience participation, which upends the traditional passive role of the viewer and places them in an active role, influencing the narrative's flow. *Bandersnatch* gives viewers control over the protagonist's choices, resulting in multiple storylines and endings. *Kaleidoscope* presents the narrative out of order, allowing viewers to piece together the story themselves. This challenges the audience to recognize patterns, identify key elements (characters, plot points), and piece together the narrative despite lacking a typical linear structure. The absence of a singular, fixed narrative highlights the effect of subjective experience on the story.

Narrative thinking is a powerful tool in design thinking as it helps us to identify and define causality or cause-and-effect relationships. Causality often depends on broader contextual understanding, and recognizing it requires a minimal empathy gap. Angus Fletcher, a neuroscientist and professor of story science at Ohio State University's Project Narrative, wrote, "Narrative is a non-logical mode of intelligence that operates by connecting causes to effects, or, more technically, by positing causal relationships between physical actors and actions."[3] Dr. Fletcher has maintained that logical thinking can discount the influence of human irrationality and impulses that impact a narrative and that storytelling is a way to develop cognitive flexibility in dynamic and uncertain environments. Imagining possible outcomes by exploring causality is essential for understanding the potential consequences of our choices. If you believe that A causes B, it may be helpful to explore what circumstances or factors you hadn't considered might make A cause C or D, instead.

Tension plays a crucial role in creating a compelling and engaging story. It is also a key concept in the world of product development, particularly when it comes to generating user stories. These "user stories" are crafted around a specific goal or task that a customer struggles to accomplish effectively, thereby introducing tension into the narrative. Identifying tension within a user story can offer valuable insights into the existing gaps in the market, presenting new opportunities for innovation. User stories that incorporate tension serve as focal points for the team, guiding them toward addressing the underlying issues. Ultimately, the primary goal is to effectively resolve the tension within the user story. Scott Belsky writes that to create disruptive innovation, you must tolerate some "necessary ruckus." He writes, "Creativity is nourished by conflict."[4]

Six-word stories are a type of narrative known as *flash fiction*. Although legend has it that Ernest Hemingway memorialized this technique of storytelling in the 1920s, there is no definitive proof the tale is true.[5] When writing these narratives, you must use only six words to tell a story that tempts the imagination. With such few words, you must ensure that each choice contributes to the narrative's impact. This strengthens your ability to filter information and make meaningful choices, just as your brain selects relevant details from a cluttered scene. For instance, if I write, "He opened the box and fainted" instead of "She opened the box and laughed," you might imagine the first story going in an entirely different direction from the latter version. And if I swap the pronouns, could that change either of the stories that these six words tell?

Even with only a half-dozen words, these narratives can be emotionally evocative. As the legend goes, Hemingway wrote, "For sale: baby shoes, never worn." Six words that take you right to the image of a grieving parent and their unborn baby. The reader's collaboration is essential in piecing together the broader narrative subtly suggested by these words, which allude to an unfulfilled event. However, there are also other interpretations; for example, the shoes were a gift from someone and were simply the wrong size or the baby's shoes were a style or design the new parents didn't like. As humans, we bring our bias and experiences to these six words, in essence co-creating the narrative with their author.

Six-word narratives serve as cognitive workouts, condensing storytelling into a format that strengthens specific mental abilities. Writing these narratives requires authors to select and organize the most essential words for maximum impact. This skill is highly valuable when formulating problem statements and evaluating solutions. Using unnecessary words when defining a design challenge or customer problem can impede creative velocity and divert attention from the core issue. Extraneous or unclear inputs can also confuse your AI partner.

Story Thinking

Psychologists and neuroscientists, such as Angus Fletcher, believe that humans are naturally wired to process and make sense of activities and encounters as stories. The data points we collect are meaningful only when captured with context. We naturally think in stories, and that process involves understanding and making sense of the world through cause-and-effect relationships. We seek meaning in the way information and experiences surround and involve us, and stories provide a coherent sequence that can make things more easily understood and remembered. As a result of this research, a framework for story thinking has emerged, along with the research that validates that story thinking enhances creativity. Fletcher outlined several key techniques to leverage story thinking to identify innovative outcomes. World-building, perspective-shifting, and action generation are key techniques in story thinking.

Since context and environment play an important role in shaping narratives and understanding human experiences, world-building provides a platform for exploring new constructs for actors and actions. For example, the film *A Quiet Place* explores a world inhabited by blind extraterrestrial creatures with an acute sense of hearing. The film's premise forces characters to think creatively and develop innovative solutions to survive. Creating this kind of world-building narrative in our professional and personal lives encourages similar creative problem-solving, enhancing cognitive flexibility. An entrepreneur like Jules Pieri might ask themselves before embarking on a risky project, "What if I lose everything in this venture?" Imagining the story of a potential future business failure made her realize she could withstand the outcome personally and professionally. Similarly, story thinking supports both inversion thinking and the premeditation of evils covered in Chapter 5, as they both benefit from well-crafted narratives around potential failures or negative outcomes.

When you prompt yourself to "imagine a world where," you begin a narrative that can lead to either creative disruption or creative destruction. For example, Waymo envisions a future without drivers. This shift could dramatically impact related industries such as insurance, public transportation, car manufacturing, real estate, and logistics. For this innovation to succeed, Waymo must anticipate the new world that will emerge when autonomous vehicles become widespread. This is when story-building can be helpful.

Akira Kurosawa's acclaimed film *Rashomon* is a classic example of perspective-shifting in storytelling. Four different characters recount the murder of a samurai, and each narrative differs significantly, showcasing the characters' personal biases, motivations, and emotional states. When the same experience is revisited from multiple points of view, the subjectivity of human perception and memory becomes apparent, which helps to close the empathy gap.

Perspective-shifting works not only when considering different people's points of view but can also benefit from shifting one's perspective of time and environment. The classic 1985 film *Back to the Future* artfully uses the time travel narrative to thoughtfully explore themes of change, causality, and the profound impact of individual choices. Understanding and appreciating these themes requires a thoughtful shift in perspective. Stories can evolve in different ways based on these additional factors, and it can be helpful to see where these shifts may impact the outcome. Researchers in Australia have also studied the application of story thinking to "technology foresight," to aid in the identification of future technology innovations. They found it was easier to "envision plausible, possible, and preferable chains of cause and effect" while enabling reflection on potential unintended consequences and conflicts.[6]

The action generation technique is particularly useful in dynamic situations requiring imaginative thinking and adaptability. The technique benefits business strategy, product development, policymaking, and any area where creative solutions are needed for complex problems and actions may have unexpected consequences. It is based on the premise of narrative theory, which states that the combination of events and characters drives a narrative forward. This technique involves creating dynamic and compelling actions within a story that challenge characters by putting them in unknown situations to test their limits or by introducing them to unexpected events or actors in a familiar environment.[7] This technique can be extremely useful when contemplating an act of creative destruction.

Story thinking also strengthens problem-solving skills by creating situations or challenges that demand resolution. The narrative formula of trigger-consequence-resolution provides an effective framework for problem-solving. The film *The Hangover* is a good example of a narrative demonstrating the action generation technique. The story is propelled by a series of events that cause the characters to react to extraordinary circumstances rather than through dialogue or exposition. In business, this technique helps test ideas and scenarios, prepare for possible outcomes, and reduce bias toward any one proposed strategy. As companies look to integrate AI into their workflows, story thinking can be used to identify clear prospective challenges that can be solved by the technology deployment and new opportunities that can now be addressed.

Story thinking is a powerful tool that can enhance scenario planning. When envisioning future states, it can be helpful to imagine the impact of potential events that could disrupt your current course. For example, using the action generation technique in story thinking could have been a valuable tool for businesses in preparing for the future disruptions caused by the pandemic. It can help a company future-proof itself by demonstrating the adaptability and resilience required to survive the unexpected. Well-crafted alternative scenario stories can help leaders question their assumptions and see the world differently.

Story thinking's bias toward action and adaptability can enhance creative velocity by increasing confidence in one's ability to respond to unplanned events, people, and environments. It enhances cognitive flexibility, improves resilience, and reduces bias. This structured approach to story thinking can help businesses identify and act on the controllable aspects of a situation while providing the mental framework to acknowledge that the unexpected can occur and to adjust when faced with uncontrollable elements.

Story thinking makes it easier to see that small things are really big things and vice versa. Since story thinking considers causality, it can highlight how small actions can have larger consequences and demonstrate how accumulating small steps, decisions, and actions can lead to significant discoveries. By considering the cause-and-effect relationships within a narrative framework, story thinking can help highlight patterns and potential connections across events, actions, and actors.

Artist's Books

I first heard about Artist's Books from my friend Kate Collins, one of the artists who introduced me to and contributed to the Exquisite Corpse illustration in Chapter 1. I became fascinated by this form of narrative. Artist's books are narrative works of art intended to share a story, express an emotion, or capture a moment. How the book is constructed—the size, scale, materials, and binding—is an important part of the art, but the essence of the work is how the narrative inside the book is told through choices the artist makes about the book's style, format, and materials. For example, a book can be merely a folded paper, revealed as an accordion, or it might be hand-bound pages. The binding can be sewn, stapled, or glued. Alternatively, the story can be told in a more elaborate pop-up structure, which unfolds a new three-dimensional scene with each page turn. Despite its name, this technique does not necessarily require the skills of an artist, and deciding the story's timeline is part of the creator's design process. When developing the concept for an artist's book, the question to address first is whether it is a snapshot in time or presents a progression from the first page to the last.

Like a Serious Play project described in Chapter 9, an artist's book can convey the story of an emotion, depict a metaphor for a feeling, or communicate a particular moment in time. This format encourages its creator to explore unconventional designs, materials, and structures beyond traditional bookbinding and two-dimensional pages. At the same time, it challenges the storyteller to craft a narrative that deliberately utilizes that structure, as the structure itself is part of the narrative. This experimentation fosters lateral thinking, as the approach is not reliant on logic and linear solutions. It also encourages multiple forms of expression, including visual, metaphorical, sensory, and emotional. Crafting an artist's book can build creative confidence by encouraging you to explore ideas and emotions. Additionally, working within the constraints of the format to build an expressive narrative requires thoughtful curation and experimentation.

This storytelling format can be liberating, as there are almost no rules for expressing oneself. Many of these books are metaphorical or abstract, and this conceptual focus encourages the creator to experiment with different ways to express an idea. Because there is no standard or "normative" way of crafting an artist's book, there also is no bar that the creator has to meet, which can make this form of expression accessible to anyone who wants to build creative confidence. What makes an artist's book great is the way it tells a narrative, not the quality of the art it presents.

As Figure 10.1 illustrates, an artist's book does not need to be constrained by standard rectangular-shaped pages, either. It can take the form of an object, in this case, a house, and the narrative associated with it gives that object meaning. While you can observe the house

Figure 10.1 Artist's book created by Leslie Grandy, ©2024.

from the perspective in the image, the back side of the image would also be used as a canvas to communicate more about the house, who lives in it, and even perhaps what makes this house a home. Is the house filled with people or just furniture? Is it neat or messy? Is this a home that contains a lot of laughter or drama? Or is there a completely different house façade on the other side? When designing the backside of this book, you might take a literal approach to mirror the spaces depicted on the front or make it an abstraction of the emotions of the people who reside there. One view of the book may be literal, and the other could be figurative. Together, they communicate a story.

The artist's book has the potential to stimulate multidimensional thinking and encourage cognitive flexibility by challenging creators to reimagine the traditional format of a book and how a story is conveyed. "Artists' books explore artistic representation of the human condition and human expression, science, life, and mortality, providing an opportunity to pause and reflect on the complex layers of human interaction and emotion in the profession."[8]

Artists' books can help develop creative problem-solving skills in several ways. Artists' books may use symbolic metaphors instead of literal representation. Interpreting these visual metaphors involves connecting the dots to combine different ideas to reveal a new perspective. This technique is key to problem-solving. Like six-word stories, the open-ended nature of artists' books leaves room for multiple interpretations, and that ambiguity encourages an open mindset. Planning and developing the theme for the book requires conceptual thinking. Considering how the pages interact with each other and how the viewer interacts with the book wholistically aids in spatial thinking. Storytelling in this format exercises multiple skills in your cognitive toolbox intimately and uniquely.

Partnering with Generative AI

Humans naturally enjoy telling stories, and social scientists and neuroscientists agree that we benefit from the activity. However, our stories can reflect our personal perceptions and biases that can impact their value as training data for AI. Researchers at Carnegie Mellon University (CMU) studied the capacity of generative AI to create compelling character backstories. When their output was reviewed by humans, they suggested it lacked nuance, cultural awareness, and the complex thought process that can drive emotional or impulsive acts. While AI can provide initial ideas and assist in the creative process, the researchers suggested that human writers remain essential for adding depth, cultural sensitivity, and ethical considerations to narratives.[9]

For example, a decision may be required by the character in a story to take an action that is good for a small segment of the community but not for everyone. Using only logic to make that decision could under-represent the specific values or ethics of the character. For example, films like *Schindler's List* and *Sophie's Choice* propose this type of dilemma. Oskar Shindler could maintain his safe financial position by using Jewish labor, or instead, he could marshal his resources and influence to save their lives. Sophie was forced to choose which child to save.

I asked Google's Gemini what choice it would make in each case. It replied to the *Shindler* quandary, "As a large language model, I can't experience emotions or have a moral compass in the same way a human does." It then proceeded to offer a list of questions, the answers to which might help me make the decision. In the *Sophie's Choice* example, Gemini replied, "As a large language model, I can't truly understand the depths of human emotions and the desperation that would come with such a horrific choice. However, based on the information I have access to and principles of ethics, here's how I would approach the situation in Sophie's Choice." The response then outlined three logical frameworks for making this decision: (1) maximizing life, (2) considering the age and needs of each child, and (3) recognizing the best way to be fair may, in fact, require the choice to be random.

These examples demonstrate a key limitation the CMU researchers highlighted when collaborating with generative AI on narrative development. It supports their recommendation that AI be viewed as a collaborative tool rather than a replacement for human creativity in storytelling and character creation because emotions in storytelling stem from lived experiences and cause irrational thoughts that AI may struggle to understand. This co-creation process requires human discernment, which must be a human commitment to assess and evolve the generative AI output based on things like societal norms, ethics, emotions, and values. Human storytellers draw on their own emotional journeys, infusing their narratives with genuine feelings and experiences. While AI can mimic emotional responses, it often lacks authenticity because it misses the mark on relatability. Humans may recognize that the best option is the one AI proposes, but they understand how it is possible to make suboptimal choices for reasons not rooted in logic.

In 2022, neuroscientist Angus Fletcher produced a controversial paper suggesting that "Computational AI Will Never Do What We Imagine It Can," in which he dispels several myths about AI's narrative capabilities. Despite AI researchers damning him for not keeping up with improvements in AI, Fletcher maintains his knowledge is indeed current and based on an understanding of deep neural networks. He warns not to be led "by the notion of 'emergent properties' into thinking that nuts and bolts can jump the laws of physics. A computer that (for example) achieved sentience would still be limited to performing computation, just as a car that achieved sentience would still be limited to driving from one place to another."[10] Said simply, we are wired differently from our AI collaborators.

Researchers continue to explore ways to overcome the limits of computational creativity today. Different constructs seek to simulate specific elements of the creative process, including character simulations, genre frameworks, stream of consciousness, and goal-based simulations. One challenge that needs to be addressed when co-creating with generative AI is maintaining the coherence of different storylines over time. Large language models frequently encounter difficulties in retaining the context over lengthy text sequences. As the narrative unfolds, earlier details or plot points may become "forgotten" or overlooked, resulting in inconsistencies or contradictions. Frequently in literature, details that may seem inconsequential at the story's beginning can be the key to solving a mystery or explaining a character's motivation. It will be critical to highlight the facts you believe should not be overlooked or should represent an outsized impact as the narrative develops. For example, suppose you are designing a product for a target persona, and developing a customer journey narrative. In that case, it may not be obvious to your generative AI partner why each detail matters, and some may be inadvertently lost over time.

While AI can analyze patterns and make predictions based on historical data, it struggles with behaviors that deviate sharply from established patterns or are driven by complex, context-specific motivations. Like characters in novels, humans often act based on emotions, spontaneous decisions, or unique personal experiences that are difficult to quantify and predict. They can be irrational, illogical, and even criminal. Generative AI systems can address some aspects of these challenges by learning from vast amounts of data and employing sophisticated algorithms. Still, without an analogous system to the brain's amygdala and hippocampus, which are involved in processing human emotions, rewards, and motivation, generative AI tools' effectiveness is limited, especially in highly dynamic or unpredictable situations.

Interview with Scott Belsky

In his own words, Scott Belsky is a builder, author, investor, and all-around product obsessive. He is currently a partner at A24, an independent film studio, after serving as Adobe's chief strategy officer and executive vice president of Design & Emerging Products. Scott co-founded Behance in 2006 and served as chief executive officer until Adobe acquired Behance in 2012. Although I have not personally worked with Scott, I have been inspired by his work for many years and have personally benefitted from his passion for building the creative confidence of all people, not just artists and designers. I also appreciate that he is a forward thinker who believes in the limitless potential of the creative mind when partnered with the right technology and tools. Some of the content Scott provided first appeared in his newsletter, *Implications*.

1. **In a world of abundant generative AI tools, what is the role of human creativity?**

In the age of abundance—and the rapid commoditization and accessibility of content and entertainment—there will be a growing human desire for authenticity and story. As every brand "floods the zone" just because it can, I am interested in the unique human desires that empower more niche and non-scalable experiences (and who benefits from providing such services). I believe that uniquely human stories and non-scalable craft will capture our imagination more than ever before in the AI era. When something seems ubiquitous and commoditized, we crave more craft and meaning. I think it is important to remember in the age of AI that *natural human tendencies always overpower technical innovations.*

There's a lot of speculation and rhetoric these days about whether AI democratizes creativity or advances it. However, it is abundantly clear to me that both are true. Humanity's creative confidence has gone up as people of all ages are able to prompt whatever is in their mind's eye and express themselves visually. We've shifted from a world where we had to find someone with the skills to tell our story to one where we can tell our own story. We've shifted from being skills-constrained to being imagination-constrained.

Until now, skills have been a major differentiator for humanity. However, in the age of AI, taste will become more important than skills as much of skill-based work

(*continued*)

and productivity is offloaded to compute. Taste seems scarcer these days and increasingly differentiating in the age of AI.

2. **If AI tools raise the ceiling of what's possible rather than superseding the need for human creativity, how can humans better prepare to co-create with technology? What should individuals, teams, and companies do to ensure they have the most significant impact when collaborating with AI?**

In short, we must outsource our productivity to compute and apply our humanity to our creativity.

When I consider the uniquely human work we will do in the era of AI, I like to start with a reminder of the weaknesses and strengths of AI. AI is a great consensus and mimicry machine, telling you "what the right answer most likely is and sounds like" or "what the image prompt entered would most likely look like." Of course, AI is leveraging all of its training data to give you an answer you'd expect while leveraging some random number generation along the way to give you something one-of-a-kind. What is lacking in AI is soul, namely the craftsmanship, the story, and the unquantifiable yet extraordinarily impactful human experience that impacts the outcomes in small ways that make a big difference.

The story and attention to detail that commands a premium for great brands and fine cuisine will extend to all life aspects. As consumers, we will crave meaning in a world of abundance. Humans much like machines, recycle all of their inputs (training data) to create solutions to problems. However, we apply our life experiences to our outputs instead of random number generation. The role of humans in the era ahead will be to inject meaning into what we make—from entertainment and software to cuisine and content of all kinds.

We must study the history of art and the creative choices and sources of the greats. We must expose people to unique and admirable demonstrations of taste and celebrate it. We must develop a desire and value for creative expression in the next generation.

3. How do you re-energize your creative spirit during periods of frustration or stagnation? Where do you find inspiration?

I seek more and new inputs in the form of experiences that both serve and develop my curiosity, and I make sure that my body is being taken care of. Creativity thrives on conflict-born emotion and abhors comfort. But conflict alone won't cut it. You need hope and a vision—something toward which you can channel the dark energy.

4. In your interview on the proofwellness.com you said you like to get your endorphins going by taking a morning run. In another interview, you noted that your mind wanders when forced to unplug. Are those two comments connected? Does running help you get into a state of creative flow? What does peak performance look and feel like to you?

In 2023, I wrote in my *Implications* blog that when you're forced to unplug, your mind is forced to wander. Our phones, schedules, and constant connection to the world as it happens around us is a tremendous burden on the spontaneity of our imagination. Even Uber rides and airplane flights have become windows for productivity at the expense of just thinking. At this point, the only two places I am forced to unplug and let my mind wander are the shower and . . . while running. The endorphins released while running and the forced period of disconnection are a godsend for me. I challenge my plans and contemplate my projects, I think of

(*continued*)

UX tweaks in products, I brew new articles to write, I develop tactics to close deals . . . and if I didn't have this window of thinking imposed on me, I'd likely just be responding to more emails and Slack messages. In the modern era, we desperately need forced windows of non-stimulation and can no longer rely on circumstance. Find something in your life that forces you to regularly disconnect, do it regularly, and open the aperture of your free-flowing imagination.

The pause between idea and action has a bounty we seldom reap. *Wait for it.* I have a lot of ideas while running, and I get obsessed with just trying to remember them, but I never let myself stop mid-run to write them down. Partly because that would be a pathetically seductive excuse to take a break. But mostly because, if I let these ideas continue to brew they actually get better. It turns out, the time and distance between when you have an idea (and feel tempted to stop and capture it) and when you wait until you finish your run is a golden period of polish that doesn't exist in the normal real-time sitting state world. That space in between is both a period of natural selection and iteration that supernaturally extends your blue-sky state at a moment when endorphins are running high. On many occasions in my life, a good idea became a great idea (or a properly discarded idea) during this period.

5. **You have said, "AI democratizing creativity" is missing the point. How?**

"AI democratizing creativity" is only half the equation. There's a lot of speculation and rhetoric these days about whether AI democratizes creativity or advances it. However, it is abundantly clear to me that both are true. On the one hand, humanity's creative confidence for humanity has gone up as people of all ages are able to prompt whatever is in their mind's eye and express themselves visually. We've shifted from a world where we had to find someone with the skills to tell our story to one where we can tell our own story. We've shifted from being skills-constrained to being imagination-constrained.

For creative professionals, AI unlocks exponentially more cycles of discovery. Exploring the full surface area of possibility for the very best solution to a problem has always been a function of time, and AI changes the game. As a result, creative professionals can cover more terrain and find better solutions . . . thus "raising the ceiling" of what is possible. Artificial intelligence actually makes creativity more viable and efficient.

As the expression of ideas becomes exponentially easier, the ideas themselves become more of the differentiator (yes, I think "Prompt Engineering" will become a discipline in and of itself!). Good ideas aren't derived solely from logic and patterns of the past; they're also the product of human traumas, mistakes of the eye, and uniquely human ingenuity.

The most rewarding path for individuals will be focusing on creativity. While productivity is about squeezing all the value out of existing resources, creativity and creative thinking are about discovering new resources: creative problem-solving that turns an obstacle into an advantage, inspiration that leads to a new product, creative reinvention that changes the course of your career.

Exercises

PLOTTING (INDIVIDUAL)

You can repeat this exercise as many times as you want. Each time, however, the subsequent round should challenge you to ask yourself, "What if?" While you can practice this activity with generative AI, remember that causality in narratives is challenging for generative AI, and computational tools are not generally trained on humans' many possible criminal, unpredictable, or irrational behaviors.

- **Round 1:** Choose a novel title on the bestseller list and be mindful to pick only a book for which you have no knowledge of the story and have not read any reviews or the book's synopsis. Imagine the novel's plot, characters, setting, and style, and write a paragraph synopsis just using the title alone.
- **Round 2:** Change one of the four elements in your synopsis—plot, characters, setting, and style—and rewrite the synopsis. Maybe the hero of the story changes or the context or setting is different; the point is to imagine what impact these modifications might have on the narrative flow. Re-plot.
- **Round 3:** Select one of the two synopses you created. Then add an implausible or fantastical event to the mix and build a new world. This addition should be as wild as you can imagine. The approach you pick should challenge your sense of logic and plausibility. "Now, imagine a world where . . ." Re-plot.

PERSPECTIVE SHIFTING (SINGLE OR GROUP)

This exercise illustrates the concept of parallel narratives or alternate realities. Take a familiar story and retell it from a different character's point of view:

1. Choose a well-known fairy tale or short story.
2. If working in a group, assign different characters to participants. If working alone, imagine the story from multiple characters' perspectives.
3. Take 15–20 minutes to rewrite a key scene from your character's perspective.
4. Identify what fuels the character's different perspective of the same story.
5. Now, alter the course of events based on a different character's perspective. How would this character intervene to affect a different outcome for the story?

WORLD BUILDING (GROUP)

This exercise allows the group to create a random set of variables that can then be used as the basis for a short narrative.

- Each group should contain five to six participants.
- Each participant randomly selects a theme from this list:
  - Cultural
  - Legal
  - Political
  - Geographical
  - Environmental
  - Social
  - Historical
- Each participant will take 10–15 minutes to create their fragment of the world individually. Use the time to fill in details that will convey your theme's most essential aspects and attributes. For example, if you pick historical, you might describe critical events that happened previously within the world. If you pick culture, you might describe the world's diversity or describe popular forms of artistic expression.
- Now, share each fragment with the group. Do not offer more details than you could during the time you were previously allotted.
- Each participant individually writes a 200-word narrative about the world based on a combination of three fragments. You do not have to use all the fragments in your narrative.

SIX-WORD STORIES (INDIVIDUAL)

Imagine at least two different narratives around these six-word stories. Write a synopsis for each.

1. Darkness is permanent, sleep eludes me.
2. Found true love. Married someone else.
3. Bird in hand, none in nest.
4. Talking dog gets reality television show.
5. He dreamed big. She dreamed bigger.

This exercise also makes a great icebreaker for teams. If you wish to do this as a group, simply ask everyone to work independently. Then, come together as a group to compare the stories for each set of six words. Were they similar or different? How were they different?

A DAY IN THE LIFE—ARTIST'S BOOK (INDIVIDUAL)

Objective: This is a hands-on exercise. Create an artist book that tells the story of "A Day in the Life" of a chosen character, object, or abstract concept. This exercise encourages you to think creatively about storytelling and visual expression.

Instructions:

1. **Choose a Subject:**
   - Select a character, object, or abstract concept to represent in your artist book. This could be a person, an animal, an object, a piece of furniture, a day of the week, an emotion, etc.

2. **Brainstorm and Plan:**
   - Spend time brainstorming the story you want to tell. Think about what happens to your subject throughout a typical day, seasonally, or as it ages.
   - Create a rough storyboard or outline of the sequence of events you want to depict in your book.

3. **Materials and Techniques:**
   - Gather materials for your artist book. This can include paper, cardboard, fabric, paint, markers, collage materials, found objects, glue, tape, string, etc.
   - Experiment with different artistic techniques like drawing, painting, collage, and mixed media to communicate your story.

4. **Create Your Pages:**
   - Design each page either to represent a different part of the day, a single significant event in your subject's life or use them all together to portray a landscape or idea. Consider how the content will flow moving from one page to the next.
   - Think about the use of color, texture, and composition to convey energy and emotions that tell the story.

5. **Construct the Book:**
   - Assemble the pages into a book format. This could be a traditional bound book, an accordion fold book, a pop-up book, flip book, or any other creative structure.

o Pay attention to how the pages interact with each other and present to the audience when the book is opened and closed.

6. **Final Touches:**

o Add any finishing touches to your book. This could include a cover, title, and any additional decorative elements.

o Ensure that your book is cohesive and that the story flows smoothly from beginning to end, front to back.

7. **Presentation and Reflection:**

o Present your artist book with friends and family. Ask for their interpretation of the work.

o Share the story behind your subject and explain your creative process.

o Reflect on what you learned during this exercise and how you applied creative thinking to produce your artist book.

Epilogue

In 2023, more than 800 companies, representing more than 11 million employees, were surveyed, and 73.2% indicated they consider "creative thinking and analytical thinking to be the skills most expected to rise in importance between 2023 and 2027."[1] Author Ray Dalio, founder of Bridgewater Associates, says when hiring, he looks for the three Cs—creativity, competence, and character. While analytical thinking is considered the top core skill by more companies than any other skill, another cognitive skill, creative thinking, ranks second.[2] The 2023 Deloitte Global Marketing Trends executive survey, conducted in June 2022, also supports that growth is a reason brands should hire for creativity. "At a time when we are seeing a shift from creative skills to analytical skills across the marketing function, high-growth brands surveyed are more frequently doing the opposite by considering creative thinking as one of the most important attributes for talent."[3] The imperative to innovate, ideate, and envision new horizons is not just a strategy but a vital lifeline in today's ever-transforming landscape.

The advent of AI has revolutionized how we approach the creative process, allowing humans to offload the more tedious and repetitive tasks to machines. This shift conserves time and energy and empowers individuals to delve deeper into the aspects of creation that demand a human touch. Tasks that bog down the creative spirit, like formatting, organizing inputs, or producing numerous variants, now fall within the realm of AI's capabilities. This delegation enhances efficiency, granting humans more space to engage in mind-wandering, lateral thinking, and critical interpretation. In this partnership, it is crucial to remember that AI is not a substitute for human creativity but rather a tool that can enhance it. The strategies outlined in the book offer numerous ways to collaborate with generative AI to accelerate your creative capacity because the real creative value comes from humans actively directing, interpreting, and contextualizing AI-generated content.

Employees with strong creative self-efficacy will be essential as AI is increasingly integrated across various industries and functions. They will not only contribute to generating novel ideas but will also play a crucial role in assessing the value and meaning of AI-generated concepts. Working together, humans and AI can achieve amazing things and unlock new levels of creativity and innovation. In our exploration, we have also addressed the potential pitfalls of relying too heavily on generative AI. Over-reliance can dilute the very essence that makes creativity so impactful—its human touch. Creativity, at its best, is deeply personal and often reflects the complexities of the human experience. AI-generated outputs can be impressive, but without a human mind's intentional curation and direction, they can lack the subtlety and intention that truly innovative ideas require.

The people I interviewed for this book share a similar view on the role of human creativity in the age of generative AI. They see AI as a tool that can streamline processes, inspire new ideas, and accelerate creative expression by lowering the barriers to entry. They emphasize that while AI can generate content quickly and efficiently, it still requires human guidance, input, and oversight. There is a strong consensus that uniquely human qualities—such as emotion, empathy, taste, authenticity, and storytelling—are irreplaceable. Scott Belsky, Scilla Andreen, and Denny Post stressed the importance of these human elements, arguing that they bring depth, meaning, and context to creativity that AI cannot replicate. Humans bring the critical "soul" to the creative process.

While all those interviewed underscored the importance of human creativity, there was a range of skepticism and optimism about what creative value they see emerging from AI output. Several people maintained that AI's most significant opportunity is to allow for quick iteration and experimentation, ultimately leading to more impactful and faster creative outputs. Scott Ehrlich and Tony Fadell highlighted how AI can speed up inspiration and visualization. More skeptically, Jules Pieri said she believes AI is not inherently creative and will always lag in capturing the forefront of human-driven artistic expression. She predicts a market division where AI-driven outputs serve mass, non-bespoke needs while human creativity continues to dominate in areas that require high-quality, custom, and authentic experiences. This outlook suggests a dual-path future where AI serves functional and scalable purposes, and human creativity remains the hallmark of bespoke and emotionally resonant work.

Whether you are an optimist or a skeptic, one thing is clear—to be effective creative partners, humans must practice their skills by honing their unique strengths that AI cannot replicate. Humans must continue to bring discernment, judgment, and refinement, and abandon fixations and biases, as AI becomes more integrated into creative processes. Regularly practicing the tools and techniques in this book will build the confidence to produce more effective prompts and then challenge and improve the machine's output.

If you are unsure where to start your creative partnership, you can provide your generative AI partner with a well-constructed problem statement and a few of your favorite techniques from this book to help you practice them. Then, observe how the methods can be applied to suggest a solution. Iterate the initial output by challenging your AI partner's assumptions or by adding or subtracting constraints. Spend time stretching the boundaries of the initial problem definition to evolve the solution further. Most importantly, throughout this process, observe how changes you make to your prompts or the AI training data can produce a pipeline of new results to evaluate.

When human creativity meets generative AI, amazing things happen. AI's ability to recognize patterns and make connections takes our brainstorming sessions to new heights. Nonetheless, it is essential to balance these advancements with efforts to preserve the diversity, originality, richness, and emotional resonance of creative expression. By developing our creative abilities, we can maximize the potential of generative AI and drive a continuous flow of inventive solutions and fresh perspectives, propelling us toward creative velocity.

Endnotes

Introduction

1. Nielsen, Jared A., Brandon A. Zielinski, Michael A. Ferguson, Janet E. Lainhart, and Jeffrey S. Anderson. 2013. "An Evaluation of the Left-Brain vs. Right-Brain Hypothesis with Resting State Functional Connectivity Magnetic Resonance Imaging." PLoS One 8, no. 8: e71275. https://doi.org/10.1371/journal.pone.0071275.
2. Mathias Benedek, Martin Karstendiek, Simon M. Ceh, Roland H. Grabner, Georg Krammer, Izabela Lebuda, Paul J. Silvia, Katherine N. Cotter, Yangping Li, Weiping Hu, Khatuna Martskvishvili, James C. Kaufman. "Creativity Myths: Prevalence and Correlates of Misconceptions on Creativity." *Personality and Individual Differences* 182 (2021). Accessed June 24, 2021. https://doi.org/10.1016/j.paid.2021.111068.
3. Livingston, Paisley. "Chapter Seven. Poincaré's 'Delicate Sieve': On Creativity And Constraints In The Arts." pp. 127–146 *The Idea of Creativity* (Leiden, The Netherlands: Brill, 2009) https://doi.org/10.1163/ej.9789004174443.i-348.46
4. Belsky, Scott. "Creating in the Era of Creative Confidence - Scott Belsky - Medium," Medium, December 24, 2022, https://scottbelsky.medium.com/creating-in-the-era-of-creative-confidence-b4e251d725f.

Chapter 1

1. Editors of Merriam-Webster. 2023. "What Does 'MacGyver' Mean? | Slang Definition of MacGyver." In. https://www.merriam-webster.com/wordplay/what-does-macgyver-mean-slang-definition.
2. "Functional Fixedness." n.d. *Oxford Reference.* https://doi.org/10.1093/oi/authority.20110810104943772.
3. Felipe Munoz-Rubke et al., "Functional Fixedness in Tool Use: Learning Modality, Limitations and Individual Differences,"

Acta Psychologica 190 (October 1, 2018): 11–26, https://doi
.org/10.1016/j.actpsy.2018.06.006.

4. Katherine O'Toole and Emőke-Ágnes Horvát, "Extending Human
Creativity With AI," *Journal of Creativity* 34, 2 (February 6, 2024):
100080, https://doi.org/10.1016/j.yjoc.2024.100080.

5. Rikke Friis Dam, "The 5 Stages in the Design Thinking Process," *The Interaction Design Foundation* (blog), June 9, 2024,
https://www.interaction-design.org/literature/article/5-stages-in-
the-design-thinking-process#stage_2:_define%E2%80%94state_
your_users'_needs_and_problems-2.

6. Tony McCaffrey, "Find Innovation Where You Least Expect
It," *Harvard Business Review*, September 10, 2020, https://hbr
.org/2015/12/find-innovation-where-you-least-expect-it.

7. Tony McCaffrey, "Innovation Relies on the Obscure: A Key to Overcoming the Classic Problem of Functional Fixedness on JSTOR,"
Www.Jstor.Org, n.d., https://www.jstor.org/stable/41441775.

8. "Exquisite Corpse | the History of Exquisite Corpse," Language
IsAVirus.com, n.d., https://www.languageisavirus.com/exquisite
corpse/corpse.php.

9. "Supermind Design Primer | MIT Center for Collective Intelli-
gence." n.d. https://cci.mit.edu/supermind-design-primer/.

10. "The Effects of Generative AI on Design Fixation and Divergent
Thinking." n.d. https://arxiv.org/html/2403.11164v1.

11. "Make Your Own Exquisite Corpse | Magazine | MoMA." n.d.
The Museum of Modern Art. https://www.moma.org/magazine/
articles/457.

Chapter 2

1. "Hume, Imagination | Internet Encyclopedia of Philosophy,"
n.d., https://iep.utm.edu/hume-ima/.

2. Brian Lowry, "Variety," *Variety*, September 15, 2015, https://
variety.com/2015/tv/reviews/scream-queens-review-ryan-
murphy-horror-series-fox-1201593058/.

3. Roger L. Martin, "How Successful Leaders Think," *Harvard Business
Review*, June 1, 2007. http://dx.doi.org/10.1108/sd.2007.05623
kad.006 https://hbr.org/2007/06/how-successful-leaders-think.

4. Maria Popova, "Networked Knowledge and Combinatorial Creativity," The Marginalian, May 6, 2022. https://www.themarginalian .org/2011/08/01/networked-knowledge-combinatorial-creativity/.

5. Wikipedia. 2024. "Printing Press." Wikimedia Foundation. Last modified February 11, 2024. https://en.wikipedia.org/wiki/ Printing_press.

6. Hyejin Youn, Deborah Strumsky, Luis M. Bettencourt, and Jose Lobo. "Invention as a Combinatorial Process: Evidence from US Patents." *Journal of the Royal Society Interface 12*, (2015). Accessed February 20, 2024. http://dx.doi.org/10.1098/ rsif.2015.0272.

7. Jamie Siminoff. "Why Reinvention Is Crucial to Ring's Innovation." The Ring Blog. November 7, 2022. https://blog.ring.com/ about-ring/why-reinvention-is-crucial-to-rings-innovation/.

8. "Teen Invents Bluetooth EKG to Help Keep Hearts Healthy | Kids Discover Online," Kids Discover Online, n.d., https:// online.kidsdiscover.com/quickread/teen-invents-bluetooth-ekg- to-help-keep-hearts-healthy.

9. Richard O'Reilly, "The Cutting Edge: COMPUTING / TECHNOLOGY / INNOVATION: Multipurpose Machine Combines Printer, Copier, Fax in a Compact Space - Los Angeles Times," *Los Angeles Times*, March 6, 2019, https://www.latimes.com/archives/la-xpm-1994-11- 16-fi-63474-story.html.

10. Jake Swearingen, "An Idea That Stuck: How George De Mestral Invented the Velcro Fastener," *New York Magazine*, November 1, 2016. https://nymag.com/vindicated/2016/11/an-idea-that- stuck-how-george-de-mestral-invented-velcro.html.

11. Gary Wolf, "Steve Jobs: The Next Insanely Great Thing," *Wired*, February 1, 1996. https://www.wired.com/1996/02/jobs-2/

Chapter 3

1. "'Seinfeld' the Voice (TV Episode 1997) ☆ 8.3 | Comedy," IMDb, October 2, 1997, https://www.imdb.com/title/tt0697806/?ref_=ttfc_ql.

2. "Wale and Jerry Seinfeld Interview (2014 Cover Story) | Complex," complex.com, n.d., https://www.complex.com/covers/ wale-seinfeld-interview-2014-cover-story/.

3. Adam Grant, "Why So Many Ideas Are Pitched as 'Uber for X'," *The Atlantic*, February 4, 2016. https://www.theatlantic.com/business/archive/2016/02/adam-grant-originals-uber-for-x/459321/

4. Lizzie O'Leary, "Do We Really Need High-Tech School Buses?," Slate Magazine, September 14, 2023, https://slate.com/technology/2023/09/high-tech-school-bus-zum.html.

5. "We Analyzed 477,358 Startup Pitches, and This Is the Shockingly Unoriginal Secret Formula," MarketWatch, March 23, 2015, accessed March 17, 2024, https://www.marketwatch.com/story/everyone-wants-to-be-like-airbnb-and-uber-2015-03-20.

6. Mark W. Moffett, "Battles among Ants Resemble Human Warfare," *Scientific American*, December 1, 2011. https://www.scientificamerican.com/article/ants-and-the-art-of-war/

7. McGuire et al., "Minimal Navigation Solution for a Swarm of Tiny Flying Robots to Explore an Unknown Environment," *Science Robotics*, 4: eaaw9710 (2019). https://doi.org/10.1126/scirobotics.aaw9710

8. K. Duncker, "On Problem Solving," *Psychological Monographs*, 58 (Whole No. 270) (1945). https://doi.org/10.1037/h0093599

9. Mary L. Gick, and Keith J. Holyoak, "Analogical Problem Solving," *Cognitive Psychology* (1980): 306–355. https://doi.org/10.1016/0010-0285(80)90013-4.

10. Nikolaus Franke, Marion K. Poetz, and Martin Schreier. "Integrating Problem Solvers from Analogous Markets in New Product Ideation," *Management Science 60*, no. 4 (2014): 1063–1081. Accessed February 19, 2024. https://doi.org/10.1287/mnsc.2013.1805.

11. D. Gentner, "Structure-Mapping: A Theoretical Framework for Analogy," *Cognitive Science,* 7, no. 2 (1983), 155–170. 10.1207/s15516709cog0702_3

12. William J. Gordon. *Synectics: The Development of Creative Capacity.* (Harper & Row, 1961).

13. Tom Hope et al., "Accelerating Innovation Through Analogy Mining," *Proceedings of the 23rd ACM SIGKDD International Conference on Knowledge Discovery and Data Mining*, August 4, 2017, https://doi.org/10.1145/3097983.3098038.

Chapter 4

1. Paraskevas Petrou, Dimitri Van Der Linden, and Oana Catalina Salcescu, "When Breaking the Rules Relates to Creativity: The Role of Creative Problem-Solving Demands and Organizational Constraints," *The Journal of Creative Behavior* 54, no. 1 (2018): 184–95, https://doi.org/10.1002/jocb.354.

2. Murray Griffin and Mark R. McDermott, "Exploring a Tripartite Relationship Between Reblliousness, Openness to Experience and Creativity," *Social Behavior and Personality* 26, no. 4 (1998): 347–56, https://doi.org/10.2224/sbp.1998.26.4.347.

3. Paraskevas Petrou, Dimitri Van Der Linden, and Oana Catalina Salcescu, "When Breaking the Rules Relates to Creativity: The Role of Creative Problem-Solving Demands and Organizational Constraints," *The Journal of Creative Behavior* 54, no. 1 (2018): 184–95, https://doi.org/10.1002/jocb.354.

4. "Deep Dive Into Marigold Engage by Sailthru's Retail Personalization Index Top 10: Best Buy," sailthru.com, September 17, 2019, https://www.sailthru.com/marketing-blog/best-buy-personalization-index/.

5. Ian, "The Evolution of Netflix Under Reed Hastings' Leadership," Pressfarm, January 8, 2024, https://press.farm/the-evolution-of-netflix-under-reed-hastings/.

6. Sharon Reier, "Half a Century Later, Economist's 'Creative Destruction' Theory Is Apt for the Internet Age: Schumpeter: The Prophet of Bust and Boom," *The New York Times*, June 10, 2000, https://www.nytimes.com/2000/06/10/your-money/IHT-half-a-century-later-economists-creative-destruction-theory-is.html?ugrp=m&unlocked_article_code=1.iU0.CPUn._QjnbyIBn3lc&smid=url-share.

7. Osborn, Alexander Faickney. Applied Imagination: Principles and Procedures of Creative Problem-solving, 1963. http://ci.nii.ac.jp/ncid/BA59671805.

8. "Scamper Method," MMM-ext, n.d., https://www.post-it.com/3M/en_US/post-it/ideas/articles/scamper-method/.

9. Maria Popova, "Combinatorial Creativity and the Myth of Originality," *Smithsonian Magazine*, November 18, 2013, https://www.smithsonianmag.com/innovation/combinatorial-creativity-and-the-myth-of-originality-114843098/.

10. "How much is a 20 ft. shipping container to buy?," EasyRelocated. https://easyrelocated.com/how-much-is-a-20ft-shipping-container-to-buy/.

11. David Kindy, "The Accidental Invention of Play-Doh," *Smithsonian Magazine*, November 11, 2019, https://www.smithsonianmag.com/innovation/accidental-invention-play-doh-180973527/.

12. Douglas Martin, "Guinter Kahn, Inventor of Baldness Remedy, Dies at 80," *The New York Times*, September 19, 2014. https://www.nytimes.com/2014/09/20/business/guinter-kahn-inventor-of-baldness-remedy-dies-at-80.html.

13. Katherine Ellen Foley, "Viagra's Famously Surprising Origin Story Is Actually a Pretty Common Way to Find New Drugs," Quartz, July 20, 2022, https://qz.com/1070732/viagras-famously-surprising-origin-story-is-actually-a-pretty-common-way-to-find-new-drugs.

Chapter 5

1. PuhPow, "Seinfeld - Inside Look of the Opposite Episode, Season 5," December 3, 2019, https://www.youtube.com/watch?v=fL9lMP0lKg0.

2. Catherine I. Phillips and Penny M. Pexman, "When Do Children Understand 'Opposite'?," *Journal of Speech, Language, and Hearing Research* 58, no. 4 (August 1, 2015): 1233–44, https://doi.org/10.1044/2015_jslhr-l-14-0222.

3. James Clear, "Inversion: The Crucial Thinking Skill Nobody Ever Taught You," James Clear, February 4, 2020, https://jamesclear.com/inversion.

4. Alan Smith Business Coach, "Charlie Munger Explains Inversion Thinking Process," January 25, 2024, https://www.youtube.com/watch?v=K_vFpa0v3Wg.

5. Stock Compounder - Brad Kaellner, "Charlie Munger on Killing Pilots #Shorts," January 7, 2022, https://www.youtube.com/watch?v=TkuQeQpnRIg.

6. Lucius Annaeus Seneca and Robin Campbell, "LETTERS FROM a STOIC," ed. Betty Radice, PENGUIN BOOKS (Penguin Books, 1969), Letter XCI page 81, https://hillelettersfromstoic.wordpress.com/wp-content/uploads/2014/10/letters-from-a-stoic_lucius-annaeus-seneca.pdf.

7. "Janusian Thinking and the Scale Insurgent," Bain, March 5, 2019, https://www.bain.com/insights/janusian-thinking-and-the-scale-insurgent-fm-blog.

8. Albert Rothenberg, "The Process of Janusian Thinking in Creativity," *Archives of General Psychiatry* 24, no. 3 (March 1, 1971): 195, https://doi.org/1E0.1001/archpsyc.1971.01750090001001.

9. Loizos Heracleous and David Robson, "Why The 'paradox Mindset' Is the Key to Success," February 25, 2022, https://www.bbc.com/worklife/article/20201109-why-the-paradox-mindset-is-the-key-to-success.

10. Matthew Rubin, Ella Miron-Spektor, and Joshua Keller, "Unlocking Creative Tensions with a Paradox Approach," in *Elsevier eBooks*, 2023, 125–45, https://doi.org/10.1016/b978-0-323-91840-4.00006-2.

11. Ella Miron-Spektor, Francesca Gino, and Linda Argote. 2011. "Paradoxical Frames and Creative Sparks: Enhancing Individual Creativity Through Conflict and Integration." *Organizational Behavior and Human Decision Processes* 116 (2): 229–40. https://doi.org/10.1016/j.obhdp.2011.03.006.

12. "Post | LinkedIn." n.d. https://www.linkedin.com/posts/nicholasxthompson_mostinterestingthingintech-activity-7128114168435523584-8Eos/?utm_source=share&utm_medium=member_desktop.

Chapter 6

1. Wu-Jing He, "Positive and Negative Affect Facilitate Creativity Motivation: Findings on the Effects of Habitual Mood and Experimentally Induced Emotion," *Frontiers in Psychology* 14 (January 26, 2023), https://doi.org/10.3389/fpsyg.2023.1014612.

2. Katie Beresford, Margaret L. Kern, and Aaron Jarden, "The Creative-being Model: The Role of Negative Emotion in Creative Flourishing and the Impact on Positive Education," *The Journal of Positive Psychology* (February 26, 2024), 1–13, https://doi.org/10.1080/17439760.2024.2322467.

3. Jason Silva, "The Relationship Between Mood, Flow and Creativity: Turns Out Flow. . .," February 19, 2018, https://www.facebook.com/watch/?v=1976175069313435.

4. Eddie Harmon-Jones, Philip A. Gable, and Tom F. Price, "The Influence of Affective States Varying in Motivational Intensity on Cognitive Scope," *Frontiers in Integrative Neuroscience* 6 (January 1, 2012), https://doi.org/10.3389/fnint.2012.00073.

5. Jiemin Yang et al., "Increased Motivational Intensity Leads to Preference for Distraction Over Reappraisal During Emotion Regulation: Mediated by Attentional Breadth," *Emotion* 22, no. 7 (October 1, 2022): 1595–1603, https://doi.org/10.1037/emo0000977.

6. Lily Yuxuan Zhu, Christopher W. Bauman, and Maia J Young, "Unlocking Creative Potential: Reappraising Emotional Events Facilitates Creativity for Conventional Thinkers," *Organizational Behavior and Human Decision Processes* 174 (January 1, 2023): 104209, https://doi.org/10.1016/j.obhdp.2022.104209.

7. Daniel Goleman, *Emotional Intelligence: Why It Can Matter More Than IQ* (Bantam, 2005).

8. Emma Schootstra, "Can 10 Minutes of Meditation Make You More Creative?," *Harvard Business Review*, August 29, 2017, https://hbr.org/2017/08/can-10-minutes-of-meditation-make-you-more-creative.

9. Zorana Ivcevic and Marc A. Brackett, "Predicting Creativity: Interactive Effects of Openness to Experience and Emotion Regulation Ability," *Psychology of Aesthetics, Creativity, and the Arts* 9, no. 4 (November 1, 2015): 480–87, https://doi.org/10.1037/a0039826.

10. Itamar Shatz, "The Empathy Gap: Why People Fail to Understand Different Perspectives," n.d., https://effectiviology.com/empathy-gap/.

11. Adam M. Grant and James W. Berry, "The Necessity of Others Is the Mother of Invention: Intrinsic and Prosocial Motivations, Perspective Taking, and Creativity," *Academy of Management Journal/ The Academy of Management Journal* 54, no. 1 (February 1, 2011): 73–96, https://doi.org/10.5465/amj.2011.59215085.

12. Lee Ross, David Greene, and Pamela House, "The 'False Consensus Effect': An Egocentric Bias in Social Perception and Attribution Processes," *Journal of Experimental Social Psychology* 13, no. 3 (May 1, 1977): 279–301, https://doi.org/10.1016/0022-1031(77)90049-x.

Chapter 7

1. Bas Verplanken, *The Psychology of Habit* (Springer eBooks, 2018), https://doi.org/10.1007/978-3-319-97529-0.

2. Charles Duhigg, *The Power of Habit: Why We Do What We Do in Life and Business*, pp. 17–18 (National Geographic Books, 2012).

3. James Clear, *Atomic Habits: An Easy & Proven Way to Build Good Habits and Break Bad Ones* (Avery, 2018), https://catalog.umj.ac.id/index.php?p=show_detail&id=62390.

4. @JasonSilvaVideo | Facebook. August 1, 2020. https://www.facebook.com/watch/?v=3212638432118997

5. Jeffrey Gish et al., "Sleep and Entrepreneurs' Abilities to Imagine and Form Initial Beliefs About New Venture Ideas," *Journal of Business Venturing* 34, no. 6 (November 1, 2019): 105943, https://doi.org/10.1016/j.jbusvent.2019.06.004.

6. Joshua J. Gooley et al., "Exposure to Room Light Before Bedtime Suppresses Melatonin Onset and Shortens Melatonin Duration in Humans," *The Journal of Clinical Endocrinology and Metabolism* 96, no. 3 (March 1, 2011): E463–72, https://doi.org/10.1210/jc.2010-2098.

7. Razzagh Rahimpoor, "Physiological and Physical Effects of Sleep Disorder Among Shift Work Nurses," (IntechOpen eBooks, 2023), https://doi.org/10.5772/intechopen.110417.

8. Yanjun Liu, Shiyong Xu, and Bainan Zhang, "Thriving at Work: How a Paradox Mindset Influences Innovative Work Behavior," *The Journal of Applied Behavioral Science* 56, no. 3 (November 13, 2019): 347–66, https://doi.org/10.1177/0021886319888267.

9. Martin Oscarsson et al., "A Large-scale Experiment on New Year's Resolutions: Approach-oriented Goals Are More Successful Than Avoidance-oriented Goals," *PLoS One* 15, no. 12 (December 9, 2020): e0234097, https://doi.org/10.1371/journal.pone.0234097.

10. "Study: Brain Battles Itself Over Short-term Rewards, Long-term Goals," n.d., https://pr.princeton.edu/news/04/q4/1014-brain.htm.

11. Phillippa Lally et al., "How Are Habits Formed: Modelling Habit Formation in the Real World," *European Journal of Social Psychology* 40, no. 6 (July 16, 2009): 998–1009, https://doi.org/10.1002/ejsp.674.

12. Maggie Seaver, "Habit Stacking Makes New Habits Last—Here's How It Works," *Real Simple*, March 24, 2024, https://www .realsimple.com/work-life/life-strategies/inspiration-motivation/ habit-stacking.

13. Charles Duhigg, *The Power of Habit: Why We Do What We Do in Life and Business,* p. 62 (National Geographic Books, 2012).

14. Marco Stojanovic, Axel Grund, and Stefan Fries, "App-Based Habit Building Reduces Motivational Impairments During Studying – An Event Sampling Study," *Frontiers in Psychology* 11 (February 7, 2020), https://doi.org/10.3389/fpsyg.2020.00167.

Chapter 8

1. John Geirland, (1996). "Go with the Flow," *Wired*, September, Issue 4.09. https://www.wired.com/1996/09/czik/

2. Susie Cranston, and Scott Keller "Increasing the 'meaning quotient' of work," McKinsey Quarterly, January 1, 2013 https://www .mckinsey.com/capabilities/people-and-organizational-performance/our-insights/increasing-the-meaning-quotient-of-work

3. James Slavet, "Five New Management Metrics You Need To Know," *Forbes*, December 13, 2011. https://www.forbes .com/sites/bruceupbin/2011/12/13/five-new-management-metrics-you-need-to-know/?sh=3ab23e5d717d.

4. "Founders' IPO Letter," Alphabet Investor Relations, n.d., https:// abc.xyz/investor/founders-letters/ipo-letter/.

5. Ann Marsh, "The Art of Work," Fast Company, 08/01/05 https:// www.fastcompany.com/53713/art-work

6. Aine Cain, "One of the best companies in America gives employees 'yay days' to take off work—but they can't be used for just anything," *Business Insider*, https://www.businessinsider .com/rei-jobs-vacation-2018-2

7. Zachary C. Irving et al., "The Shower Effect: Mind Wandering Facilitates Creative Incubation During Moderately Engaging Activities," *Psychology of Aesthetics, Creativity, and the Arts* (September 29, 2022), https://doi.org/10.1037/aca0000516.

8. Apple Podcasts. 2024. "Fly on the Wall With Dana Carvey and David Spade on Apple Podcasts." May 10, 2024. https://

podcasts.apple.com/us/podcast/jerry-seinfeld/id1603639502?
i=1000654895619.

9. James A. Roberts and Meredith E. David, "Instagram and Tik-Tok Flow States and Their Association With Psychological Well-Being," *Cyberpsychology, Behavior and Social Networking* 26 no. 2 (2023): 80–89. https://doi.org/10.1089/cyber.2022.0117.

10. Ashwin Seshagiri et al., "How TikTok Changed America," *The New York Times*, May 4, 2024, https://www.nytimes.com/interactive/2024/04/18/business/media/tiktok-ban-american-culture.html.

11. Paul Verhaeghen, Alexandra N. Trani, and Shelley N. Aikman, "On Being Found: How Habitual Patterns of Thought Influence Creative Interest, Behavior, and Ability," *Creativity Research Journal* 29, no. 1 (January 2, 2017): 1–9, https://doi.org/10.1080/10400419.2017.1263504.

12. Kosuke Kaida and Kazuhisa Niki, "Total Sleep Deprivation Decreases Flow Experience and Mood Status," *Neuropsychiatric Disease and Treatment* 19 (December 1, 2013), https://doi.org/10.2147/ndt.s53633.

13. Valeria Drago et al., "The Correlation Between Sleep and Creativity," *Nature Precedings* (March 9, 2010), https://doi.org/10.1038/npre.2010.4266.1.

14. Jeffrey Kluger, "How to Wake up to Your Creativity," *TIME*, April 30, 2017, https://time.com/4737596/sleep-brain-creativity/.

15. Rasha Aridi, "Need a Creative Boost? Nap Like Thomas Edison and Salvador Dalí," *Smithsonian Magazine*, December 13, 2021, https://www.smithsonianmag.com/smart-news/the-first-stage-of-sleep-is-a-creative-sweet-spot-180979211/.

16. Adam Haar Horowitz, "Dreaming and Creativity – MIT Media Lab," MIT Media Lab, n.d., https://www.media.mit.edu/posts/dreams-and-creativity/#faq-what-are-the-main-findings-of-this-study.

17. Zach Baron and Levon Baird, "The Return of James Cameron, Box Office King," *GQ*, November 21, 2022, https://www.gq.com/story/james-cameron-profile-men-of-the-year-2022.

18. Wikipedia contributors, "Elias Howe," Wikipedia, February 8, 2024, https://en.wikipedia.org/wiki/Elias_Howe.

19. Mauricio Sierra-Siegert et al., "Minding the Dreamer Within: An Experimental Study on the Effects of Enhanced Dream Recall on Creative Thinking," *The Journal of Creative Behavior* 53, no. 1 (October 31, 2016): 83–96, https://doi.org/10.1002/jocb.168.

20. Steven Kotler, "The best way to maximize the power of the HUMAN-AI cooperation? It's all about FLOW!," July 28, 2024, https://www.linkedin.com/posts/stevenkotler_the-best-way-to-maximize-the-power-of-the-activity-7223376511628648448-w-j4?utm_source=share&utm_medium=member_desktop.

Chapter 9

1. "Fostering Intrinsic Motivation in the Early Years." n.d. https://www.cela.org.au/publications/amplify!-blog/sep-2023/why-fostering-intrinsic-motivation-in-early-years.

2. Sandra W. Russ, "Pretend Play: Antecedent of Adult Creativity," *New Directions for Child and Adolescent Development* 2016, no. 151 (March 1, 2016): 21–32, https://doi.org/10.1002/cad.20154.

3. Video Arts, "John Cleese on Creativity in Management," June 21, 2017, https://www.youtube.com/watch?v=Pb5oIIPO62g.

4. Michael Schrage, *Serious Play: How the World's Best Companies Simulate to Innovate* (Harvard Business Press, 2000).

5. Matt Statler, Loizos Heracleous, and Claus D. Jacobs, "Serious Play as a Practice of Paradox," *The Journal of Applied Behavioral Science* 47, no. 2 (May 3, 2011): 236–56, https://doi.org/10.1177/0021886311398453.

6. The LEGO® Group. n.d. "The LEGO® Group." https://www.lego.com/en-us/themes/serious-play/background.

7. Jackie Andrade, "What Does Doodling Do?," *Applied Cognitive Psychology* 24, no. 1 (February 27, 2009): 100–106, https://doi.org/10.1002/acp.1561.

8. Gd Schott, "Doodling and the Default Network of the Brain," *Lancet* 378, no. 9797 (September 1, 2011): 1133–34, https://doi.org/10.1016/s0140-6736(11)61496-7.

9. Patrick Bateson, "Play, Playfulness, Creativity and Innovation," *Animal Behavior and Cognition* 2, no. 2 (January 1, 2014): 99, https://doi.org/10.12966/abc.05.02.2014.

10. Patrick Bateson, "Playfulness and Creativity," *Current Biology* 25, no. 1 (January 1, 2015): R12–16, https://doi.org/10.1016/j.cub.2014.09.009.

11. Micah Solomon, "Three Wow Customer Service Stories From Zappos, Southwest Airlines and Nordstrom," *Forbes*, August 3, 2017, https://www.forbes.com/sites/micahsolomon/2017/08/01/three-wow-customer-service-stories-from-zappos-southwest-airlines-and-nordstrom/?sh=57d022d12aba.

12. Pier Vittorio Mannucci, Davide C. Orazi, and Kristine De Valck, "Developing Improvisation Skills: The Influence of Individual Orientations," *Administrative Science Quarterly* (November 23, 2020), https://doi.org/10.1177/0001839220975697.

Chapter 10

1. Scott Belsky, "On Escape Velocity, Necessary Ruckus, & Working at the Edge of Reason: 6 Thoughts," *Implications, by Scott Belsky (blog)*, November 5, 2015, https://www.implications.com/p/on-escape-velocity-necessary-ruckus-working-at-the-edge-of-reason-1a85d9bc36aa.

2. AAAI, "Narrative Intelligence - AAAI," October 16, 2023, https://aaai.org/papers/0001-fs99-01-001-narrative-intelligence/.

3. Angus Fletcher, "The Limits of Logic: Why Narrative Thinking Is Better Suited to the Demands of Modern Combat - Modern War Institute," Modern War Institute, August 23, 2023, https://mwi.westpoint.edu/the-limits-of-logic-why-narrative-thinking-is-better-suited-to-the-demands-of-modern-combat/.

4. Behance, "Blog :: Creativity Is Nourished by Conflict," 2024 Behance, n.d., https://www.behance.net/blog/creativity-is-nourished-by-conflict.

5. Quoteresearch, "For Sale, Baby Shoes, Never Worn – Quote Investigator®," January 28, 2013, https://quoteinvestigator.com/2013/01/28/baby-shoes/.

6. Helen Marshall, Kim Wilkins, and Lisa Bennett, "Story Thinking for Technology Foresight," *Futures* 146 (February 1, 2023): 103098, https://doi.org/10.1016/j.futures.2023.103098.

7. Angus Fletcher and Mike Benveniste, "A New Method for Training Creativity: Narrative as an Alternative to Divergent Thinking,"

Annals of the New York Academy of Sciences 1512, no. 1 (March 10, 2022): 29–45, https://doi.org/10.1111/nyas.14763.

8. Jane Carlin and Sha Towers, "The Power of Artists' Books: Catalysts for Creative Thinking Across the Curriculum," Carlin | College & Research Libraries News, May 7, 2024, https://crln.acrl.org/index.php/crlnews/article/view/26335/34276.

9. Anna Kasunic and Geoff Kaufman, "Learning to Listen: Critically Considering the Role of AI in Human Storytelling and Character Creation," *Proceedings of the First Workshop on Storytelling*, January 1, 2018, https://doi.org/10.18653/v1/w18-1501.

10. Angus Fletcher, "Why Computer AI Will Never Do What We Imagine It Can," *Narrative* 30, no. 1 (2022): 114–137. https://doi.org/10.1353/nar.2022.0006.

Epilogue

1. Ahmed Sherif, "Skills Expected to Rise in Importance from 2023 to 2027." Statista. September 4, 2023. https://www.statista.com/statistics/1383183/skills-on-the-rise/.

2. "The Future of Jobs Report 2023," World Economic Forum, n.d., https://www.weforum.org/publications/the-future-of-jobs-report-2023/in-full/4-skills-outlook/.

3. Mark Singer and Rory McCallum, "Creativity as a Force for Growth," Deloitte Insights, April 20, 2023, https://www2.deloitte.com/us/en/insights/topics/marketing-and-sales-operations/global-marketing-trends/2023/creativity-to-solve-marketing-challenges.html.

Puzzle Answers

Chapter 1

INSIGHT PROBLEM

There is no missing dollar. The problem lies in the challenge question, which is intentionally misleading and suggests adding the $2 kept by the bellhop to the $27 paid by the guests. That total is $29, but it has no bearing on the problem itself.

The correct way to think about it is as follows:

- $30 (initial payment) = $25 (correct room cost) + $2 (kept by the bellhop) + $3 (returned to the guests).

The math is consistent:

- Initial amount paid: $30.
- The correct cost of the room is $25.
- Money kept by the bellhop: $2.
- Money paid by the guests: $27 (correct cost plus the amount retained by bellhop).
- Money returned to the guests: $3.

Chapter 3

FIND CONNECTIONS PUZZLE 1

1. **Things you'd find underground:** MINE, WELL, SPRING, GOLD
2. **Words that end in a body part:** ALARM, BEAR, SLIP, AHEAD
3. **Banking-related things:** DEPOSIT, CHECK, INTEREST, CARD
4. **Sports equipment:** HELMET, BAT, CLUB, NET

FIND CONNECTIONS PUZZLE 2

1. **Famous Chucks:** BERRY, BARRIS, NORRIS, JONES
2. **Cuts of meat:** CHOP, CHUCK, LOIN, SHANK
3. **To make fun of:** SKEWER, JAB, RIB, POKE
4. **Body_____:** GUARD, CAM, SUIT, LANGUAGE

CREATE CONNECTIONS

1. door, gentle, sand, and ___handy_____ plus ____man_____
2. battle, corn, play, and ____mine____ plus ____field_____
3. light, dog, green, and ___out_____ plus ___house_____
4. foot, hand, eye, and ____pin_____ plus ____ball_____
5. hump, play, out, and __feed_____plus ____back_____

FILL IN THE ANALOGY

Here is just one possible answer for each pair. There are multiple answers that will work.

1. Petal is to Flower as ___Spoke_____ is to ___Wheel_____.
2. Chapter is to Book as ____Ingredient___ is to ____Recipe_____.
3. Heart is to Circulation as __Battery_____ is to ___Electrical Power_____.
4. Day is to Night as ___Hot____is to ____Cold____.
5. Desk is to School as __ Counter_____ is to ___Jewelry Store___.
6. Flame is to Candle as ___Spotlight____ is to ____Lighthouse_____.
7. Whisper is to Shout as ___Chuckle____ is to ___Guffaw_____.
8. Cereal is to Supermarket as ___Tool___ is to ___Hardware Store_____.
9. Goose is to Swan as ____Pig___ is to ___Boar_____.
10. Chef is to Kitchen as __Conductor_____ is to ____Orchestra_____.

Chapter 8:

Three Houses Puzzle

Let's analyze the clues one at a time:

1. **Doctor—yellow:** We know this confirms the yellow house is occupied by the doctor.
2. **Blue—dog:** The blue house has the dog as a resident.
3. **Lawyer—red (neighbor):** The lawyer lives next to the red house.
4. **Parrot—not with fish:** The parrot doesn't live in the same house as the fish.
5. **Tea drinker—red:** The red house has the tea drinker as an occupant.
6. **Lawyer—music lover (neighbor):** The lawyer lives next to the music lover.
7. **Teacher—no music:** The teacher dislikes music.
8. **Teacher—right of parrot:** The teacher lives to the right of the parrot.
9. **Music lover—coffee:** The music lover enjoys coffee.
10. **Doctor—dog (neighbor):** The doctor lives next door to the dog.
11. **Dog—left of tea drinker:** The dog lives to the left of the tea drinker (meaning the red house).
12. **Fish—not coffee drinker:** The fish doesn't live with someone who drinks coffee.
13. **Coffee drinker—not parrot owner:** The coffee drinker doesn't own the parrot.
14. **The parrot is left of the teacher.**

Now, let's use this information to solve the puzzle:

- We know the doctor (yellow) and dog (blue) are neighbors.
- Since the teacher dislikes music and the music lover drinks coffee, the teacher cannot be the coffee drinker.
- The lawyer lives next to the music lover, and the teacher is to the lawyer's right. So the order is doctor, lawyer, teacher. Yellow-Blue-Red.

- The coffee drinker is not the parrot owner or the fish owner.
- The lawyer owns the dog since the tea drinker lives in the red house, and the dog is to the left of the tea drinker.
- If the teacher lives in the red house and the parrot lives to the teacher's left, then the parrot and dog live in the blue house with the lawyer.
- Since the parrot and fish don't live together and the fish doesn't live with the coffee drinker, then the fish must live in the red house with the teacher.

Solution: Fish lives in: Red house

- **Yellow house:** Doctor, music lover, coffee drinker.
- **Blue house:** Lawyer with the dog and the parrot.
- **Red house:** Teacher owns the fish and drinks tea.

House Colors and Professions:

- Yellow—Doctor
- Blue—Lawyer
- Red—Teacher

Magic Square Puzzle

15	16	22	3	9
8	14	20	21	2
1	7	13	19	25
24	5	6	12	18
17	23	4	10	11

Acknowledgments

As a first-time author, I depended on the help of a group of talented individuals to navigate my way to the finish line. I wouldn't be here if it weren't for Christina Rudloff, who acquired my book for Wiley and whose support has been unflagging since the first day we met. Thanks to my team of superwomen at Wiley, notably Purvi Patel, who has always been ready and willing to help whenever I have needed her, and Julie Kerr, whose consistent encouragement has been the fuel I needed to get the job done. I owe a special shout-out to Dan Olsen, whose counsel and support were invaluable to me at the starting line and who I can always count on to share the tough love I need to hear. And a big thank-you to Kate Collins, who was kind enough to share her art in this book and who has been a sounding board and a personal inspiration to me since we met more than 20 years ago.

I am also grateful for the inspiration, insights, and advice I have received throughout my career from the accomplished and creative people I interviewed for this book. They offered me their time and perspective without asking for anything in return, and for that, I am honored. To show my gratitude, I have made charitable donations in their honor to the nonprofit organizations of their choice. The following list represents the causes and organizations that received these donations to thank these incredibly generous and esteemed individuals.

Chapter 1: Kerry Lenhart and John Sakmar – Bags and Grace
Chapter 2: Tony Fadell – Environmental Defense Fund, Methane Sat
Chapter 3: Denny Post – Foreseeable Future Foundation
Chapter 4: Scott Ehrlich – American Museum of Ceramic Arts
Chapter 5: Jay Samit – Doctors without Borders

Chapter 6: Scilla Andreen – Impactful Fund

Chapter 7: Jules Pieri – Navy Yard Garden & Art

Chapter 8: Jason Silva – MAPS.org

Chapter 9: Pat Copeland – Little Bit Therapeutic

Chapter 10: Scott Belsky – Museum of Modern Art Education Fund

About the Author

Leslie Grandy is a speaker, CEO advisor, and product executive who guides companies, teams, and business leaders to expand their creative capacity to innovate for customers, accelerate growth, transform operations, and maintain relevance in a fast-changing world.

From a successful career in the film industry in Los Angeles as a member of the Directors Guild of America to becoming an executive at iconic brands such as Amazon, Discovery, T-Mobile, Best Buy, and Apple, Leslie has built and led teams from the ground up and pioneered multiple first-to-market products, including co-authoring a patent for the earliest digital media subscription services that Intel acquired. In multiple corporate roles, Leslie has guided internal innovation teams as an IDEO-trained leader in Design Thinking.

Leslie coaches and mentors leaders through the advisory firm she founded, The Product Guild, the University of Michigan College of Engineering's Center for Entrepreneurship, and the University of Washington Foster School of Business. She co-created and serves as the Lead Executive in Residence in the Product Management Leadership Accelerator of the Foster School's Executive Education program.

Index